Kenneth Roberts

Twayne's United States Authors Series

Joseph M. Flora, Editor

University of North Carolina

TUSAS 626

KENNETH ROBERTS.
Photograph courtesy of Virginia Mosser.

Kenneth Roberts

Jack Bales

Mary Washington College

Twayne Publishers • New York
Maxwell Macmillan Canada • Toronto
Maxwell Macmillan International • New York Oxford Singapore Sydney

Kenneth Roberts
Jack Bales

Twayne Publishers
Macmillan Publishing Company
866 Third Avenue
New York, New York 10022

Maxwell Macmillan Canada, Inc.
1200 Eglinton Avenue East
Suite 200
Don Mills, Ontario M3C 3N1

Library of Congress Cataloging-in-Publication Data

Bales, Jack.
    Kenneth Roberts / by Jack Bales.
      p.   cm.— (Twayne's United States authors series; TUSAS 626)
    Includes bibliographical references and index.
    ISBN 0-8057-7643-5 (alk. paper)
    1. Roberts, Kenneth Lewis, 1885-1957—Criticism and interpretation. 2. Historical
fiction, American—History and criticism. 3. United States—Historiography. I. Title.
II. Series.
PS3535.O176Z59   1993
813'.52—dc20   93-4000
                                                                                          CIP

The paper used in this publication meets the minimum requirements of American
National Standard for Information Sciences—Permanence of Paper for Printed Library
Materials, ANSI Z39.48-1984.∞ TM

10 9 8 7 6 5 4 3 2 1

Printed in the United States of America.

"I wish you good things, . . . only good things."
—Herman Raucher

To Patrick and Laura
For helping me manage
and to D.
For helping me with just about everything else that matters

Contents

Preface

From the late 1930s to his death in 1957, Kenneth Roberts was one of the most popular historical novelists in the United States. In a 1938 survey conducted by the American Institute of Public Opinion, Americans were asked, "What is the most interesting book you have ever read?" Roberts's *Northwest Passage* ranked eighth in a list of the top 20 titles selected.[1] This book and several of his other novels have each sold more than 100,000 copies; the rest have sold at least 50,000 copies each. All of his novels have been translated into foreign languages in countries around the world. Shortly before he died he was awarded a special Pulitzer Prize for this collective body of work that spanned nearly three decades.

Although Roberts's books have been praised by reviewers in the popular press, the author has been ignored by most scholarly critics and virtually all biographers. A private individual who preferred the company of a few close friends rather than numerous acquaintances, Roberts did not encourage researchers interested in his work. Although his 1949 memoir, *I Wanted to Write*, is simply a chronicle of his years as a journalist and novelist from 1904 to 1947, he preferred that it stand as the official record of his life and career. Thus, with the exception of a cursory 72-page essay in a 1989 biobibliography, no account of his life has been published.[2]

The purpose of this book is to present a thorough review and analysis of Roberts's fiction and nonfiction within the framework of a biographical narrative. Each of the six chapters is devoted to a period in Roberts's life with reference to the works he produced during that period. Chapter 1 discusses his childhood and youth, his editorship of Cornell University's humor magazine, and his brief career as a reporter for the *Boston Post* and contributor to *Puck, Judge*, and the old *Life*. Chapter 2 centers on his years as an international correspondent for the *Saturday Evening Post*. Chapter 3 marks the transition between Roberts leaving the *Post* and his branching off on his own as a novelist, and the next chapter focuses on him at the top of his craft as one of the country's most successful authors. Chapter 5 explores an aspect of his life that has never before been studied: his passion for water dowsing and his three books on the subject. Chapter 6 concentrates on what he wrote during the last few years of his life and includes descriptions of some of the projects he was working on at the time of his death.

While completing this literary biography, I have read thousands of letters both to and from Roberts that are preserved in libraries across the country. In addition, I have made lengthy and repeated research trips to such major Roberts repositories of primary material as the Library of Congress, Dartmouth College, Colby College, and institutions in Roberts's hometown, Kennebunkport, Maine, and in nearby Kennebunk.

I have also found his many diaries in the Roberts collection at Dartmouth's Baker Library to be both fascinating and invaluable. Roberts depended on the candid observations and reflections in these diaries, covering the years 1912 to 1935, while he worked on *I Wanted to Write*. Although donor restrictions preclude citation or quotation of the diaries, I have carefully documented my other sources for the benefit of subsequent researchers.

The first citation of a given work appears in the Notes, with subsequent references cited parenthetically in the text. Because several of Roberts's novels were published in revised editions, each citation to *Arundel*, *The Lively Lady*, and *Rabble in Arms* includes both chapter number and page number, separated by a slash (/).

Acknowledgments

Researching and writing this book on Kenneth Roberts and his works has indebted me to many people and institutions, and I am grateful to all for their help and interest. I especially wish to express my appreciation to faculty and staff members of Mary Washington College. In the college library Carla Bailey secured countless books and articles through interlibrary loan, and Linda Thompson never failed to assist with last-minute typing or other projects. Elizabeth S. Perkins offered numerous suggestions on the manuscript at various stages, and Library Director Roy Strohl provided constant support and release-time from professional duties. College President William M. Anderson, Jr., and Dean Philip L. Hall gave me more than one faculty development grant as well as a summer-long sabbatical, and the library's reference staff generously filled in for me while I was away. Personnel in the college bookstore ordered reference books and other volumes I needed.

I am grateful to John I. Kitch, Jr., the dean of Roberts scholars, who carefully read this book in manuscript form and shared with me his irreplaceable research material as well as his critical judgment. Also, Phyllis S. Bales and Richard F. Bales, for meticulous criticism of the manuscript; Stacy Birkenstock; military historian Harrison K. Bird; Mary Bryant; Joyce Butler and the staff of the Brick Store Museum, Kennebunk, Maine; Cheryl Cole; William B. Edgar; Donald R. Eldred; Karen Duffy; Glenys Gifford; Stephen L. Jacobs; Kevin Kelly; the Library of Congress, Manuscript Division; Robert Ludlum; former Doubleday editor in chief Kenneth D. McCormick; Mark McManus; Ellen Menk; James A. Michener; Jacob and Polly Mosser; Donald and Margie Nurnberg; Lee Pfeiffer; Jana Perkins; Jessica Perkins; Sandra Severance; Earle G. Shettleworth, Jr.; Robert and Cathy Steinkamp; John Tebbel, biographer of George Horace Lorimer; Willard M. Wallace, biographer of Benedict Arnold; Nicholas Westbrook, director, Fort Ticonderoga; Edward Winston; Eleanor W. Woodman; James Woodress, biographer of Booth Tarkington; and Edith Zimmerman.

I am grateful to Joseph M. Flora for helpful advice in the preparation of the manuscript of this book. I would also like to thank my editor, Barbara Sutton, for having copyedited the manuscript so masterfully. It is greatly appreciated.

I am especially indebted to the following persons and institutions for permission to quote from published and unpublished material. These include:

John B. Barney, Vice President and Counsel, Key Trust Company of Maine, successor as personal representative for the Estate of Kenneth Roberts to the Canal National Bank, Portland, Maine, for permission to quote from *March to Quebec* and Roberts's unpublished letters. Also, the Estate of Kenneth Roberts and Anna M. Roberts for permission to quote from *I Wanted to Write*. I am also grateful to Virginia Mosser, Kenneth Roberts's niece and personal representative for the estate of Marjorie Mosser Ellis, for permission to quote from *Good Maine Food* and for supplying me with the photograph of Roberts used for this book's frontispiece.

Also, Special Collections, Colby College, Waterville, Maine, and Patience-Anne W. Lenk, Special Collections Librarian; Allan Nevins Papers, Richard L. Simon Papers, Rare Book and Manuscript Library, Columbia University, New York City; Department of Manuscripts and University Archives, Cornell University, Ithaca, New York, and Gould P. Colman, University Archivist; Dartmouth College Library, Hanover, New Hampshire, and Philip N. Cronenwett, Chief of Special Collections.

Also, the Lilly Library, Indiana University, Bloomington, Indiana; the Maine State Library, Augusta, Maine; Special Collections Department, Northwestern University Library, Evanston, Illinois; Phillips Exeter Academy Library, Exeter, New Hampshire; Syracuse University Library, Syracuse, New York.

Also, Carol Christiansen, Copyright and Permission Department, Doubleday, a division of Bantam, Doubleday, Dell Publishing Group, Inc., for permission to quote from the following works by Kenneth Roberts:

Arundel, by Kenneth Roberts. Copyright 1930, 1933, 1956 by Kenneth Roberts. Used by permission of Doubleday, a division of Bantam, Doubleday, Dell Publishing Group, Inc.

The Battle of Cowpens, by Kenneth Roberts. Copyright 1957 by Anna M. Roberts and the Canal National Bank of Portland, Portland, Maine, executors of the Estate of Kenneth Roberts and Anna M. Roberts. Used by permission of Doubleday, a division of Bantam, Doubleday, Dell Publishing Group, Inc.

Boon Island, by Kenneth Roberts. Copyright 1955 by Kenneth Roberts and Anna M. Roberts. Used by permission of Doubleday, a division of Bantam, Doubleday, Dell Publishing Group, Inc.

For Authors Only, and Other Gloomy Essays, by Kenneth Roberts. Copyright 1935 by Kenneth Roberts. Used by permission of Doubleday, a division of Bantam, Doubleday, Dell Publishing Group, Inc.

Henry Gross and His Dowsing Rod, by Kenneth Roberts. Copyright 1951 by Kenneth Roberts. Used by permission of Doubleday, a division of Bantam, Doubleday, Dell Publishing Group, Inc.

The Lively Lady, by Kenneth Roberts. Copyright 1931, 1935 by Kenneth Roberts. Used by permission of Doubleday, a division of Bantam, Doubleday, Dell Publishing Group, Inc.

Lydia Bailey, by Kenneth Roberts. Copyright 1947 by Kenneth Roberts and Anna M. Roberts. Used by permission of Doubleday, a division of Bantam, Doubleday, Dell Publishing Group, Inc.

Northwest Passage, by Kenneth Roberts. Copyright 1937 by Kenneth Roberts. Used by permission of Doubleday, a division of Bantam, Doubleday, Dell Publishing Group, Inc.

Oliver Wiswell, by Kenneth Roberts. Copyright 1940 by Kenneth Roberts. Used by permission of Doubleday, a division of Bantam, Doubleday, Dell Publishing Group, Inc.

Rabble in Arms, by Kenneth Roberts. Copyright 1933, 1947 by Kenneth Roberts. Used by permission of Doubleday, a division of Bantam, Doubleday, Dell Publishing Group, Inc.

The Seventh Sense, by Kenneth Roberts. Copyright 1953 by Kenneth Roberts. Used by permission of Doubleday, a division of Bantam, Doubleday, Dell Publishing Group, Inc.

Trending into Maine, by Kenneth Roberts. Copyright 1944 by Kenneth Roberts. Used by permission of Doubleday, a division of Bantam, Doubleday, Dell Publishing Group, Inc.

Water Unlimited, by Kenneth Roberts. Copyright 1957 by Kenneth Roberts. Used by permission of Doubleday, a division of Bantam, Doubleday, Dell Publishing Group, Inc.

Passages from *The Collector's Whatnot*, by Kenneth Roberts, Booth Tarkington, and Hugh MacNair Kahler, copyright 1923, are reprinted by permission of Houghton Mifflin Company. Passages from the letters of Kenneth Roberts are published by permission of the Houghton Library, Harvard University. Passages from the letters of Kenneth Roberts are published by permission of the Princeton University Library, Princeton, New Jersey.

Chronology

1885 Kenneth Lewis Roberts born 8 December in Kennebunk, Maine, the only child of Frank Lewis and Grace Mary Tibbets Roberts.

1902 Publishes four limericks in high school literary magazine.

1904-1908 Attends Cornell University, graduating in 1908 with an A.B. in the arts; edits college humor magazine, the *Cornell Widow*, from 1905 to 1908; writes lyrics for Cornell musical comedy *Panatela*, presented in January 1907.

1908-1909 Assistant office boy in a Boston leather firm.

1909-1917 Reporter for the *Boston Post*.

1911 Marries Anna Seiberling Mosser of Roxbury, Massachusetts, on 14 February.

1915-1918 Holds editorial positions at *Life* (1915-18) and *Puck* (1916-17) magazines.

1918-1919 Captain, Intelligence Section, Siberian Expeditionary Force, U.S. Army.

1919-1928 Staff correspondent for the *Saturday Evening Post*. Publishes eight books based on *Post* articles: *Europe's Morning After* (1921), *Why Europe Leaves Home* (1922), *Sun Hunting* (1922), *Black Magic* (1924), *Concentrated New England* (1924), *Florida Loafing* (1925), *Florida* (1926), *Antiquamania* (1928).

1923 *The Collector's Whatnot*, with Booth Tarkington and Hugh MacNair Kahler.

1930 *Arundel*, his first historical novel.

1931 *The Lively Lady*.

1933 *Rabble in Arms*.

1934 *Captain Caution* and *The Brotherhood of Man* (one-act play from the *Saturday Evening Post*). Receives honorary doctor of letters from Dartmouth College.

1935   Is elected to the National Institute of Arts and Letters; receives honorary doctor of letters from Colby College. *For Author's Only, and Other Gloomy Essays* (articles from the *Saturday Evening Post*).

1936   *It Must Be Your Tonsils* (article from the *Saturday Evening Post*).

1937   *Northwest Passage.* Receives honorary membership in Phi Beta Kappa at Dartmouth College.

1938   *Trending into Maine* and *March to Quebec.* Receives honorary doctor of literature from Middlebury College and honorary doctor of letters from Bowdoin College.

1940   *Oliver Wiswell.*

1945   *The Kenneth Roberts Reader.* Receives honorary doctor of literature from Northeastern University.

1947   *Lydia Bailey* and *Moreau de St. Mery's American Journey (1793-1798).*

1949   *I Wanted to Write*, his literary autobiography.

1950-1953   Forms the corporation Water Unlimited in 1950 to promote study of dowsing; writes the dowsing books *Henry Gross and His Dowsing Rod* (1951) and *The Seventh Sense* (1953).

1951   *Don't Say That about Maine!* (article from the *Saturday Evening Post*).

1956   *Boon Island.*

1957   Receives special Pulitzer Prize on 6 May "for his historical novels which have long contributed to the creation of greater interest in our early American history"; dies on 21 July and is buried in Arlington National Cemetery, Arlington, Virginia. *Water Unlimited* published posthumously.

1958   *The Battle of Cowpens.* Water Unlimited corporation dissolved.

Chapter One

The Early Years

On 27 November 1935, a few months after Colby College awarded Kenneth Roberts an honorary degree, he wrote to a friend who had wondered how he had become interested in writing historical novels. "I've had a theory for a great many years," Roberts explained, "that a writer can write [more] effectively about his own people than he can about people that aren't in his blood. . . . My people have always lived in Maine. All of twenty years ago I started mousing around for something to write that would have my own sort of people in it."[1]

Roberts's "own sort of people" were frequently his ancestors who had served in various American wars and campaigns. Some family members had belonged to the New England regiments that had fought in the French and Indian Wars Roberts dramatized in *Northwest Passage* (1937). His great-great-great-grandfather, Joshua Nason, helped capture Louisburg from the French in 1745 and commanded a company in the battles at White Plains and Saratoga during the American Revolution. Roberts's *Arundel* (1930) and *Rabble in Arms* (1933) chronicled the campaigns of Benedict Arnold and the Northern Army during the Revolution, and principal characters in each novel were modeled after Joshua Nason and his descendants. Roberts's great-grandfather, Daniel Nason—who, as Richard Nason, is the central character and narrator of *The Lively Lady*—was sailing master of the privateer *MacDonough* during the War of 1812. The British captured the ship in 1814 and sentenced Nason and his crew to Dartmoor Prison in England for the duration of the war. While researching *The Lively Lady* Roberts made a special trip to Dartmoor to visualize the suffering of his ancestor and the other American prisoners. When an interviewer a few years later asked about his great-grandfather, he observed respectfully, "The old boy had a pretty tough time of it from what I hear."[2]

Beginnings

Although Roberts wrote a great deal about his ancestors, he had little to say throughout his life about his immediate family. The scattered

1

available information indicates that his father, Frank Lewis Roberts (1860-1911), was a Boston traveling salesman, the son of Millett W. and Hannah A. Butler Roberts of Acton, Maine. Frank Roberts married Grace Mary Tibbets (1858-1948) on 15 April 1884. She was the daughter of Ebenezer A. and Jane A. Nason Tibbets of Great Falls (now Somersworth), New Hampshire.

Jane Tibbets grew up in Kennebunk, Maine, where her family was prominent and well-established. After the Robertses' marriage the couple moved to Kennebunk, and on 8 December 1885 their only child, Kenneth Lewis Roberts, was born in the house they were renting on Storer Street. Kenneth was not at all close to his father and never mentioned him in any of his articles or books. His mother, on the other hand, was different: he frequently wrote about her family—particularly in his essay collection *Trending into Maine*—and during his youth he enjoyed visits with the Tibbetses in Great Falls and vacations at Kennebunk Beach, where they owned a summer house.[3] As he recalled years later, "Various . . . members of my family lived in the same New Hampshire town, and I remember with gratitude that is tearfully sincere the help and the guidance I received from them. One aunt broke me of sucking my thumb. A little later she offered a standing reward of five cents for each of Longfellow's poems that I would translate into readable prose. To another aunt I am indebted for a large part of my so-called higher education."[4]

At the time young Kenneth was enjoying these visits with his relatives, the Roberts family was living in the Boston suburb of Malden, where the youth attended grammar school and the first part of high school. He participated in many sports, including baseball, football, and hockey, and spent hours exploring the Maine woods while hunting and fishing. Roberts always maintained that his longtime familiarity with Maine's wilderness was crucial to the successful writing of his books: "No one, in my opinion, should undertake a historical novel without being thoroughly familiar with the locality in which the action takes place. I was born and brought up around here. As a boy I hunted and fished and sailed the waters. I shot my first deer when I was 13 years old and I have been lost in the almost impenetrable brush such as Arnold's expedition encountered on the Height of Land."[5]

Kenneth Roberts grew up with a fondness for books as well as for the outdoors, and in letters to his relatives he often commented on the volumes he was reading, which included *Ben Hur*, *Oliver Twist*, Doyle's tales of Sherlock Holmes, the Bible, *Arabian Nights' Entertainments*, and various boys' books by G. A. Henty. His mother frequently read to him at night, and she was largely responsible for her son's interest in books. Katharine Mosser Pediconi, Roberts's sister-in-law, recalled almost a decade after his death that "his mother was a chain reader and he was an only child, two excellent ingredients to make a child a reader."[6]

His literary pursuits also included creative writing, and he contributed at least one work to the *Oracle*, the Malden High School literary magazine. "Four Songs of the Heart," a collection of four limericks revealing a typical adolescent's sense of humor, was published on the first page of the 25 September 1902 issue. The first poem reads:

> *A gallant young middy named Bou*
> *Was once called on deck by his crou;*
> *They said: "For a treat*
> *We want something to eat,"*
> *So he gave them the toe of his shou.*

Roberts's letters suggest that he was a fairly good student in the Malden public schools. He completed high school, however, at Charles Wellington Stone's preparatory school in Boston, "to which I repaired after being ejected from High School for telling my Geometry teacher that Geometry gave me a pain in the neck."[7] Frank Roberts's income as a traveling salesman apparently could not cover all his family's bills. His son's private school tuition, as well as his college expenses, were paid by his aunt, Lucy Tibbets Russell (Kitch, 17).

College Days and the *Cornell Widow*

Roberts entered Cornell University in the fall of 1904. During his four years at Cornell he was—as one of his roommates recalled years later—a member of "practically every club or society" on campus.[8] He was a cheerleader and wrote the words to two popular football songs, "Fight for Cornell" and "Carnelian and White." He was also active in the Masque and Savage clubs, two organizations that presented light musical entertainment. One of the Masque club's most popular productions was *Panatela*, a three-act musical comedy presented in January 1907, for which Roberts wrote most of the lyrics. He belonged to the Chi Psi fraternity, several campus committees, Undine (a social club), Dunstan (a club for sophomores), the Mummy Club (for upperclassmen), Aleph Samach (for juniors), and Quill and Dagger (for seniors). The *Cornell Class Book* observes that if Roberts "were to wear all his club and society

pins at one time, there would be such a decided list to port that everything would spill out of his pockets."[9]

Unfortunately, Roberts's academic accomplishments were not nearly
as notable as his extracurricular activities, and his college transcript
reveals mediocre grades. "Overall, his record is unremarkable," according to the current university archivist.[10] Indeed, even Roberts admitted
years after he left college that "I never understood how I contrived to
accumulate sufficient information on the side to cope with examinations
and acquire a degree."[11] Asked about Roberts, one of his Chi Psi fraternity brothers remembered that "he was *very* popular with students," and
that he "raised h—l" around the fraternity house, singing until midnight
with his friends.[12] From 1907 to 1908 Roberts was president of the
Kappa Beta Phi society, a campus drinking club. Its aims, Roberts
acknowledged years later, "were avowedly the opposite of Phi Beta
Kappa's: candidates for admission were required to prove they had been
ejected (busted, in Cornell phraseology) from at least one collegiate
course, and were obliged to drink a bottle of Younger's Scotch Ale (as
effervescent as it was potent) through a straw; then display sufficient
control over the churning fumes within them to walk one hundred feet
along a curbstone without stumbling" (*IWW*, 47).

Despite Roberts's "unremarkable" academic record and apparent
commitment to frivolity and collegiate high jinks, he pursued one of his
interests with a sense of determination that would later characterize his
essays and novels. Soon after he arrived on campus he started writing for
the *Cornell Widow*, the college humor magazine. Within a few months he
was elected to the publication's editorial board and became editor in
chief during his sophomore year by persuading the underclassmen on the
board to vote for him as a bloc. He remained as editor until his graduation in 1908.[13]

The *Cornell Widow* was modeled after the old *Life* (a national weekly
humor magazine) and contained jokes, cartoons, poems, and literary par-
odies. Naturally, the humor seems hopelessly dated by today's standards,
as these jokes from the October 1907 *Widow* illustrate: "PIKER: 'Did
the Prof in Photography 23 accept that picture you took of the Bowery
Burlesquers?' HIKER: 'Naw, he said it was over exposed!'" Also, "MR.
PORT: 'Your honor, I got drunk merely for the experience.' JUDGE:
'Ten days! You have too great a thirst for knowledge.'"

Because none of the pieces in the *Widow* were signed, it is impossible
to single out Roberts's material. His contributions, however, were not
limited to poetry and light prose. Even as a college freshman he was

drawn to controversial topics and did not hesitate to write articles attacking or satirizing the college administration and its policies. Although the *Widow*'s editorial board refused to publish some of Roberts's articles, a few of them, as his longtime friend and former *Widow* editor Romeyn Berry remembered in 1940, "managed to squeeze through the editorial mesh" (Berry, 149). After one such essay appeared the university's dean, Thomas "Teefy" F. Crane, reprimanded the board: "I doubt if I, as Dean, possess the power to abolish the Cornell Widow. But there can be no doubt of my full power—nor of my present inclination to exercise it—of my full power, I repeat, to abolish you and every other member of the board, including the unlicked cub who wrote that peculiarly offensive attack on the management of the Forest City Livery and Boarding Stables" (Berry, 149).

Some of the *Widow*'s favorite targets included other university publications, especially the campus newspaper, the *Cornell Daily Sun*. While the monthly *Widow* posed little threat to this daily newspaper, the magazine constantly ridiculed the *Sun*'s editorials, news stories, journalistic mistakes, and typographical errors. In 1906, for Cornell's Spring Day festivities, Roberts began a campus tradition by publishing an eight-page parody of the *Cornell Daily Sun*, titled the *Cornell Daily Sin*. In succeeding years the *Widow* published at least seven full-length *Sun* spoofs and several smaller ones.[14]

The *Widow*'s editor in chief and business manager traditionally divided the profits at the end of the academic year, consequently, the spring of 1908 found Roberts with $5,000 in his pocket, as well as an A.B. in the arts, a desire to write, and valuable writing and editorial experience.[15] Furthermore, characteristics that people would always identify with him were fostered and developed during his four years at Cornell. These included his conservative political views and his ready willingness to investigate and to write about controversial subjects. His warm sense of humor, however, was occasionally obscured by his strong, forceful personality and outspokenness, traits that in later years led some to label him "the irascible Mr. Roberts." In 1964, for example, one of his fraternity roommates, Edgar S. Wheelan, remembered how Roberts once wanted him to vote for a particular student to take over the editorship of the *Widow* after he graduated. Wheelan had already promised to support another student in the election, and he refused to change his vote. "Rarely have I seen a man as angry as Roberts got," Wheelan recalled. "He called me every name in the book" (Wheelan; Bales 1989, 7).

Literary Apprenticeship

Roberts's first job after graduating from Cornell was with a Boston wholesale leather firm, where he earned $4 a week as an assistant office boy. The position, however, only succeeded in fueling his literary ambitions, as he despised his duties and low salary and detested the smell of leather (*IWW*, 12-15). Fortunately, he was able both to supplement his income and to gain some writing experience during his spare time. His first project was a series of "fairy tales" that a chair manufacturing company requested, for which he received $180, as well as praise for his writing ability: "With reference to series of Fairy Tales that you wrote for our trade papers, I would say they are entirely satisfactory to us and that our advertising agencies have complimented us on the quality of these Fairy Tales. . . . Up to the present time, we have had all our trade paper material written by men of extremely high standing in New York City so that we feel it is somewhat of a compliment to have your work accepted."[16] He next wrote "Some Cornell Professors," his humorous reminiscences of student life at his alma mater, which brought him $45 and publication in the June 1909 issue of the *Bohemian Magazine*.[17]

Roberts finally got the opportunity to write full time in late 1909, when he joined the staff of the *Boston Post* at a salary of $18 a week. At the newspaper he learned how to gather facts and organize them into a smooth-flowing and accurate story, as well as "how to ask questions about things that interested me until I understood them and got at the truth about them" (Morgan). Roberts's sense of humor was soon discovered. As he wrote years later to a close friend,

> I got my keenest pleasure out of little stories that had no news value— stories like a man losing a pair of pants on a trip to a tailor shop. . . . It has always been my contention that if you write details—little intimate details that nobody else bothers with—into a thing, you will get something that is extremely humorous. At any rate, I got something out of these stories that was unexpected, because even on crowded days, when blackjackings and piano-factory-fires were getting 600 words, my column-and-a-half stories would be run in full. . . . I never took the pleasure in big stories that I did in little ones, because I couldn't get the space to write in the little things, and then up would come the feeling that I was being dull and boring people.[18]

One day in 1911 Roberts added "little intimate details" to a story and came up with the most famous humorous character he ever created for the *Boston Post*. Asked to write an article about a 71-pound, record-breaking codfish caught off a Boston wharf, he contributed a fictitious interview with Morton Kilgallen, "the eminent authority on fish." So cleverly conceived was the Kilgallen story that many people believed the loquacious professor to be a real person. After the story appeared in the *Post*, the editor of the *New York World* sent a telegram to the paper's Boston correspondent, rebuking him for not getting the interview first. Soon the popular Kilgallen became a noted fixture in the newspaper, and Roberts timed the professor's marriage on 14 February 1911—dutifully reported in the *Post*—to coincide with his own marriage to Anna Seiberling Mosser, of the Boston suburb Roxbury.[19]

Because the daily *Boston Post* already had a humor column, titled "All Sorts," Roberts was not allowed one of his own, but during the "All Sorts" editor's vacations he was permitted "to fill his column with odds and ends of a frivolous nature" (*IWW*, 53). In early 1912 Roberts's salary jumped to $40 a week after his promotion to the *Boston Sunday Post*, where he was responsible for an entire page of humor. Calling it "All Around Boston-Town," he wrote stories, parodies, jokes, political satires, and humorous essays. He was also proficient in writing light verse, and although his humor, like that in the *Cornell Widow*, may seem outdated, the following poem, "The Unreasonable Ball-Player," from the 18 January 1914 *Boston Sunday Post* could easily have been written 75 years later:

> There was a baseball player once
>   Who made the magnates sore
> By asking them for lots of coin,
>   And smiling at their roar.
>
> "Kick in," said he, "with what I want,
>   And cause me no fatigue;
> Else I will jump your dog-goned club
>   And join the Federal league!
>
> "You see I'm human, after all,
>   And hate to take a loss:
> I care for nobody, no, not I,
>   Unless he comes across!"

Roberts admitted that although time prevented him from rewriting any of his work—material that he conceded years later to be "something pretty awful in the line of literature" (Morgan)—at least he was able to write every day on a regular basis: "It wasn't the sort of writing that I vaguely hoped to do; but it was sustained work, and it's my conviction that no one can become a writer of any standing unless he learns to drive himself incessantly and ruthlessly" (*IWW*, 56). His arduous writing schedule quickly increased, as did his salary, when he learned in 1915 that the weekly magazine *Life* welcomed submissions. Soon he was writing between 10,000 and 12,000 words a week, besides holding editorial positions on *Life* (from 1915 to 1918) and on *Puck* (1916 to 1917), as well as publishing material in *Judge*. As he recalled in 1945, "I wrote a page [for the *Boston Post*], and finally that page, as I recall it, became the repository for stuff that was rejected for *Life*, *Puck*, and *Judge*. I would spend one day a week writing for *Life*, *Puck*, and *Judge*, and what was over, when those rejection slips came back, would go into my page, plus what I wrote in the other six days of the week. Not very satisfactory" (Blackington; see also *IWW*, 59-63).

One source of Roberts's dissatisfaction was that he had not yet settled on his literary career, and another stemmed from the strain of writing so much every week. He admitted a few years later that "two years of it made me so nervous and jumpy that I would bark like a dog whenever anybody said 'Boo'!" ("Autobiography"). Because the extra income he earned in 1916 from *Life*, *Puck*, and *Judge* was more than $1,850, he felt that by working full time as a freelance writer he could still manage to support himself and his wife while he "gambled on another sort of writing—just what sort I didn't know" (*IWW*, 68). Thus in March 1917 he left the *Boston Sunday Post*, parting amiably with its editor and publisher, Edwin A. Grozier. He would never return to newspaper writing (*IWW*, 64-67).

Just as his work for the *Cornell Widow* had given him valuable experience, so had his writing for the newspaper. He had polished the techniques of working within a deadline and of fitting his material into specified column lengths. Besides general reporting, he had had ample opportunity to try his hand at a wide variety of prose and verse and was well prepared to try something new.

After leaving the *Post* Roberts and his wife moved to Kennebunk Beach, Maine, where they owned a remodeled stable, named "Stall Hall," that they had purchased from his aunt, Lucy Tibbets Russell. He continued submitting material to *Life*, *Puck*, and *Judge* and in 1917 wrote some 550 sketches, playlets, short essays, and poems, of which more than 300 were published. A brief news item in the *Boston Transcript* gave him the basic idea for his first short story, a Christmas tale about a confidence man that featured a surprise ending in the style of O. Henry. After finishing the story Roberts sent it to a New York literary agent, who immediately sold it to the *Saturday Evening Post* for $300. Shortly thereafter the magazine paid $350 for another story, increasing Roberts's income for 1917 to more than $5,000. A third story, rejected by the *Post* and other leading magazines, was eventually purchased by *Collier's* for $400.

Despite his efforts, however, many of Roberts's submissions were rejected. "I learned a lot from that hard work in 1917," he reminisced decades later. "The most important thing I learned was that I knew far too little about anything, and that I must thoroughly investigate everything about which I wanted to write, just as a reporter might cover a news story, only more exhaustively. . . . I learned that any sort of writing was the most absorbing pursuit in which I could indulge: that I'd been having too good a time, for too long a time, playing at writing, and that I couldn't delay much longer if I intended to get anywhere."[20]

World War I

In 1918 while thousands of American men enlisted in the armed forces to fight Germany, Roberts joined the army for a different reason— to gain more writing experience. Because he "was distinctly and unmistakably told that the army was urgently in need of investigators trained to collect accurate and unbiased information of a military nature, and to report it quickly," he requested a commission as a captain in military intelligence (*IWW*, 70). Soon after receiving it, he reported for duty in Washington, D.C.

Roberts soon became both amused and irritated with military life. Instead of learning military investigative techniques and writing reports, he chafed under red tape, bureaucracy, and the army's regimentation. He also had the not unusual civilian air of intellectual superiority to all things military. He and other frustrated writers formed a group they called the General Hind Quarters, which privately ridiculed the army and its operations. What particularly annoyed Roberts and his friends was the regulation forbidding personnel to write for publication under penalty of dishonorable discharge. Roberts, however, managed to circumvent this rule by writing for *Life* under the pseudonym Laurence Kane, a name whose syllables—if slurred together—are a sort of acrostic of the letters L, R, and K, Roberts's initials (*IWW*, 71-79; Kitch, 22).

But this limited writing opportunity did little to allay Roberts's bore-
dom, and when the opportunity came for service in Siberia in the
Military Intelligence Division of the American Expeditionary Force,
Roberts quickly volunteered. Just before leaving for his post in
Vladivostok, he wired George Horace Lorimer, the widely respected editor of the *Saturday Evening Post*, and inquired whether he would be interested in an article on his Siberian experiences. Replying by telegram on
13 August 1918 (Roberts received it when he returned to the United
States), Lorimer said that he was "very much interested," thus beginning
a personal and professional relationship that was to last almost two
decades.[21]

Although Roberts eventually received permission from the army to
write for publication, all his work was subject to censorship, a situation
that greatly exasperated him. As Roberts scholar John I. Kitch, Jr.,
explains,

> In Japan, his first stop on the way to Vladivostok, Roberts found things
> pleasant and the people amiable, an opinion he reversed when he arrived
> in Siberia, saw the activities of the Japanese Army there, and became con-
> vinced of Japanese expansionist designs on the Asiatic mainland. As one
> of the officers responsible for military censorship in Siberia—hardly the
> job for a censored writer—he became involved in a persistent battle with
> his superiors over censorship policy: he felt only items of military signifi-
> cance ought to be checked, while his superiors thought anything going
> out of Siberia needed censoring. He found the morale of American troops
> quite low as they sat back and watched the Bolsheviks slowly beat back
> the allied forces and the Japanese just as inevitably take over. For Roberts
> the whole Siberian campaign was a mistake, a series of blunders from the
> start. (Kitch, 23)

On 17 January 1919 Roberts received his orders to return to the
United States. On his way to San Francisco he stopped and "nosed
around Manila" to add some notes about the Philippines to those he had
already taken on Siberia, the Bolsheviks, and the Japanese. Arriving in
San Francisco, he collected his back pay as well as a $60 bonus, and on
24 March 1919 got his honorable discharge. Only then did he mail to
the *Saturday Evening Post* the article on his Siberian experiences, thereby
neatly bypassing any problems of censorship and clearance (*IWW*, 117-
25; Kitch, 24).

About a week later Roberts went to the *Post*'s offices in Philadelphia
to call on Lorimer for the first time. Much to Roberts's delight, the

editor offered him $1,000 for his 22,000-word article critical of the American army's Siberian campaign, along with a position on the magazine. Before the meeting ended Roberts had interested Lorimer in two more articles: one an account of the inept Bolshevik rule in Russia and Siberia, and another criticizing Emilio Aguinaldo and the Philippine independence movement. Lorimer also tentatively accepted a one-act play dramatizing the final hours of the Russian royal family in 1918. By early autumn the author had written several more articles for the *Post* and some shorter pieces for *Life*, resulting in an income of $7,700 during the first seven months since his return from Siberia (*IWW*, 125-27, 132).

Clearly, Roberts had found his literary niche—at least for the time being—and Lorimer's respect for him increased along with the author's published manuscripts. That both Roberts and Lorimer had made the right decisions is corroborated by a note the editor wrote to a mutual friend on 20 May 1919: "Roberts is a real one and we hope to have him in the Post often. I have three more articles by him that are coming along in early numbers."[22]

Chapter Two

"In a Sense, You Have a Roving Commission"

By the time Kenneth Roberts joined its staff, the *Saturday Evening Post*, with its steadily increasing circulation of more than 2 million, had become the largest weekly magazine in the world. As literary historian James Playsted Wood acknowledged in his *Magazines in the United States*, "It was seen and read everywhere. People came to know it as they knew their own names. Its influence was pervasive and immeasurable, spreading simultaneously in many directions."[1]

The magazine's popularity largely stemmed from its championship of American democracy, nationalism, free enterprise, and the status quo, as well as its avoidance of anything esoteric or sensational—a philosophy that neatly dovetailed with Roberts's conservative, middle-class values. This "America first" doctrine particularly found a receptive audience in the years immediately following World War I. As thousands of immigrants from war-ravaged Europe sought refuge and employment in the United States, editorial writers and other Americans complained that the influx would not only contribute to an already depressed labor market but also flood the country with undesirable barbarians.[2]

The *Post* expressed similar opinions on its editorial pages, as George Horace Lorimer was convinced that the United States could not assimilate the peoples of Europe.[3] Roberts also voiced his own xenophobic sentiments soon after his byline began appearing in the *Post*. In his article criticizing the drive for Philippine independence, for example, he referred to the Tagalogs on the island of Luzon as "illiterate, extremely superstitious, impractical, illogical, uninquisitive, unimaginative, uninventive, unresourceful."[4]

Although Lorimer did not specify in the brief note he wrote in May 1919 what made Roberts "a real one," he did soon decide that his new contributor would be the ideal person to write a series of articles on America's immigration problem. Three months after the Philippine article was published, Lorimer called Roberts to Philadelphia to give him this first major assignment, subsequently outlining his instructions in a letter dated 31 October 1919:

> The prime object of your trip is to secure a series of articles for us on immigration. Of course, it is not possible to lay out this series in any detail as it will depend entirely on the character and the abundance of the material. It should, however, be approached from two slants: First, you should get in touch with as many aliens recently returned from America as possible and get their reactions on the situation that they find at home and their intentions as to settling down in Europe or returning to America. Secondly, we want to find out to just what extent aliens are planning or hoping to emigrate to America; the causes behind their decision; whether they are going to make a stake with the idea of returning to Europe and settling down there or whether it is their plan to become citizens of the United States. Also, find out whether the larger number of these would-be immigrants hope to settle in the United States or some other country, particularly the direction that emigration from the Central Empire is likely to take and whether they will go in big numbers to Latin American countries. The character, trades and desirability of these would-be immigrants should be determined.[5]

Lorimer also asked Roberts to examine European business, political, and social conditions and to "dig up some new stuff" about Bolshevism. Although the editor carefully detailed in these instructions what he wanted, he also indicated that Roberts would have considerable latitude once overseas: "In a sense, you have a roving commission as the way in which the articles shape up and their number depend entirely on what you find from actual investigation."

The First Trip, 1919-1920

A week after he received Lorimer's letter Roberts boarded an ocean liner headed for England. From there he journeyed through Ireland and then on to the Continent—France, Germany, Poland, Austria, Czechoslovakia, Bohemia, Moravia, Hungary, Italy, Albania, and Yugoslavia—interviewing hundreds of people and working from 12 to 20 hours a day, eventually completing 13 articles that were published in the *Post* between February and October 1920. In England alone he talked with 282 persons, and his extensive notes on Britain's and Ireland's political and social conditions were the basis of his first two articles.[6]

"The Rising Irish Tide" and "How Cousin John's Getting Along" were generally favorable postwar surveys of Ireland and England. "The English," Roberts proclaimed in his second article, "are great people with whom to forgather. They speak our language, and they fight well and cleanly. They are wonderful people to do business with, because their word is as good as their bond and they are steadfast in their associations."[7]

In his essay on Ireland Roberts presented his personal feelings—and prejudices—on immigration, contrasting the characteristics of "old" and "new" immigrants. He wrote that prior to 1883 four-fifths of American immigrants were from Western Europe, with the majority able to read and write. Because they migrated to the United States with the idea of settling down and becoming American citizens, they easily assimilated into the population. Since 1883, however, nearly four-fifths of the immigrants were from Eastern and Southern Europe, with over a third unable to read or write English. Before Roberts had even visited this area of the Continent he maintained that its citizens came to the United States solely to earn as much money as possible in as short a time as possible, and then return to their respective homelands. Because they kept to themselves, spoke their own languages, preserved their own habits and customs, and read foreign language newspapers ("which in many instances have been extremely anti-American"), they proved difficult to assimilate.[8]

While Roberts singled out the Irish as "among the very best of our immigrants" ("Irish," 61), he had no use for the American "hotbeds of discontent, unrest, sedition and anarchy" in which lived the immigrants of Austria, Hungary, Bulgaria, Czechoslovakia, Greece, Italy, Yugoslavia, Poland, Portugal, Romania, Russia, Spain, and Turkey: "If the United States is the melting pot something is wrong with the heating system; for an inconveniently large portion of the new immigration floats round in unsightly indigestible lumps. Of recent years the contents of the melting pot have stood badly in need of straining, in order that the refuse might be removed and deposited in the customary receptacle for such things" ("Irish," 4).

Roberts's repugnance for Central Europe and its inhabitants is unmistakable in his *Saturday Evening Post* articles. Throughout "Schieber Land," an unfavorable report on postwar Germany, Roberts related "tales of starving Germany" and maintained that the country "is using her poorly nourished children as political propaganda to create sympathy in the outside world."[9] In "Husks" he asserted that "Austria is a husk of a country—an empty shell. The nation itself is nothing but an unnatural boundary line surrounding a mass of land insufficiently large to feed its people, and without sufficient industries to support them."[10] In "Almost Sunny Italy," which Roberts completed while sailing back to the United States, he criticized the internal confusion and turmoil in postwar Italy, sarcastically noting, for example, that "the Italian laborer has succeeded thoroughly in grasping the deep, soul-stirring joy which lies in striking and making everyone, including himself, excessively uncomfortable."[11]

In all the other countries Roberts visited only Poland and France received from him any words of commendation—Poland in particular because of its fight against the Bolsheviks. The other nations, he argued, were clearly unfit to govern themselves, and he maintained that the strikes, riots, and other symptoms of internal chaos provided ample reason for the United States to pursue an isolationist policy (Kitch, 25). His conservative viewpoint is perhaps most apparent and unqualified in "Husks," the lead article in the 1 May 1920 issue of the *Post*: "Central Europe is the greatest political, social and economic mess, with the single exception of Bolshevik Russia, that any man now living has ever seen. The situation is so fantastic and so incredible that any person who attempts to tell even a small part of it will automatically be doubted by all persons accustomed to a sane and ordered existence" ("Husks," 4).

Eight of the 13 articles Roberts wrote were later published in book form by Harper & Brothers in 1921 under the title *Europe's Morning After*.[12] As he later admitted, because "I never thought of revising the articles that had been printed in the *Post*," the book chapters vary little from the magazine versions (*IWW*, 145).

The Second Trip, 1920-1921

When Roberts docked in New York on 23 May 1920 he had not only pages of notes for his remaining articles on the postwar chaos in Europe but also material for some half-dozen articles specifically on Central European immigration. "We've got to hammer at immigration," Lorimer told him that summer, "until Washington and the country at large wake up to what's happening. Go on back again, and this time start with the emigrants at their homes and go right down to the ships with them" (*IWW*, 145). Roberts left for Europe later that year, and combed the slums of England, Scotland, France, Belgium, Holland, Poland, Italy, Turkey, and Greece for additional material for the *Post* before returning to the United States in May 1921 ("Statement," 98).

Just as Roberts's outspokenness and conservatism were hallmarks of his association with the *Cornell Widow*, so were these traits similarly recognized while he was a roving correspondent for the *Saturday Evening Post*. His first attack on unrestricted immigration was the scathing "The Goal of Central Europeans," published in the 6 November 1920 *Post*. Unlike Emma Lazarus and the Statue of Liberty, who welcomed "the wretched refuse of your teeming shore," Roberts pointedly declared that the likelihood of the United States being able to assimilate all of its immigrants "is even less than a humming bird's chances of assimilating a box of tacks."[13] Although he conceded that as individuals most of them were "hard-working, well-meaning, [and] likable," he rejoined that, when viewed collectively, "it is no more possible to make Americans out of a great many of them than it is possible to make a race horse out of a pug dog" ("Goal," 61).

Roberts also charged that because the newcomers lived and worked only with people of their own race or with other foreigners, they came in contact with virtually no Americanizing influences. Furthermore, he contended that this segregation fostered not a love of the United States but a devotion to their respective homelands: "Given a cause on which to unite, they have no hesitation in pursuing an emphatically un-American course. Many of them would be overjoyed to embroil America in a war with a foreign country if by so doing they could further the interests of the country of their origin" ("Goal," 62).

Roberts relied on his firsthand observations to buttress his arguments. In one of his most significant articles, "The Existence of an Emergency," he related how an American consulate in Warsaw, Poland, was continually besieged with "howling, fighting, frantic crowds" clamoring for visas. To accommodate the mob, the consulate set up quarters in a kosher meat market. "From half past three in the afternoon till night it is filled with yelling, shrieking butchers and meat sellers and meat buyers. Beeves hang from the hooks of movable racks and the floor is slippery with blood. From nine in the morning until three in the afternoon it is the visa office of the American consulate."[14]

In sections of the article vividly titled "Delousing Future Americans," "Professional Vermin Fighters," and "The Menace of the Filth Peril," Roberts luridly described his visit to the Troyl delousing camp near the city of Danzig, Poland. After the emigrants' arrival to the camp their baggage and outer coats were "heavily gassed in order to destroy the lice and the germs that are usually present" ("Existence," 90). Their clothes were put into boilers, "which kills the vermin in them with live steam." All men had to have their heads clipped, and they sat on chairs placed in pans filled with creosote. As Roberts graphically recounted, the clipped hair fell into the creosote, killing the head lice:

> There is always a frightful outcry at the head clipping. I have stood in the head-clipping room and heard man after man swear by all that he held near and dear that he hadn't a louse on him and had never had a louse on him, and beg the American public health officer to exempt him from having his head clipped. The officer explained to me that it wasn't neces-sary to examine them in order to prove that they were lying, but that since I was present he would do so. So he examined man after man as the protests were lodged; and on each protester he showed me one or more nits—and he never had to hunt longer than five seconds to find one. ("Existence," 93)

All emigrants had to take hot showers. "Apparently," Roberts conjec-tured unnecessarily, "it is the first bath that some of them have ever had in their lives." Many of the women, he further caustically noted, had "bathed so seldom that their skins are almost battleship gray in color" ("Existence," 93).

Roberts often corroborated his findings with the testimony of govern-ment and consular officials. One young American consular officer with tears in his eyes told him, "When I think that these people are going to America to have a voice in the future of that country, it makes me see red!"[15] When the consul general in Rotterdam told Roberts that numer-ous emigrants bound for the United States had fraudulent passports, Roberts asked if he could quote him. "'You certainly can,' said Mr. Anderson, 'if anything that I say can help to convince the people in America that the continuation of the present immigration is a very bad thing for the country and a very bad thing for the American people'" ("Existence," 94).

Roberts also relied on the theories of pseudoscientific racists. Two of the leading proponents of Nordic superiority over the inferior races were Madison Grant (*The Passing of the Great Race*, 1916) and Lothrop Stoddard (*The Rising Tide of Color against White-World Supremacy*, 1920). Roberts not only had read their books but had met both men; in fact, his arguments were occasionally just mere paraphrases of passages from their works. For example, Grant claimed in *The Passing of the Great Race* that "the Nordics are, all over the world, a race of soldiers, sailors,

adventurers, and explorers." In "Ports of Embarkation" Roberts echoed
that the Nordic people were "the world's voluntary explorers, pioneers,
soldiers, sailors and adventurers."[16]

Photographs and drawings accompanying his articles dramatized
Roberts's perception of the Central European immigrant as being
untrustworthy, lazy, dirty, and immoral; thus he felt they were totally
undesirable U.S. citizens. On the first page of "The Goal of Central
Europeans," above the caption "Rusinian Peasants," is a photograph of
five disheveled men, their clothes in shreds. Published with "Plain
Remarks on Immigration for Plain Americans" is a half-page political
cartoon of a tattered, bearded, and swarthy street peddler, identified as a
"Red" and an "Undesirable Alien." As he offers bottles labeled "100
Proof Strike," "Discontent," "Labor Trouble," and "Strife" to a skeptical
American businessman holding a briefcase bearing the word "Labor," a
stalwart policeman with "US" emblazoned on his hat and belt buckle
approaches, massive nightstick in hand. The drawing's caption: "100%
Impure."[17]

Roberts's series of immigration articles appeared in the *Saturday
Evening Post* from November 1920 to February 1922, with 11 of the articles subsequently revised and published as his second book, *Why Europe
Leaves Home*.[18] *Post* editor Lorimer not only shared Roberts's restrictionist views but publicly championed them in his magazine. Two weeks
after the *Post* featured "The Existence of an Emergency" Lorimer editori-
alized that the "Americanization" of immigrants was more of a biological
problem than a social process: "A change of air, of scene and of job cannot change the fundamental facts of heredity, and it is on these that a
race is built. . . . The trouble with our Americanization program is that
a large part of our recent immigrants can never become Americans.
They will always be Americanski—near-Americans with un-American
ideas and ideals."[19]

On 3 June 1921, less than three weeks after Lorimer railed about
"Americanski," the Three Percent Law went into effect. This temporary
quota statute stipulated that the number of aliens of any nationality
admitted into the United States from 3 June 1921 to 30 June 1922
would be limited to 3 percent of the number of foreign-born persons of
each nationality present in the United States at the time of the last
(1910) census. This would restrict European immigration to about
300,000 persons. Although Roberts conceded the Three Percent Law to
be "a pretty good law" as it reduced the number of immigrants, he contended in "Shutting the Sea Gates" that "it is no more fitted to deal with

the immigration problem than a pair of sugar tongs is fitted to handle a barge load of cannel coal."[20]

In the fall of 1921 Roberts temporarily moved to Washington, D.C., to serve as the Capitol correspondent for the *Post* (Kitch, 28). His letters indicate that he spent countless hours lobbying members of the House and Senate Committees on Immigration and Naturalization, urging them to read and endorse his articles and *Why Europe Leaves Home*. Albert Johnson, chairman of the House committee, befriended Roberts, and Johnson's private secretary of many years recalled decades later that Roberts spent nearly every day at the committee's offices while working on his *Post* articles (Higham, 313; *IWW*, 149).

Roberts's tireless lobbying on Capitol Hill (along with such Congress-bashing articles as "Lest We Forget") paid off handsomely: *Why Europe Leaves Home* was praised as "a splendid book" in a pamphlet picturing the members of the Senate Committee on Immigration and Naturalization.[21] Also, on 14 December 1921, six months after the Three Percent Law went into effect, Roberts testified as an expert witness before the House Committee on Immigration and Naturalization, relating what he had observed in Europe ("Statement," 97-106).

On 26 May 1924 President Calvin Coolidge signed the Immigration Act (the Johnson Bill), which drastically restricted immigration by reducing the nationality quota percentage from three to two, based on the 1890 census. In addition, immigration from Southern and Eastern Europe was limited. This new statute "erected a formidable wall" against foreigners, according to historian John Higham, and the restrictionists claimed a solid victory. William W. Husband, commissioner general of immigration, credited passage of the law to Roberts's works in the *Saturday Evening Post*, and given the magazine's vast circulation and the prominence accorded the articles within the *Post*'s pages, it would be difficult to argue that Roberts did not have considerable influence in shaping public opinion. Indeed, a reviewer of *Why Europe Leaves Home*, writing in the *New Republic*, complained that "Mr. Roberts' views are usually proclaimed from the columns of a magazine which insures them a greater American circulation in a week than that which, say Bertrand Russell's *Roads to Freedom* can hope to attain in ten years."[22]

"A Desire to Protect This Country"

Roberts's xenophobia and deep-seated prejudices unquestionably shaped and distorted his views on immigration restriction, although he was quick to deny this to anyone who questioned him. As he told a newspaper reporter a month after he returned from his second trip abroad, "If you print what I say, watch for the howl. . . . [People will] call me a bigot, and you know me well enough to know how absurd that is. If being an American and fighting for the people who are here now and their children constitutes bigotry, then I am a bigot."[23]

Contrary to his self-righteous indignation, however, Roberts's note-books, letters, and personal papers contain numerous derogatory comments and stereotypical observations. Italians were invariably called "wops," and he often referred to his sister-in-law's Italian husband as his "wop relative."[24] While in Yugoslavia in 1920, he recorded in his note-book that "the customs officials argued for 10 minutes over my type-writer at Longatico, the wop frontier."[25] In another notebook he protested that the "only people in Central Europe who are working and working disinterestedly and honestly are Americans. Everyone else loafing, cheating, grafting—or starving or debauching."[26]

While traveling in Mexico for a series of articles on Mexican immigrants, published in 1928, Roberts wrote in his notebook that "Mexicans are great wife-abandoners" and "all mining towns lousy with wet Mex, as is Detroit."[27] He angrily told his editor in 1937 that "I don't like Limeys."[28] In 1956 he scrawled on the title page of the German edition of one of his books, "Trust these Kraut bastards: they left out dedication, references, biblio notes and ads of other books."[29]

Roberts singled out African-Americans in his diatribes as well. Bermuda was "a good place to work," he acknowledged in 1948, "but not much good for anything else. Too many niggers: niggers too god-damned self-satisfied."[30] After reading an article in the *Post* on the Ku Klux Klan in Alabama he noted privately that the group's activities did not particularly bother him, as its members stood for the same principles that most respectable people believed in.

Anti-Semitic slurs also permeated Roberts's correspondence and other writings. While relaxing by the ocean at Kennebunk Beach one August day he recoiled with horror at seeing some Jews. Soon after the publication of *Why Europe Leaves Home*, U.S. Representative Adolph Sabath (D-Illinois), who was Jewish, protested on the House floor that the book "contains more unjustifiable, unwarranted charges and more libel than any other thing ever written by anyone who had the courage to publish it under his own name."[31] On hearing Sabath's charges, Roberts fired off an angry letter to his publisher, calling Sabath "a dirty Jew from Chi[cago]."[32]

As is evident in his *Post* essays, Roberts was essentially an apologist for his "own sort" of political and social conservatives—individuals who supported the status quo who in turn financially supported the magazine and him. His prejudices—particularly his anti-Semitism—are best summarized by John I. Kitch, Jr., in his dissertation, "From History to Fiction: Kenneth Roberts as an Historical Novelist." Kitch observed that Roberts's articles reflected the general xenophobia and nativism of the decade—fears that were unique neither to him nor the *Post*:

> The anti-Semitic tone of Roberts' statements is most likely explained by his "downeast" prejudices. Despite living in Malden, a Boston suburb, during his youth and in Boston itself when working for the newspaper, he consistently betrayed the feelings of a conservative, rural New Englander who was uncomfortable around anyone more foreign than the British. Roberts was essentially anti-foreign and evidently viewed the Jews as the most foreign, the least American, of any he had observed in Europe. Foreigners were simply not Roberts' "own people," and he could not view them dispassionately. In his desire to save his country from the hordes of Central Europe, he undoubtedly overstated his case for effect; however, in so doing he was voicing the feelings of many Americans of the period, and the desire to restrict immigration was by no means limited to the *Post*. (Kitch, 28)

Even George Horace Lorimer, as much as he endorsed the views of his roving correspondent, felt it necessary to blue-pencil much of Roberts's blatant racism. A comparison of Roberts's manuscripts and published articles reveals the numerous changes, which in turn explains why the *Post* articles differ from the versions published in *Why Europe Leaves Home*: although the articles for *Europe's Morning After* were taken directly from the pages of the *Post*, Roberts returned to his original manuscripts while working on *Why Europe Leaves Home*. Some examples that corroborate this conclusion follow.

Passage from "The Existence of an Emergency," original manuscript, Library of Congress:

> Any ordinary quarters in Warsaw are quite incapable of accommodating the howling, fighting, frantic crowds that have been known to besiege the American consulate. There is always a mob, ranging in numbers each day from one thousand to fifteen hundred; but it is seldom panic-stricken nowadays. During the Bolshevik advance in the summer of 1920, crowds of 5000 Hebrews, mad with fear of what the Bolsheviks and the Poles together might do to them and made doubly unmanageable by

their incredible and ruthless selfishness, almost wrecked the consulate repeatedly. In order to get this crowd under cover, the consulate secured an enormous cement-floored, glass-roofed market known as St. George's Bazaar.

Passage from "The Existence of an Emergency," *Saturday Evening Post*, 30 April 1921, page 89:

Any ordinary quarters in Warsaw are quite incapable of accommodating the howling, fighting, frantic crowds that have been known to besiege the American consulate. There is always a mob, ranging in numbers each day from a thousand to fifteen hundred. In order to get this crowd under cover the consulate secured an enormous cement-floored, glass-roofed market known as St. George's Bazaar.

Passage from "The Existence of an Emergency," in *Why Europe Leaves Home*, page 85:

Any ordinary quarters in Warsaw are quite incapable of accommodating the howling, fighting, frantic crowds that have been known to besiege the American consulate. During the Bolshevik advance in the summer of 1920, crowds of five thousand Jews, mad with fear of what the Bolsheviks and the Poles together might do to them, and made doubly unmanageable by their incredible and ruthless selfishness, almost wrecked the consulate repeatedly. In order to get this crowd under cover, the consulate secured an enormous cement-floored, glass-roofed market known as St. George's Bazaar.

The book version differs only slightly from Roberts's original handwritten manuscript. The second sentence in the manuscript is not present in the book because Roberts probably thought it would date the work. The word *Hebrews* in the manuscript's third sentence reads as *Jews* in *Why Europe Leaves Home*—a name change that Roberts frequently made while editing the essay for book publication. Roberts once privately complained that Lorimer refused to print the words *Jews* or *Jewish* in the *Post*, and the editor often deleted the two from his correspondent's manuscripts.

Lorimer also tempered much of Roberts's inflammatory rhetoric in "The Goal of Central Europeans." The following paragraph, while not present in the article, appears in chapter 1 of *Why Europe Leaves Home*:

Races cannot be cross-bred without mongrelization, any more than breeds of dogs can be cross-bred without mongrelization. The American nation was founded and developed by the Nordic race, but if a few more million members of the Alpine, Mediterranean and Semitic races are poured among us, the result must inevitably be a hybrid race of people as worthless and futile as the good-for-nothing mongrels of Central America and Southeastern Europe (*Why Europe Leaves Home*, 22).

The letters and records Roberts wrote during this period reveal his frustration at what he called Lorimer's "emasculation" of his articles. Although the author seldom publicly expressed his displeasure, in 1924 he made the mistake of answering a letter from a man he had befriended in Siberia during World War I. Herman Bernstein, editor of the Polish newspaper *Polish Everybody's Daily* (*Dziennick dla Wszystkich*) of Buffalo, New York, had protested Roberts's use of the word "Poles" in his article "East Is East." Roberts wrote back what he considered a personal reply, stating that it was originally "Polish Jews," but that the *Post* had changed the words to "Poles," an alteration that "made me look like an ignorant ass and rotten reporter."[33]

After Bernstein sent Roberts's letter to Lorimer and attacked both Roberts and the *Post* in his newspaper, Lorimer sent Roberts a terse note, asking if he had indeed criticized the magazine's policies. When Roberts replied that he had, a rift occurred between the two men that lasted until Roberts came to Lorimer's office to apologize (Tebbel 1948, 216-17; Cary, 115-16).

Hereafter Roberts shared his complaints with only his wife and a few close friends. One such diatribe, written to fellow *Post* contributor Julian Street, is particularly significant as it illustrates not only Roberts's prejudices and depth of his zealotry concerning immigration but also his ongoing frustration at what he considered to be the uncalled-for tampering of his manuscripts by Lorimer and the *Saturday Evening Post*:

Prof. R[obert] DeCourcy Ward of Harvard wrote recently, taking me mildly to task for going after Congressmen too hard. He has been an ardent and militant immigration restrictionist for many years. Yet he advocates pussyfooting so that the feelings of dumb Congressmen wont [*sic*] be injured. I have been trying to convince him that the only way to get respect is to hit 'em with both fists and then kick them violently in the stomach. I wont admit that a desire to protect this country against a lot of damned half-negro Italians, half-Mongol Jews and thoroughly bastardized Greeks and Levantines is selfishness or narrow-mindedness. I say that the people who want to open up to them are mush-heads; and by God if they're mush-heads, I'm not narrow-minded to buck them. Of course [the *Post*] cut out your tables. The Post cut out my tables showing that 60 percent of our present immigrants from Italy, Russia and Poland are straight morons. They cut out the stuff about 2000 and more straight idiots being admitted under the Three Percent Law, as well as the horrible results which will result from that as proved by the record of the Kallikak family. Down with everything. I get so damned mad over the whole business that I can't spit.[34]

More *Post* Assignments and Books

Roberts's conservatism, as well as his disdain for Washington, D.C. ("that fount of fat-headedness"), is evident in the other articles he wrote for the *Post* during the five years he served as the magazine's Washington correspondent (*IWW*, 162, 175). "Pepper," for example, was a favorable feature story on the U.S. senator with "common sense," George Wharton Pepper of Pennsylvania. President Calvin Coolidge received high praise for "his sincerity, his honesty, his modesty, his reliability, [and] his determination to do what is right." Conversely, Roberts ticked off numerous weaknesses of the House of Representatives in his "The Troubles of the House," and particularly stressed that most congressmen were "boobs," "boneheads," "animated windbags," "small-bore politicians," and "perfect specimen[s] of the dodo family."

In "The Tribulations of the Senate" Roberts focused on the "boring ability" of U.S. senators, a skill he found especially annoying and one he vowed never to emulate. Thus 11 years after he left Washington, when asked to give a speech discussing his latest book, *Northwest Passage* (1937), he replied, "Long addresses are things that I have consistently refused to make ever since the days when I sat in the Senate press gallery and heard senators talk for hours on end about nothing. I made up my mind at that time that no matter what happened, I'd never behave like a senator."[35]

Some of his articles were diatribes against liberals, reformers, and other progressives, such as "Retrogressives and Others," "The Progressives—What They Stand for and Want," and "The Common-Sense Serum." Still others criticized sacred cows on Capitol Hill that Roberts considered to be notable examples of governmental inefficiency and waste. "Senators and What-Not" lambasted pork barreling, "Filibusters" criticized the time-honored practice of filibustering, and

"Done in the District of Columbia" ridiculed his "fat-headed" Washington, D.C. Perhaps his most significant contribution to political satire was the creation of politician David Augustus Flack, the practical and judicious ex-minister to Bessarabia who acted as Roberts's alter ego and spokesman on public issues.[36]

By the spring of 1923 Roberts was so tired of the "tumult, turmoil, waste, constant telephone ringing and political ineffectuality of Washington" (*IWW*, 151) that he pleaded with Lorimer to send him to Europe for a change of pace. Lorimer agreed to do so and assigned him to obtain some additional material on immigration and to investigate the spread of fascism in Italy and Germany.

Although Roberts labeled Benito Mussolini a "highly offensive character" in his 1949 literary autobiography (*IWW*, 153), in 1923 he wrote a series of articles in which he lauded the Italian Fascisti movement as anti-Communist and an inevitable reaction against left-wing politics and anarchy. (He slightly revised these four articles and published them with two other *Post* essays a year later in his 1924 book, *Black Magic*).[37]

In his first article, "The Ambush of Italy," Roberts described the "intolerable condition" of Italy prior to the advent of "common sense" and the Fascisti movement. In his second, "The Fight of the Black Shirts," he defended Mussolini's dictatorship of Italy and commended his rabid nationalism, strength, and integrity. Roberts told *Post* readers that "there has never been a word uttered against his absolute sincerity and honesty. Whatever the cause on which he is embarked, he is a natural-born leader and a gluttonous worker."[38] Roberts also presented a sympathetic account of the governmental system's beginnings:

> Fascism wasn't started by Mussolini, properly speaking. It was largely a state of mind, and it started by itself. It was the opposite of wild ideas, of lawlessness, of injustice, of cowardice, of treason, of crime, of class warfare, of special privilege; and it represented square dealing, patriotism and common sense—particularly the sort of common sense that saw what needed to be done and then went ahead and did it without hedging, dodging or delaying. ("Fight," 162)

Roberts's misconceptions of fascism are understandable; he was not a fascist himself, but his innate conservatism, coupled with his disgust of the political chaos in post–World War I Europe and the "socialists, communists, anarchists, [and] syndicalists" in Italy ("Fight," 19), prompted him to support Mussolini because of the seeming stability, efficiency, and prosperity he brought to the country. Ironically, in his article "Suds,"

Roberts dismissed Hitler as a loud braggart and a mere "talker" and contended that his Bavarian Fascisti "bears almost the same relation to Mussolini's Italian Fascisti that a last year's duck's egg bears to a golf ball."

In 1927 Lorimer sent Roberts back to Italy to meet with Mussolini so that he could ghostwrite Il Duce's autobiography for the *Post*. Roberts, who was skeptical of the proposal from the beginning, was not surprised when the project fell through. The trip was worthwhile, however, in that he saw firsthand the effects of Mussolini's empire building, and after his return to the United States he wrote of the eye-opening experience to his close friend, U.S. Vice President Charles G. Dawes: "I had a terrible trip to Italy. . . . The Fascisti government, as it has worked out, is the sourest and most dangerous thing that I have ever seen. I was a great enthusiast for him and his methods when I wrote the story in 1923; but I'm harder agin [*sic*] him and his rotten damned government at the present time than I've ever been agin anything."[39]

The year 1923 also saw the publication of Roberts's first book that was not a collection of his *Saturday Evening Post* articles. Roberts and Lorimer were both antique collectors and together they often scoured out-of-the-way shops and barns for glass, porcelain, Early American furniture, and other items. Roberts occasionally wrote humorous articles about antique collecting for the *Post* and one of them, "A Tour of the Bottlefields," memorialized a lengthy antique-hunting expedition made by the two men and two of their friends.[40]

On the appearance in the 21 January 1922 *Post* of "Notes on an Antique Weevil" Houghton Mifflin publisher Roger L. Scaife wrote Roberts, complimented him on the article, and suggested that he write a spoof of antique collecting. Roberts liked the idea, and he replied that as soon as he finished some work on *Why Europe Leaves Home* for Bobbs-Merrill and completed a few articles for the *Post* he would start the book, enlisting the aid of his friends, fellow *Post* contributors Booth Tarkington and Hugh MacNair Kahler. As he concluded in his letter, "What you want, I suppose, is the nut who goes mad over an old Colonial pump and places it in the middle of his living-room merely because it is old and Colonial."[41]

Because *The Collector's Whatnot* was not intended to be a serious work the three men used pseudonyms. Roberts resurrected his old friend from the *Boston Post*, Milton Kilgallen, and gave him a brother named Morton to be one of the "authors." Tarkington adopted the name Cornelius Obenchain Van Loot and Kahler became Murgatroyd Elphinstone.

The volume's preface (written by Roberts) clearly indicates that the men intended the book to be a burlesque on antiques. The first paragraph recognizes that "the American Academy for the Popularization of Antiquities was formed on February 14, 1911 [Roberts's wedding day], by Eben S. Twitchett, B.B.S., Cornelius Obenchain Van Loot, D.A., C.O.J., Raymond L. Pry, A.B., A.M., S.I.W., and Professor Milton Kilgallen, F.R.S., of Balliol College. The present volume is largely made up of the papers delivered by these distinguished pedants before their equally distinguished society."[42]

Besides the preface, *The Collector's Whatnot* contains seven chapters, of which Roberts wrote "The Secret of Success" and "The European Field." Roberts was also responsible for the concluding eight pages of farcical advertisements titled "Other Books for the Antique-Lover." These ads are especially humorous because they feature excerpts from fanciful reviews. C. Von Whistelberry's *Autographs and Antimacassars*, for example, received this review from the *Sunday School Times*: "This would make a charming and welcome gift for children who are just old enough to learn about and be interested in forging and other autograph features" (*CW*, [153]).

The Collector's Whatnot is further enhanced by photographs and Tarkington's ink sketches. The caption beneath a photograph of a statue of a bearded man (actually a small statue of Ulysses S. Grant owned by the Kahler family) notes that the monument was "erected to Professor Kilgallen in Floral Park City, Florida, by grateful citizens of that community" (*CW*, opp. 42). One line drawing showing ordinary garden and hand tools is labeled "Professor Kilgallen's magnificent collection of early American utensils, all hand-wrought, and some obtained from the descendants of the families in which the articles had been handed down from father to son" (*CW*, opp. 81).

When Houghton Mifflin proposed publishing a second edition of *The Collector's Whatnot*, Roberts wrote the firm that he, Tarkington, and Kahler were "all willing to have our names used for publicity, but we don't care to have them put on the title page."[43] Thus the new edition, published in 1928, revealed on the dust jacket (and only on the dust jacket) that Van Loot, Kilgallen, and Elphinstone were "better known as—Booth Tarkington, Kenneth L. Roberts, and Hugh M. Kahler."

The identification of the three authors did not notably increase sales of the book, and Roberts admitted that both editions "followed the pattern of [my] previous books by selling 3,782 copies" (*IWW*, 152). He evidently felt, however, that there was strong public interest in the

book's subject, for in 1928 he, Tarkington, and Kilgallen again collabo-
rated on a book—the humorous *Antiquamania: The Collected Papers of
Professor Milton Kilgallen*, "with further illustrations, elucidations and
wood-cuts done on feather-edged boards by Booth Tarkington."
Although Roberts is noted as the editor of the volume he was, in fact,
the author; the book includes some of his revised *Saturday Evening Post*
articles on antique collecting, as well as a few original pieces.[44]

Roberts continued to write for the *Saturday Evening Post* throughout
the 1920s and, as was his practice, occasionally focused a series of articles
around one subject. In 1924 he traveled throughout the southwestern
United States, producing such articles as "Patient Pimas," "Navaho
Land," "Fruits of the Desert," and "First Families of America." Although
in these articles he praised the intelligence, efficiency, and strong work
ethic of America's native Americans, he had few words of commendation
for the Mexican immigrants who were profiled in another series four
years later. "Wet and Other Mexicans," his first of the three articles,
included other stereotypical observations and comments besides the one
in its title: "Some say that [the Mexican peon] is naturally dirty and gets
a bath twice during his lifetime—once when he is born and once when
he dies. Others say that he is naturally clean. . . . Some believe that he
responds quickly to schooling; others are equally sure that his dumbness
in educational matters can scarcely be exceeded by that of the water
buffalo."[45]

Another *Post* series focused on the Florida real-estate boom of the
1920s. The state's rapid population growth began in the 1890s after
railroad construction opened up the southern part of the state. The
drainage of the Everglades, begun in 1907, drew more people, and the
advent of Henry Ford's automobile suddenly enabled countless middle-
class Americans to enjoy winter vacations far from snow. After the state
ratified an amendment in November 1924 prohibiting income and
inheritance taxes investors particularly found Florida attractive. Not surprisingly, therefore, nationwide high-pressure advertising by newspapers,
businesses, and chambers of commerce seduced thousands of speculators.

Lorimer sent Roberts to Florida to investigate the land boom, and in
"Florida Loafing," published in the 17 May 1924 *Post*, he dazzled readers
by recounting success stories of those who had profited in the speculative
frenzy. He was quick however, to point out the risks involved:

> The great danger of relating these glittering stories of sudden riches that
> have been acquired in Florida real estate lies in the fact that persons with

small capital in many parts of the North, without any knowledge whatever of Florida conditions, may pick up the idea that they can rush to Florida, drop all their money into the first thing that is offered to them and meet with nothing but success. Many persons, lured by talk of quick returns and large crops, have sunk all their savings into Florida farmlands or real-estate projects that were insufficiently developed. Sometimes this land has been under water. Sometimes it has been shrouded in palmetto scrub and jungle, which is about as easy to clear—for an inexperienced agriculturist without resources—as for a Filipino to clear a twenty-acre polar tract of snow and ice with a bolo.[46]

"Florida Loafing" was expanded and published in hardcover the following year. Between December 1925 and February 1926 Roberts wrote six more articles on the state's wildcat real-estate speculation that were also published in book form.[47] Although he boasted in *I Wanted to Write* that "the articles in the *Post* had hastened the collapse of the Florida boom" (*IWW*, 175), numerous business executives and dozens of publications had predicted as early as mid-1925 that the land bubble would soon explode. In August that year railroad lines needing to make urgent repairs to their tracks declared an embargo on all construction materials, and mother nature delivered the boom's knock-out punch on 18 September 1926 with a hurricane that devastated the southeast Florida coast.[48]

Although Roberts continued to write part time for the *Saturday Evening Post* for another decade, he decided it was time to leave his position as the magazine's roving correspondent. "By mid-1924," he recalled in *I Wanted to Write*, "I could see that I was making no progress—except financially" (*IWW*, 165). His choice of literary careers would be a dramatic departure from his previous writing experiences, one that would establish a new international reputation for him.

Chapter Three

"I Want to Do Lasting Pictures"

Kenneth Roberts's *Saturday Evening Post* articles brought him financial success as well as worldwide recognition. In 1924 editor George Horace Lorimer raised his salary from $1,500 for each article to $1,750 (*IWW*, 166), giving him an annual income of $26,500 that year and $32,400 the following year (as compared with about $2,500 in 1917).

Despite these rewards, however, Roberts no longer enjoyed working for the magazine. Not only did Lorimer continue to edit his manuscripts, but occasionally he rejected some commissioned articles outright while offering no assistance on how they could be improved. Roberts also resented having to stay in Washington instead of being allowed to gather material abroad for articles of an international nature. He consequently suffered long bouts of depression, unable to concentrate on his writing. In late summer 1926, a few days before he and Lorimer left together on an antique-hunting expedition, Roberts vented his discontent to his close friend, Ben Ames Williams: "I hope that my disposition during the coming winter will be adjusted on this trip, and that I shall find out whether I am to be sold into slavery in Washington again, or sent to foreign parts for a further broadening of the mind."[1]

Roberts was not surprised when Lorimer did not award him the sought-after trip to Europe, but by this time he was determined to abandon article writing and become a novelist, a career he had contemplated ever since his graduation from Cornell. In 1919, for example, he thought about writing a book about spies in Siberia (*IWW*, 132). While employed as the *Post*'s Capitol correspondent, Roberts envisioned a novel based on his Washington experiences, and in 1925 he considered writing a sweeping historical work, one that would begin with the Louisburg expedition in 1745 and conclude with Benedict Arnold's march to Quebec with New England and Virginia troops in 1775. Unfortunately, his magazine assignments prevented all three of these plots from progressing past the outline stage.[2]

By the mid-1920s, however, Roberts knew that he wanted to incorporate the experiences of several of his ancestors in a novel. In his youth he had often asked family members about his forebears, who had emigrated from Stratford, England, to Kittery, Maine in 1639. Although many had played prominent roles in the development of the United States, none of the relatives Roberts talked to knew much about them or their exploits. Fiercely proud of his Maine heritage, Roberts not only wanted to research and immortalize his family but also capture a sense of New England history that was swiftly disappearing. In 1931, soon after the publication of *The Lively Lady*, Roberts reflected on this sense of pride that encouraged him to launch a career as a historical novelist while at the zenith of his profession as a *Post* correspondent:

There was another thing I was extremely anxious to do in these books . . . and that was to preserve the speech, the events, the customs and the appearance of this section of New England—and you have no idea how rapidly those things are vanishing. . . . These coastal ship-building, ship-captain towns of Maine were pretty hot stuff in the old days, and so were the people in them. . . . I have bundles of letters written from foreign ports by greatuncles [*sic*], greataunts, etc.: ship-captains and their wives. They're grand: beautiful things: colloquial: chatty: splendid letters. Yet knowledge of those days has been almost completely lost. You have to travel all over hell's kitchen to find anyone who knows what they did and how they did it. Knowledge of the Maine Indians has been long lost. Knowledge of Maine's shipbuilding days has practically gone. Here's a case in point: My greatgrandfather was sailing master of a privateer out of Arundel in the War of 1812. He was captured, with his entire crew: sent first to Halifax, and then to Dartmoor. The whole crew came from Arundel—the whole damned crew. In the town today there are hundreds of people descended from the crew of that vessel. Not one of them—not *one* of them—knew that their ancestors had been captured and sent to Dartmoor. When I was a boy, my grandmother told me just once that my greatgrandfather had been in Dartmoor prison. That was all I knew. Nobody else in the family knew about it. I tried to look up his record and couldn't find it in the Navy list or the Canadian list. I turned Gen. [Charles G.] Dawes loose on it, and with the assistance of the Superintendant [*sic*] of Public Records in England he was located on the Dartmoor entry books, together with the entire crew of the privateer. . . . And not one of their descendants here in Kennebunkport knew a damned thing about it.

. . . I want to do lasting pictures of early days in the section I know about, and of the people of those days, and I want the pictures to be something more than just ordinary romances in which the feller marries the girl.[3]

How Historical Novels Suited Roberts

Roberts's writing experiences, coupled with his personality, illustrate that his decision to write historical fiction was a natural choice for him. The genre did not limit him; it fit him perfectly.

As longtime friend Herbert Faulkner West recalled in 1962, by the time Roberts left the *Post* he was "an accurate reporter" who "had become a craftsman through long years of writing."[4] His various positions on the *Cornell Widow*, the *Boston Post*, *Life*, *Puck*, and *Judge* had given him valuable experience with various types of writing, including short stories, essays, poems, humorous anecdotes, and playlets. By 1929 he had written some 165 feature articles for the *Saturday Evening Post* and some 30 editorials and brief biographical sketches for the magazine's "Who's Who—and Why" column (Kitch, 32).

Although Roberts had never written a novel or other lengthy work, he was familiar with journalistic research techniques and had always striven to follow the tenet of the *Boston Post*, a directive emblazoned on signs in the newspaper's city room in 80-point-type capital letters: "ACCURACY, ACCURACY, ACCURACY" (*IWW*, 26). Thus a fidelity to fact and historical events complemented both his abilities as a researcher and his integrity as a reporter.

Roberts's life-long conservatism and adherence to New England "down east" traditions stimulated his desire to write about Maine and his ancestors. Even a cursory reading of his *Saturday Evening Post* articles confirms the high regard Roberts ("a dyed-in-the-wool Maine conservative," according to Herbert Faulkner West) placed on middle-class values (West 1962, 91).

For example, in "The Existence of an Emergency" Roberts contended that "starting around 1880 the immigrants who swarmed into the United States were of an entirely different breed from the people who had discovered the country, colonized it, made its laws and developed it" ("Existence," 3). In "A Patient Waiter" he attributed the effectiveness of Commissioner General of Immigration William W. Husband to "one of those New England upbringings that seem to coat the possessor with a sort of adamantine varnish that offers no point of entry or exit for free verse, garrulousness, unwise money spending, loose thinking or kindred barbed irritants."[5]

Just as Roberts's "capacity for indignation" (his "most conspicuous trait" according to Ben Ames Williams)[6] proved to be a principle motivator behind his newspaper and magazine writing, so would this characteristic and his resolute nonconformity determine to some degree the subjects of his historical novels. In a 1945 interview, when asked why he chose in his books to write about certain types of people, Roberts replied, "I am not interested in the guy that has been fried, baked, and embalmed in a thousand ways, probably correctly. Now if they [authors] have done it correctly, why cut in on another fellow's field? . . . Certain things interest me. A fellow that has been a stinker [Tobias Lear, *Lydia Bailey*] interests me very much, or a fellow who has got a bum deal [Benedict Arnold, *Arundel* and *Rabble in Arms*] interests me very much" (Blackington).

This same indignation helped motivate Roberts to write novels based on true historical events, correcting the errors he found in history books. When he began researching the military campaigns in which his ancestors and other Arundel residents participated, he discovered that none of the works he read contained the details he wanted, and all of them were boring, unimaginative, and inaccurate:

> I had tried to get some of these things straightened out in my mind by reading histories that purported to explain them; but in every case—not in most cases, but in *every* case—I found that the books explained nothing fully or satisfactorily. They were drab, dull, unconvincing, rich in omissions, and crowded with statements that couldn't possibly be true. The people in them were generals and statesmen and important personages: cardboard people, flat, unreal, bloodless, lifeless, behaving without rhyme or reason. The little people like my great-great-grandfathers and all those other men from Maine, who sailed the ships and stopped the bullets and cursed the rotten food and stole chickens and wanted to get the hell out of there and go home—they just didn't exist at all." (*IWW*, 167)

Roberts's disdain for the "cardboard people" in history books was also reflected in his contempt of historical fiction. "I have always had a profound aversion to most historical novels," he wrote in *I Wanted to Write*, "because the people in them aren't real people, and neither act nor talk like anyone I've ever known" (*IWW*, 168). In March 1932, for instance, he stopped reading Harold Frederic's *In the Valley* (1890), a novel about the Revolutionary War's Battle of Oriskany, "when I encountered a love passage in which the hero explains how pure he is, not even allowing himself to touch the heroine's skirt. I wish it could be distinctly understood that I do *not* write historical novels" (*IWW*, 233).

In 1935 after he had published four works of fiction, Roberts explained to a friend that this desire to write books that were realistic, historically accurate, and enjoyable to read both inspired him to begin to write novels and encouraged him when he became depressed and felt like quitting: "It was the realization of the slovenly manner in which these things had been treated in history that made me willing to go ahead, and that kept me working when I was damned near dead from discouragement" (Letter to Leonard, 27 November 1935).

As Sylvia Choate Whitman observed in her master's thesis, historical novels "not only maximized [Roberts's] strengths, but [they] minimized his weaknesses" (Whitman 1989, 84, 65). As a journalist Roberts had never been overly concerned about establishing a narrative to his reportage, and as a novelist he admitted that he had difficulties working out characterization and plot. Soon after he began publishing novels he acknowledged that "the stuff might be badly written, might be dull, [and] might fail in character-work" (Letter to Leonard, 27 November 1935). In 1928, during an unsuccessful attempt with Ben Ames Williams to write a play, he made it clear that he depended on his friend to come up with a story line: "You, of course, are a dirty bum not to give me a plot idea. You are old John D. Plot himself, while plots are as alien to me as is diplomacy or fly-casting."[7]

Also, while Roberts had the journalist's ability to research his articles, he seldom viewed any issue from more than one perspective, and he rarely scrutinized his data to find the significance of the facts he had uncovered. He seldom rewrote his articles, and his journalistic style and syntax were by no means adaptable to those needed by a novelist. Furthermore, his articles were frequently cluttered with "cute" expressions and comparisons. In one of his immigration articles, for example, he wrote that "an ostrich could assimilate a croquet ball or a cobble stone with about the same ease that America assimilated her newcomers from Central and Southeastern Europe" ("Goal," 12).

Roberts was able to offset these weaknesses, however, when he began researching and writing novels. He obtained plots and other story lines from historical events, and he drew on local histories and genealogies for suitable characters. By researching in both secondary and primary sources, he was able to examine the past from a historian's perspective, and through constant revision he acquired a tighter, more polished writing style.

Arundel

The *Saturday Evening Post*'s purchase of his first short story, "Good Will and Almond Shells," in 1917 largely inspired Roberts to contemplate writing historical fiction ("Truth," 29). He was further encouraged a year later by the former president, Theodore Roosevelt. After Roosevelt admitted in an interview that he could not recall either the title or author of a book he had read, Roberts in reply wrote a poem that was published in the 13 April 1918 issue of the *New York Evening Sun*. In "To Col. Roosevelt, a Letter of Protest" Roberts humorously argued that an author's works cannot sell unless the reading public is familiar with both the titles and the writer's name:

> *And if you, sir, forget these things,*
>   *Won't lesser minds forget them also?*
> *Indeed they will! 'Tis that which stings,*
>   *And stirs my gall so!*
>
> *So, speaking for the writing crew,*
>   *I pray that henceforth you'll be heeding*
> *The author and the title too*
>   *Of what you're reading.*[8]

Ethel Derby, Roosevelt's daughter, read the verses to him and asked about the book he had recently finished. As she wrote to Roberts two days later, he did manage to recall its plot, and she deduced that the volume was Louis Vance's *The Lone Wolf* (1914), which her father "rapturously acknowledged to be the correct title" (Beith, 11).

An exchange of letters led to a meeting between the two men. Roberts confided that he wanted to write historical novels set in Maine but could not afford to stop working to do all of the necessary research, let alone complete the actual writing of the books. Roosevelt, a writer himself, reportedly replied to him, "I want to see those books written! I'll provide you with a ton of material. I'm going to watch you until you write those books. I want to have some more talks with you about them" (Beith, 11).

Unfortunately, subsequent conversations were never held, as the would-be novelist enlisted in the army a few months after the two men's initial meeting, and by the time he received his discharge, Roosevelt had died. Throughout Roberts's writing career, however, he remained grateful to the former president for his advice and support. In 1931, for instance, he told his friend Julian Street that he got the idea for his first novel "back in the days of Roosevelt *pere*, because he encouraged me tremendously. I'd been reading reference books for years" (Letter to Street, 1931?).

Roberts's reference books and other resource material for his novel focused on one of the major campaigns during the first year of the American Revolution: Benedict Arnold's ill-fated expedition through the Maine and Canadian wilderness to capture Quebec. Roberts had originally intended to include in this book the 1745 siege of Louisburg on Cape Breton Island (in which several of his forebears had participated) but soon realized that the Arnold expedition was worth a story in itself and decided to confine the novel to that alone (*IWW*, 182; "Truth," 29).

Roberts's ancestors, however, would still figure prominently in the novel. His maternal great-great-grandfather, Edward Nason, and several other men from the town of Arundel, Maine (now Kennebunkport), had accompanied Arnold to Quebec. Another resident of Arundel, though not a Revolutionary soldier, was Stephen Harding, a well-known Maine woodsman whom Roberts had read about in local histories. Roberts wanted to tell the story of the Canadian expedition from the viewpoint of one resident of this Maine village; thus by blending the characteristics of Edward Nason and Stephen Harding he created Steven Nason, his book's protagonist and narrator. Because the novel would also describe the lives and experiences of the town's citizens, he named it *Arundel*.[9]

By 1926 Roberts was devoting most of his spare time to research for his book, but he still needed an "escape from city turmoil, summer vacationers, idlers, politicians and cocktail parties" (*IWW*, 176). He found such a location in 1927. While on a fruitless trip to Italy to ghostwrite Mussolini's autobiography for the *Post*, he visited his sister-in-law and her husband, an Italian doctor and head of the San Gallicano Hospital in Rome. In the summer the couple lived in a nineteenth-century stone farmhouse on 15 acres of land on a hilltop near Porto Santo Stefano, a small fishing village on the Tuscan coast, halfway between Rome and Leghorn and abreast of the southern tip of Elba.

This was an ideal setting for an author, Roberts realized, a place "where there are no telephones, no automobiles, no golf links, no bridge players, no friends to drop in for a weekend—not even anyone who speaks English" ("Truth," 98). He also knew that living expenses in Italy would be less than in the United States (a major factor as he was considering giving up the *Post*'s lucrative salary), and his in-laws agreed that if he had a wing built onto the house he and his wife could spend every winter there.[10]

Ironically, Roberts wrote his series on Mexican immigrants to pay for the L-shaped addition to his new Italian home. After the articles were completed in the spring of 1928 he told Lorimer that he wanted to leave the *Post* to begin work full time on his novel. Although the editor viewed the prospect of losing one of his leading contributors with little enthusiasm, he wished Roberts good luck, telling him that if he ever needed money, "we'll work out some light papers and a few side trips for you from time to time" (*IWW*, 181).

By mid-1928 Roberts had collected some 70 reference works for his book, including histories of the American Revolution; biographies of Benedict Arnold and related diaries, journals, documents, and letters; research material relating to the Abenaki Indians; and histories of many Maine towns. He had also followed Arnold's path to Quebec several times, using the journals of the men who had accompanied the military leader as guidebooks. With most of the research completed, Roberts began to outline his novel (*IWW*, 183-84; *Trending*, 305-6, "Truth," 98).

Before he started writing, however, he turned to his Kennebunkport neighbor, Booth Tarkington, whom he had met in 1919 after returning to Maine following his World War I service. Tarkington—16 years older than Roberts—was by the late 1920s at the height of his literary career, having written some three dozen works, including *The Gentleman from Indiana* (1899), *Monsieur Beaucaire* (1900), *Penrod* (1914), *Penrod and Sam* and *Seventeen* (1916), *The Midlander* (1923), and his two Pulitzer Prize–winning novels, *The Magnificent Ambersons* (1918) and *Alice Adams* (1921). On 4 September 1928 while Roberts and his wife were having dinner at the Tarkington home, Roberts mentioned that he had been having problems outlining the plot of his novel. "You'd better tell me something about it," Tarkington modestly replied. "I've had a little experience at working out plots" (*IWW*, 182).

Roberts began discussing his book with him, and from then until Tarkington's death in 1946, the older author was Roberts's literary mentor, advisor, critic—and probably closest friend. Not only did Tarkington help Roberts with the story line of *Arundel* before he began writing it, but in the summer of 1929, after Roberts completed the first draft, Tarkington substantially aided him in revising the manuscript. Later that summer he helped Roberts plan his next three novels and assisted him with subsequent books as well. In fact, Tarkington spent so many evenings editing *Northwest Passage* (1937) that Roberts offered him joint authorship and half the royalties. Although Tarkington refused to consider the idea, Roberts showed his appreciation by dedicating the book to him, just as he had dedicated *Rabble in Arms* (1933) and would later inscribe *Oliver Wiswell* (1940).[11]

As his biographer observed, Tarkington's patient assistance while the younger author struggled with his first novel was particularly unselfish of him, as during these months he was coping with his own problems. Since the early 1920s cataracts had increasingly impaired his vision, and by the end of 1928 he could barely see at all. Thus, while Tarkington was generously helping Roberts make the transition from nonfiction to fiction by listening to chapters of *Arundel* being read aloud, he was also anxiously learning to dictate his prose so he could continue his own literary career.

In the summer of 1930 Tarkington lost what little vision he had left. As James Woodress wrote in *Booth Tarkington: Gentleman from Indiana*, however, the novelist's thoughts were on Roberts's new book: "While Mrs. Tarkington made hurried arrangements for a special [railroad] car to rush her husband to Baltimore [for eye operations], Tarkington put aside his own despair and concerned himself with Roberts' problems. The last thing he did before leaving Kennebunkport for Johns Hopkins, Roberts remembers, was to dictate suggestions for using material cut out of *The Lively Lady*" (Woodress 1954, 277; see also *IWW*, 205).

Tarkington provided friendship as well as literary assistance, and the two men, both political conservatives, often socialized together. One of Roberts's close friends once remarked that a clear father-son relationship existed between the men and that Tarkington might have been the father that Roberts had seldom recognized (Kitch, 76). In any case, throughout his life Roberts gratefully acknowledged the help and encouragement the more established author unfailingly gave him. The year after *Arundel* was published he wrote to a mutual friend, "I doubt that I'd have got at [the book] when I did if it hadn't been for Booth, who saw the chances in ARUNDEL at once, and kept at me and kept at me until I'd started: then guided me until I'd got the thing to moving properly. What I'd have done without him I don't know: nothing, I guess."[12]

Besides helping him with his manuscript, Tarkington introduced Roberts to the publisher of his own books, Russell Doubleday, of Doubleday, Doran & Company. In December 1928 Roberts gave the first six chapters of *Arundel* to Doubleday, who in return handed him a $1,000 advance and a contract. Later that month Roberts finished a series of articles on American colleges for the *Post*, and with the remodeling of his new retreat completed, he sailed with his wife to Italy. As he jubilantly wrote to his friend, Vice President Charles G. Dawes, "Having disposed of the college series with fair success, I am taking my book in hand, one-fifth finished, and beating it to our Italian hill-top with 87 tons of reference books."[13]

Roberts arrived in Porto Santo Stefano on 10 January 1929 and for nearly four months wrote—and revised—most of *Arundel*, with his wife typing the manuscript after the third longhand revision. They left Italy the first week of May, and Roberts finished the book in Maine three weeks later, on the twenty-fourth. By the middle of June he had revised the book a fourth time, and after Tarkington returned from Indianapolis to his summer home in Kennebunkport on 16 June the two men revised it again, completing the task on the twenty-seventh. The final manuscript was sent to the publisher the following day (*IWW*, 187-91; "Truth," 98, 102).

In *Arundel*'s prologue narrator Steven Nason, of the town of Arundel, Maine, informs the reader that he intends to "set down the truth, as I saw it, of certain occurrences connected in various ways with this neighborhood."[14] Before he proceeds, however, he relates how his family came to Arundel and discusses his ancestors, parents, and other family members. Nason reports that his father, born in Wells, Maine, was by the age of 17 a skilled blacksmith, gunsmith, and hunter. He was also a trader, well respected for his honesty by the local Indians. He had built a log garrison house in Arundel at the mouth of the Arundel River that served as a home for the Nason family, an inn for weary travelers, and, in times of peril, a fort for all.

Nason describes in minute detail his family farm, their inn and blacksmith shop, the ferry they operated at the mouth of the river, the nearby ocean, and the town and its residents. "The truth," he affirms, "is I love the place; and if I seem to talk overmuch of it, it is because I would like those who read about it to see it as I saw it, and to know the sweet smell of it and to love it as I do" (*Arundel*, 7). Here Roberts makes it clear that the book's episodes will be told from the viewpoint of a young Maine native who participated in them. Not so evident to the reader, however, is that because Roberts researched local histories, family genealogies, and other primary sources, much of his novel is based on actual history.

We see Roberts's use of history in comparing passages from *Arundel* with sections from the reference works the author consulted. For example, this is Roberts's explanation of why Benjamin Nason, Steven

Nason's grandfather, moved from Kittery, Maine, to Wells: "In order to obtain a blacksmith, the town of Wells, in 1670, sent to my grandfather a paper, which I still have in my small green seaman's chest, guaranteeing him two hundred acres of upland and ten acres of marsh if he would settle in Wells within three months, remain there for five years, and do the blacksmith work for the inhabitants for such current pay as the town could produce" (*Arundel*, 4). This sentence, neatly woven into Nason's introductory comments, is derived from a biographical sketch of Stephen Harding appearing in Daniel Remich's *History of Kennebunk* (1911), which begins, "Harding, Stephen, was the son of Israel Harding, to whom the town of Wells, September 12, 1670, granted two hundred acres of upland and ten acres of marsh, on condition that he should come into Wells, as an inhabitant, within three months, continue as such five years and do the blacksmith work for the inhabitants 'for such currant [*sic*] pay as the town doath produce.'"

Remich's Harding and Roberts's Nason possess other similar characteristics. Remich noted that Harding "built a garrison house sufficiently large to enable him to entertain travelers; also a blacksmith's shop. He was a man of powerful frame, an excellent marksman, a hunter, shrewd and dauntless, and of course was regarded as a most valuable citizen by his townsmen" (Remich, 518-19; see also Bradbury, 99-100; *Trending*, 70-72).

The nine chapters of *Arundel*'s book 1 cover events of September and October 1759, and as Roberts relates the experiences of Steven Nason during these two months he sets in motion incidents that 16 years later will take Nason and Benedict Arnold to Quebec. In this section Roberts also introduces a number of historical and fictitious characters, including Mary Mallinson, who kisses young Steven Nason on his twelfth birthday, promptly inspiring him to fall in love with her. Because of his infatuation with Mary, neighbor Phoebe Marvin teases Nason unmercifully throughout the book, and while the reader early on suspects that Steven will eventually marry this "girl next door," the youth affirms that he "had long misliked the girl Phoebe, who was noisy and previous, dark and thin and so quick in her jumping about that one never knew where she was" (*Arundel*, 4/43).

The major antagonist in *Arundel* is the dark and sinister Henri Guerlac de Sabrevois, whom Roberts modeled after a Canadian French official named Jacques Charles de Sabrevois (Kitch, 109). A villain almost as devious is the Reverend Ezekiel Hook, who pretends to be a

Boston missionary sent into the woods to convert Indians to Christianity but who is actually a British spy named John Treeworgy.

One of Roberts's most memorable characters is Cap Huff, who provides comic relief throughout the novel. The Abenaki Indians from Maine also play significant roles, especially one named Natanis who becomes the friend and guide of Steven Nason, Jr. Near the end of book 1, in chapter 8, the Nasons meet Benedict Arnold, then a druggist's apprentice and schooner captain for the Lathrop firm in Norwich, Connecticut. The historic Arnold was famous for his athletic prowess, and Roberts soon has him impress Steven, Jr., with his strength and agility: "The young man seized the [schooner's] ratlines on the inside and went up them hand over hand, not moving his feet: as quick and agile as the monkeys that Spanish sailors carry. At the top he swung his leg over, and in a second was clinging to the mast, smiling down at us" (*Arundel*, 8/101).

While Roberts studied numerous primary sources so he could write an accurate portrayal of Benedict Arnold, he also researched other fictitious characters besides his narrator, Steven Nason, Jr. Many of these figures and their historical counterparts are outlined in chapter 22 of *I Wanted to Write* and in "Anthology of a Small Town," a chapter in Roberts's *Trending into Maine*. Phoebe Marvin, for example, is a composite of two young women mentioned in Charles Bradbury's *History of Kennebunk Port* (1837) and Mabel Littlefield, profiled in Daniel Remich's *History of Kennebunk*. Like Mabel, Phoebe is an experienced sailor with a weakness for jewelry (*IWW*, 184-85; *Trending*, 69-70; Remich, 509; Bradbury, 117-18). Mary Mallinson is based on Mary Storer, who, according to Edward E. Bourne's *History of Wells and Kennebunk* (1875), was captured by French-led Indians at age 18 and carried to Canada, where she married a Frenchman (*Trending*, 79; Bourne, 250-51).

Cap Huff's name is loosely derived from the John Burks family of Kennebunk, whose children were named "Much Experience," "Little to Depend Upon," and "Great Deliverance." When Roberts was first discussing *Arundel* with Booth Tarkington in 1928, he told him that he wanted one of the book's characters to be a "noisy oaf," because in all the military troops he had ever seen there was "at least one noisy clown, constantly in trouble and eager to steal anything that he or his friends needed" (*IWW*, 182). After Roberts mentioned to Tarkington the children's peculiar names he had read about in Remich's research work, his friend suggested that he change the surname to Huff and that the family have a fourth child: "Why couldn't your man have been given the name of

Saved From Captivity? Shorten it up to Cap Huff. I can see him now, all
sweaty and smelling of rum" (*IWW*, 183, 185; see also Remich, 511-12).

Even young Steven's pet seal, Eunice, who constantly followed him, is
based on an actual tamed seal. In 1921 a local youth named William
Babine found a seal on the ocean rocks and tamed it so that the animal
would even follow the boy into his home at the edge of a cove, where it
would track sand in the kitchen and anger the youth's mother. In an
attempt to lose the seal Babine twice took it out to sea in his motorboat,
but, as Roberts noted in his personal copy of *Arundel*, "on each occasion,
when dropped overboard, it beat him home."[15]

Arundel's book 1, "Red and White," focuses on Mary Mallinson, who
is kidnapped by Indians and taken to Quebec, thereby meeting the same
fate as her historical twin. While Steven Nason and his father pursue
Guerlac and the other kidnappers, they are helped by friendly Abenaki
Indians. As the young man watches his new friends and learns tracking
techniques and other wilderness survival skills, he reflects that over the
years the peaceful Indians had been victimized by unscrupulous settlers—the white men responsible for most of the bloodshed during
clashes between the two races. He also observes that Indians by nature
are collectively much more generous and honorable than white men, and
especially more trustworthy than the white "lustful, foul-mouthed
traders and trappers who fattened on them" (*Arundel*, 6/69).

Roberts's favorable opinion of Indians in *Arundel* echoes the views
expressed in his 1924 series of articles on the Southwest American
Indians for the *Saturday Evening Post*. Also, as John I. Kitch, Jr., has indicated, one of the author's themes in *Arundel* and in its successor, *Rabble
in Arms*, is that the colonists' antagonism toward the Indians cost the
Americans the support of what could have been a significant ally (Kitch,
111). Steven Nason, Jr., charges that "it has been one of the peculiarities
of our colonists that they have never kept faith with Indians. They have
either stolen their lands outright, or made the Indians drunk and persuaded them to sell vast stretches of territory for a few beads and a little
rum and a musket or two; and they have made treaty after treaty with
them—treaties which have always favored the white men; and never has
there been a treaty that the white men haven't broken" (*Arundel*, 4/52).

Besides including Nason's convictions on the superiority of Indians
over whites, book 1 also encompasses his—and correspondingly
Roberts's—views on religion, particularly the Boston Puritanism of
Jonathan Edwards. After failing to seize Mary Mallinson from Guerlac as
he and her other captors travel up the Kennebec River to Quebec, the

two Nasons are on their way back to Arundel when they stop at Swan Island in the lower part of the river. While relaxing with their Abenaki Indian friends, they meet the Reverend Ezekiel Hook, who "was thin and hunched, so that he looked like a heron waiting for a fish" (*Arundel*, 9/103).

Reverend Hook tells the Americans that he is a Boston missionary and that he has advised the Indians that unless they embrace the white man's Great Spirit, they will never be happy. He and Nason, Sr., argue about his interpretation of religion, with Nason condemning the Plymouth Company's sanctimoniousness and its intolerably rigid control over the New England settlers: "We're sick of your Boston God, and we're sick of your Boston merchants with their special privileges we common people can't have; with their money bags filled out of wars we little people make; with their yowling and yelping that we who want a voice in the affairs of the colony are thieves and rascals!" (*Arundel*, 9/105).

Roberts's opinion of Puritanism (and probably organized religion in general) matched Nason's in its vehemence. In *Trending into Maine*, while relating how two of his ancestors were hanged and another was banished from Massachusetts during the Salem witch trials, Roberts refers to the "malignant ferocity" of the Massachusetts Puritans and denounces his ancestors' accusers as "a group of the coldest-blooded and most malignant brats ever spawned" (*Trending*, 101, 95). In the 1950s, while writing his dowsing books, Roberts again brings up the Salem witch trials and compares those who label dowsers as witches with the persecutors of his ancestors. His third book on dowsing, *Water Unlimited*, is dedicated to Rebecca Nurse, one of his two ancestors hanged during the trials.

Although Roberts attended church services every Sunday in his youth, he was not a churchgoer in later life, and his apparent antipathy toward religion is reflected in his novels. While many Americans during the periods he wrote about were deeply religious, none of his characters (either historical or fictional) display this trait, even though some of the journals Roberts used were written by persons with strong religious convictions. For instance, while researching *Arundel* Roberts read the journal of one Abner Stocking, who was 22 when he left Connecticut to accompany Arnold to Quebec. After Stocking returned home he thanked God for helping to see him safely through the ordeal: "When wandering through the wilderness, hungry, faint and weary, God was my support, and did not suffer me like others to fall by the way—when sick and in prison he visited me—when a captive he set me free! May I ever be grateful to my Divine Protector, and my future life be devoted to his service!"[16]

Book 2, appropriately titled "Thunderheads," covers the years 1759-75 and focuses on the growing animosity between England and the American colonies. Changes also occur in Steven Nason, Jr. When his father dies after saving the Reverend Hook from drowning (he had fallen backwards into the water while stupidly trying to stand up in the Nasons' ferry), the young man assumes the responsibilities of the family's inn, blacksmith shop, and ferry. While managing the inn he hears numerous tirades against the English, which become increasingly more strident as days pass. Although Nason is obviously no coward (he finds his forge-hardened muscles useful in quelling disturbances at the inn), his conservative nature prevents him from violently rebelling against the British crown; moreover, he is opposed to following the lead of a passionate, drunken mob (Kitch, 113-15). This theme of the quiet men of courage and competence being overshadowed by loud braggarts is a significant subplot of both *Arundel* and *Rabble in Arms*:

> When it seemed as though the unrest and cantankerousness of our farmers and fishermen could grow no more, there began to be even louder rantings over a damnable business called the Stamp Tax, and bitter complaints concerning press gangs from English ships of war, which were coming into any port and snatching up our seamen to round out their crews. In talking of these things the talkers raked up all the other matters concerning which they had been ranting since the fall of Quebec—the need of paper currency; the Sugar Act. . . . It seemed as though every man had a bitter grievance for which he longed to bash someone over the head; and through all the talk there ran the moan that our liberty was being taken from us, and that no nation or people had the right to steal liberty from other people.
>
> I could not help but see that those who talked the loudest about their loss of liberty were those who had lost the least, or had the least to lose, being the poorest and wretchedest of our people, with little land, less money and no vote. Yet I learned from travelers that this was the way of it throughout New England. (*Arundel*, 10/123)

Another subplot that Roberts brings out in book 2 is the Steven Nason–Phoebe Marvin relationship. At the end of book 1, after Nason and his father return to Arundel aboard Benedict Arnold's schooner *Black Duck*, Arnold promises the boy that he will look for Mary Mallinson the next time he is in Quebec. As the years pass Nason continues to daydream about his absent sweetheart, even though he sees Phoebe virtually every day as she works in the family inn and sails along the Arundel coast. While he continues to be exasperated with her "rudeness and jeers," he concedes that she is a hard and diligent worker, as well as a superb sailor:

> All the day she was in the water or on it, fishing from a crazy skiff she had dug from the mud and patched with pitch and rotten canvas, and calked with rags and old rope. In this fearful craft she sailed in and out of the river and around the reefs until every seaman in the place threw up his hands and swore that by rights she should have been drowned ten times each month. Because of this, doubtless, she was a golden color on those portions of her that could be seen, as well, I suspected, as on several portions that could not be seen: a most unmaidenly color, wholly unlike the beautiful whiteness of Mary. (*Arundel*, 10/122)

Soon after the Battles of Lexington and Concord of 19 April 1775, Benedict Arnold asks 27-year-old Nason to meet with him at General George Washington's headquarters in Cambridge. Fort Ticonderoga on Lake Champlain had fallen to Arnold and Ethan Allen a month earlier, and the American army felt that by keeping control of the lake and seizing the British-held city of Quebec it would counter any British plans to attack from the North. At the meeting the men—along with Cap Huff—plan an attack on Quebec by way of the Kennebec and Chaudiere rivers, and Nason is pleased when General Washington offers him the opportunity to serve under Arnold as a scout and counselor.

While Steven Nason and his friends praise Arnold and his inspiring leadership throughout the novel, it is after this meeting that the reader sees the officer from a different angle. When Nason and Cap Huff tell him that they had heard of his "brave attack on Ticonderoga," Arnold bitterly relates his side of the controversy surrounding the disputed command between him and Ethan Allen at this first American offensive action of the Revolution. Each man was authorized to lead an expedition against the fort, and when neither would yield his position they agreed on a joint command. Allen, however, claimed credit for the victory, and he and his supporters did their utmost to discredit their rival. As Arnold protests to Nason and Huff,

> "By God!" he said, "it was I who suggested taking Ticonderoga; but because I waited to be commissioned by the Massachusetts Congress, so to do it legally and in order, I found the Bennington mob ahead of me,

acting on money supplied by Connecticut. A mob: that's what it was: without commissions or standing, and headed by three of the greatest boors that ever lived—Ethan Allen, James Easton, and John Brown! The Green Mountain Party, they called themselves, and they fired on me twice, by God, for refusing to obey their thieving orders. Rum and loot was what they wanted. (*Arundel*, 14/176)

Arnold's humiliation at Fort Ticonderoga marks just the first of many military frustrations that he would have to endure at the hands of his countrymen. While the reader of *Arundel* realizes before finishing the novel's first page that the author is obviously partisan toward Arnold, Roberts uses the Ticonderoga episode and others to illustrate that he believes the controversies surrounding the soldier's life were largely based on innuendoes, gossip, and petty jealousies. This passionate defense of Benedict Arnold as a daring military genius is a central theme of both *Arundel* and *Rabble in Arms*.

Most scholars agree with the novelist's interpretation of Ethan Allen's and his friends' behavior before, during, and after the capture of Fort Ticonderoga. Willard Sterne Randall, in his exhaustive biography, *Benedict Arnold: Patriot and Traitor* (1990), observes that Allen's version of the report of the attack "not only assured his place in history but served to help his friends and harm his rival, Arnold. His accounts varied from day to day. For four years he continued to embellish them, ultimately publishing an unabashedly purple memoir."[17]

Books 1 and 2 foreshadow the Northern Army's campaign in books 3 and 4 as well as establish the novel's characters, setting, plot, and various subplots. The first two parts, however, suffer from Roberts's tendency to overwrite, a weakness he admitted to Ben Ames Williams soon after *Arundel*'s publication: "Booth [Tarkington] has had me do a little cutting where I get too informative—a criticism that you made."[18] Although Roberts shortened both sections when revising *Arundel*, they still slow the pace and unnecessarily delay the action of book 3. This problem, not uncommon in first novels, is corrected somewhat in his later works, for in none of them does he devote as many chapters to preliminary narrative (Kitch, 119-20).

Roberts's years of experience as a researcher and well-trained journalist are evident throughout books 3 and 4, as he describes with graphic historical accuracy the ragged and half-starved Northern Army's long and arduous expedition to Quebec in the middle of winter. His dates, characters, events, and even minuscule incidents and details all correspond to historical facts in the primary sources he consulted. The work is a stirring creative accomplishment as well, as Christopher Ward acknowledged in his 1952 two-volume history, *The War of the Revolution*: "Roberts follows closely the actual events of the march and illuminates it with his remarkably vivid imagination, re-creating as truly as the novelist can its scenes and characters" (Ward, 1: 448).

Roberts's "re-creation" of Arnold's march can best be appreciated by comparing his contemporary sources with *Arundel*. For example, 24-year-old Captain Henry Dearborn brought along his huge dog to keep him company on the expedition, but on 1 November 1775 the starving soldiers proposed a better use for him. Dearborn's journal entry for that day reads: "This day Capt. Goodrich's Company Kill'd my Dog, and another dog, and Eat them, I remain very unwell" (*March*, 139). Dr. Isaac Senter, the young surgeon of the army, wrote the following on the same day: "In company was a poor dog, [who had] hitherto lived through all the tribulations, became a prey for the sustenance of the assassinators. This poor animal was instantly devoured, without leaving any vestige of the sacrifice" (*March*, 219).

From these and other historical accounts Roberts was able to create one of the novel's most memorable scenes:

"Captain," said Asa, "this dog of yours, he's a fine dog. We'd like for you to give him to us."

The dog, clumsy, fond creature, galloped up to us with his tongue lolling out, and blowing pleased, audible breaths. He pranced a little before Dearborn and then went over to grin amiably at Asa and Flood.

"Why," Dearborn said, "I wouldn't—do you mean to eat?"

"Damn you," said Ayres, "get out of here! You'll have food in the morning! Can't you see the captain's sick?"

"Captain," Asa said, watching Ayres warily, "I think some of us might die to-night if we can't get something into us. That dog, he'd feed thirty men. Maybe fifty. We think you ought to let us have him."

"Why, dear, dear," Captain Dearborn said, "dear, dear! He's been with us all the way! I'd no more eat him than I'd eat one of you! Why, bless me, my boy, you don't want to eat *him*!"

"Captain," said Asa, "we'd eat anything! We tried moose hide and moccasins, but they ain't no good."

"If you could only wait until to-morrow—"

"It's *now* we want food! Captain, let us have him."

I think Ayres must have made some move to go for Asa; for Dearborn stopped him. "We can't be judges," he said to Ayres. "Just because we can hold out is no sign others can. What we can do we must do." He put his hand around the dog's nose, pressing it weakly, and the dog looked up at him, grateful and loving. "Take him, my boy," he said to Asa, "but take him a long way off, and be—be merciful." (*Arundel*, 26/348)

After General Richard Montgomery dies early in the attack, unheroic Lieutenant Colonel Donald Campbell retreats, and Arnold is wounded, Nason and Cap Huff blame both Campbell's cowardice and a lack of leadership for the failure of the Northern Army to capture Quebec. Although Arnold tells them to shrug off these "fortunes of war," the two are not easily appeased. For them Campbell symbolizes all incompetents and cowards who prevent daring and resourceful leaders like Arnold from accomplishing their goals.

By the end of book 4 Roberts resolves his other subplots. Nason, for example, discovers that he has loved Phoebe for years and takes her with him back to Arundel. But while the wounded Arnold recuperates in Quebec, impatient to get back to the war, Roberts foreshadows that the controversies surrounding this "great soldier" will continue, and that his story is far from over:

> In none of my readings have I ever learned of anyone so persecuted and disappointed and unrewarded as this same brave and gallant gentleman. If the commissioning of officers had been in the hands of General Washington, where it should have been, instead of in the hands of the petty little argufiers of Congress, Benedict Arnold would never have suffered the cruel injustices that were heaped on him until, weakened by wounds, he was coaxed or driven to his awful crime. (*Arundel*, 36/476)

After Doubleday brought out *Arundel* on 10 January 1930 (the official date of publication, however, is 18 November 1929) the book received enthusiastic reviews in many national magazines and newspapers. The *New York Times Book Review* claimed that in *Arundel* "Kenneth Roberts has succeeded splendidly in capturing a fragrance belonging to the past, a faint but indispensable aroma which is the chief charm of a historical novel, and which most American historical novels have notably lacked."[19] The *Boston Evening Transcript* trumpeted similar words of praise: "The biggest achievement of the book is the manner in which Mr. Roberts makes the experiences of this march so vivid that we hope and suffer and strain onward with these men and women whose only chance of living lies in their ability to endure to the end of the march."[20]

Despite these and other laudatory reviews, sales of *Arundel* were not at all strong. During its first year it sold only 9,266 copies, "which returned," Roberts sarcastically observed, "to its happy author, a trifle more than would one article in the *Saturday Evening Post*" (*IWW*, 192). Two years after the book's publication he was "a little, but only a little, cheered" to learn that sales were steady at 70 to 120 copies a week, and that around the state the book was regarded as a sort of "Maine bible." But as Roberts glumly noted, "That, however, butters few, if any, parsnips" (Letter to Street, 1931?).

Roberts's letters and other papers indicate that during the late 1920s and early 1930s he did consider abandoning his fledgling career as a novelist, for he was often in desperate financial difficulties. In July 1928, while working on *Arundel*, he told Ben Ames Williams that as he was "shockingly poor" and "on the verge of bankruptcy," he had to finish two articles for the *Post*.[21] In June 1929 his mother suggested that he leave the writing field and become a bond salesman. A few months after the publication of *Arundel* he wrote Williams again, confessing that "this past year has been by far the worst that I have had since 1919, and when I say worst I don't mean maybe."[22]

What did encourage him, however, were letters from enthusiastic readers of *Arundel*. Although he admitted that the letters were disproportionate to the book's sales, "I'd a damned sight rather just barely subsist by writing books than make three times as much doing magazine articles" (*IWW*, 206). Thus, less than a month after he had sent the finished *Arundel* to his publisher, he was hard at work on another book. "I am blocking out a novel that needs, for a part of its background, the experiences of a Maine ship-captain in Dartmoor Prison in 1815—during, that is to say, the War of 1812," he wrote to the director of the Maine State Library. "I would be very grateful if you would look through your shelves and see if you can locate some books that might be valuable to me."[23]

The Lively Lady and *Captain Caution*

Roberts originally had several ideas for his second novel, including a sequel to *Arundel* that would complete the story of Benedict Arnold's Northern Army. Booth Tarkington, however, suggested to his friend that he wait four or five years before tackling such a book. Tarkington felt that if he started it immediately after finishing *Arundel*, using by necessity many of the same characters that had appeared in the first story, Roberts might acquire "bad habits" (*IWW*, 195).

In his four "Chronicles of Arundel" Roberts wanted to relate certain events of the Revolutionary War and the War of 1812 from the viewpoints of his ancestors and other residents of Arundel, Maine. Thus in *The Lively Lady*, his story about "the experiences of a Maine ship-captain," he focused on the next generation of the Nason family, Richard, the son of *Arundel*'s Steven and Phoebe Nason.[24]

The Lively Lady tells of the courage of American privateersmen and impressed sailors during the War of 1812 and the bitter sufferings of thousands of American prisoners of war in England's infamous Dartmoor Prison. As he did with *Arundel*, Roberts included here his ancestors' experiences. Narrator Richard Nason is modeled after his great-grandfather, Daniel Nason, who was sailing master of the privateer *MacDonough* during the War of 1812. After the ship was captured in 1814 by the British frigate *Bacchante*, Nason and his men were imprisoned in Dartmoor for the duration of the war—incidents that similarly befall the fictitious Richard Nason and crew in Roberts's novel (*IWW*, 199; *Trending*, 83-86).

Once again Roberts researched primary and other historical sources. Because most of the privateers during the war were brigs, he had to learn how one was sailed, so while at his retreat in Porto Santo Stefano he spent days watching brigs, brigantines, barques, barkentines and other vessels, as well as reading books on nineteenth-century sailing (*IWW*, 198; *Trending*, 186-88). Among the many documents he needed for his research were Dartmoor's records for his great-grandfather and the other men from Arundel who had sailed with him on the *MacDonough*. When he could not find them in U.S. Navy files, his friend Charles G. Dawes, then ambassador to the court of St. James, immediately sent his nephew to England's Public Record Office, where he located the prison ledger (*IWW*, 199-200).

In attempting to reconstruct the march to Quebec while writing his first book, Roberts retraced the path of the Northern Army, following what he called the "Arnold trail."[25] So that he would be able to visualize and write about the hardships of the American seamen imprisoned in Dartmoor, he traveled to England. As he wrote to his friend Julian Street, he believed that this attention to every detail was necessary to ensure historical accuracy in *Arundel* and *The Lively Lady*:

> The sections I describe are as near right as I can make them. I shot deer on the Height of Land when I was thirteen and could barely hoist a 30-30 rifle. I've travelled that country both in summer and in winter, and I know it pretty well. I've prowled along the Kennebec, the Chaudiere and the St. Lawrence in all sorts of temperatures. . . . I even made a special

trip to Dartmoor Prison to make sure of getting the proper picture of the prisoners' march from Plymouth to Dartmoor. (Letter to Street, 1931?)

As necessary as Roberts thought this firsthand research was, he did admit to longtime friend Chilson H. Leonard, an English teacher at Phillips Exeter Academy from 1932 to 1967, that perhaps during his trip to Dartmoor he carried his desire for authenticity and realism too far. Although he had permission in writing from the superintendent of prisons to visit Dartmoor, he was reluctant to go inside and thought he would simply stop his car at the prison entrance and ask some questions. He had no sooner stepped out of his car when a guard, brandishing a rifle, ordered him to leave. "I decided that things hadn't changed much since [Captain Thomas] Shortland's day [the former commandant of Dartmoor], and that I was willing to let my great-grandfather be the only one in our family to have any dealings with the Depot."[26]

Besides including authentic historical events in *The Lively Lady*, Roberts also carefully incorporated passages reminiscent of episodes and characters from his first novel. Thus Phoebe Nason, while not managing the family inn anymore, still lives in it and still has the habit of twisting her fingers in the string of cat's-eyes that she wears at her throat. Independent as always, she chastises her son for his reluctance to view seriously the possibility of a war with England, just as she readily used to berate his father:

> "To be frank," I said, "I see no sense to this talk of war. We're making a living out of our brig; but if we fight England, we'll have no living at all, for we'll have to lay her up. You'll never get me into a war with England. England's the only nation that defends the world's freedom against Bonaparte."
>
> My mother stood up, her hands on her hips and her new shawl clinging to her arms and her flat shoulders as if she had backed her topsail to give us a chance to come up with her.
>
> "Yes, indeed!" she said ironically. "England's always been a great hand to defend freedom! She's as eager to defend freedom as to cut her own throat!" She made a derisive sound in her nose. "Can't you tell the difference between right and wrong? Can't you get in a rage when the British and French do things to us that they shouldn't?"
>
> "They never did anything to me."
>
> "Oh, my Land, Richard! The French never did anything to your grandfather, but he fought them at Louisburg! The English never did anything to your father, but he fought them at Quebec and Saratoga; and a good thing for you and all of us that he did!"[27]

Richard Nason's pacifism disappears after he is impressed into the British Navy and taken aboard a sloop-of-war and flogged. Slipping overboard in Halifax harbor, he returns to Arundel, where, with his mother's expert help, he outfits a sloop so that he can harass British shipping on the Atlantic Ocean. With the green dress of Emily Ransome in mind, he christens his green-sided privateer *The Lively Lady* and manages to seize a number of British "prizes" before he is captured and sent to Dartmoor. With Lady Ransome's help he escapes but is recaptured and confined to the Cachot, the prison's Black Hole. Because no ships are available to take the prisoners home, he is forced to stay in Dartmoor even after the war ends; eventually, however, he is freed and is reunited with Emily Ransome.

As with *Arundel*, Roberts included a great deal of extraneous writing in *The Lively Lady*, but with Tarkington's help he managed to whittle the book from 275,000 words down to 150,000 (Tebbel 1948, 95). This leftover material became the nucleus of *Captain Caution*, a novel that was finished in 1931 but not published until 1934 after Roberts had written *Rabble in Arms*.[28]

Captain Caution is another privateering story of the War of 1812. The hero, Daniel Marvin, is first mate on the American merchant barque *Olive Branch*, captained by Oliver Dorman of Arundel. The captain's daughter, Corunna Dorman, gives Marvin the derisive nickname Captain Caution when, during a sea fight, he surrenders the ship to a British brig when her father is killed by an explosion of one of his own guns. Imprisoned on the British war brig *Beetle*, Marvin meets fellow prisoners Lucien Argandeau, a French privateer captain, and Lurman Slade, the captain of an American slave brig. When the *Beetle* is attacked by an American schooner, the prisoners overpower their English captors and escape, using weapons that Corunna had smuggled to them. Corunna, determined to sell her cargo in France, assumes command of the *Olive Branch* and hires Slade as first mate, demoting Marvin to bosun. When Slade arranges to have the *Olive Branch* recaptured by the British in return for one-half of its condemnation value, Marvin learns of his treachery, captures him with the aid of Argandeau, and is reconciled with Corunna.

Neither *The Lively Lady* nor *Captain Caution* measure up to the standards set by Roberts in *Arundel* and *Rabble in Arms*, and each is simply a series of loosely connected sea adventures with no central theme and with little of the action taking place in Arundel, Maine. Although Janet Harris contends in *A Century of American History in Fiction: Kenneth*

Roberts' Novels (1976) that a theme implied in the two books is the "growth of national pride" and the "unification of the United States," it could be argued that this is a motif in virtually all of the author's novels.[29] Herbert Faulkner West, who studied Roberts's books for decades, regarded both novels as "minor works" and believed that they were "products of a lot of historical material [Roberts] had left over and which fitted into his scheme of writing four books about Arundel" (West 1962, 95). Another critic, Carlos Baker, voiced a similar opinion: "The War of 1812 obviously holds second place to the Revolution in Robert's [*sic*] affections, and his heart is in neither [*The Lively Lady*] nor in *Captain Caution* (1934), though both are better than average historical novels."[30]

Although many reviewers enjoyed the two books, they, like Baker, were at the same time also disappointed in them. The *New York Times Book Review* observed that in *The Lively Lady* "the adventures of Richard Nason are broken into two parts—first, his privateering, and second, his imprisonment in Dartmoor. There is little beyond the element of romance to weave them together. This lack of unity weakens what is otherwise an excellent novel."[31] William Rose Benét, writing in the *Saturday Review of Literature*, regretted that *Captain Caution* was not the panoramic saga that *Rabble in Arms* was: "As usual the critics have gone off the deep end about Mr. Roberts's work, and my own enthusiasm for *Rabble in Arms* was genuine, but in *Captain Caution* he has written a new novel neither of the scope of the former extremely powerful book nor of its depth and richness."[32]

Although these two novels should not be criticized because they are more restricted in scope and plot than Roberts's previous books, they do suffer from inferior characterization, particularly *Captain Caution*. Because Roberts wanted to experiment with a "compressed method" of writing, the story is told from the third-person omniscient point of view rather than the author's usual first person (*IWW*, 206). Thus the reader is not drawn into the novel's action and does not feel directly involved with its protagonist. Even while writing *Captain Caution* Roberts admitted that the third-person point of view was unnatural to him, noting in his diary that "this experiment of abandoning the first person seems awkward and unwieldy—not enough opportunity to spread out" (*IWW*, 207). Roberts's inability to "spread out" is substantiated by the lack in both books of the intricately woven pattern of subplots and themes that helped to strengthen the characterization in *Arundel* and in later books.

Although his historical novels often feature representative types of persons rather than characters memorable in their own right, Roberts felt that dramatic action was more important than characterization. Herschel Brickell recognized this in *The Lively Lady*, praising Roberts's narratives in his review: "The story is the thing, and he can make a story get up and step along." He also criticized the novel, however, for its "stock characters": "Mr. Roberts has helped himself to a perfectly conventional plot, in which there are a Hero, a Heroine, a Villain and a Comic Relief, all old, old friends."[33]

Rabble in Arms

Roberts was as concerned about accuracy in his published books as he was when they were in manuscript form and would carefully check each novel for errors as soon as he received it from Doubleday. He was in Italy working on *The Lively Lady* when he received the first copy of *Arundel* on 6 January 1930, and he immediately cabled to his publishers some 20 minor corrections for the book's next printing (*IWW*, 191-92). After Doubleday allowed him to revise the book for a new edition, he shortened it by some 40,000 words and in July 1933 declared that "a greatly improved edition of *Arundel* is somewhere in the offing. . . . The type is better, and I spent a year revising the text, so to eliminate as much dead wood as possible. I think I worked harder revising it than I did writing it."[34]

While Roberts was revising *Arundel*, he was also writing its sequel, *Rabble in Arms*, which takes its title from British general John Burgoyne's contemptuous description of the American troops who had fought at Bunker Hill: "A rabble in arms, flushed with success and insolence." Beginning where *Arundel* left off, the book completes the story of Arnold's Northern Army after the defeat at Quebec, describing the retreat of the half-dead Americans southward from Quebec in May 1776; the hasty building of a fleet on Lake Champlain and the battle of Valcour Island; the flight from Ticonderoga before General Burgoyne's advance; and the Second Battle of Saratoga at Bemis Heights in which the ragged army defeats Burgoyne in October 1777.

Although many characters from *Arundel* reappear in this sequel— Steven and Phoebe Nason (now married), Cap Huff, Marie de Sabrevois (formerly Mary Mallinson), and, of course, the dashing Benedict Arnold—Roberts uses a new narrator. Two principal characters who account for the success of Roberts's various subplots in the novel are Peter and Nathaniel Merrill, sons of a well-to-do Arundel shipbuilder; Roberts has the older brother, Peter, narrate the story.

Roberts's development as a novelist in the years since he wrote *Arundel* is easily seen in the opening chapters of *Rabble in Arms*. He wastes no time with a lengthy introduction but instead focuses directly on his story: while Peter and Nathaniel are in England to sell their father's ship, they meet Marie de Sabrevois and the man she introduces as her uncle, Mr. Leonard, who is really Charles Louis de Lanaudiere, a French-Canadian fighting for England. Because Peter and Nathaniel are in England, people in Arundel suspect the Merrill family of being Loyalists, and the young men's father asks them to come home. To prove their loyalty to the patriot cause, they both enlist in the American army.

Roberts is not as wedded to his reference books as he was a few years earlier. For example, although he was a descendant of the Merrill family and Peter and Nathaniel Merrill are derived from historical counterparts, Roberts does not systematically follow family history as he did in his first book. With *Rabble in Arms* he has matured as a creative artist, and he clearly does not feel the need to rely on historical and genealogical sources for the purely fictitious sections of his book (Bales 1989, 251-54; Kitch, 135-36).

He is, however, still meticulous about historical details. The bibliography for *Rabble in Arms* of just his principle sources numbers some 80 titles, and Roberts consulted primary manuscript material both in the United States and abroad. Not content, for example, with naval expert Admiral Alfred Thayer Mahan's contention that it was impossible to know how the American ships at the battle of Valcour Island were rigged, he consulted records at the British Admiralty and found drawings of the galleys.[35]

The many conflicting historical accounts also contributed to Roberts's difficulties with this episode, yet he realized that the battle at Valcour, a critical engagement for the Northern Army, needed to be accurately represented. While struggling with these chapters, he wrote to two friends, "Rabble in Arms has started to move along again, though I'm not yet through with the building of the fleet. I feel like a fool, going into such detail over it, but it's a feature that has never been properly developed; and if it hadn't been for the fleet, there'd never have been any battle of Saratoga, and the American Revolution would have come to an abrupt end in 1777."[36]

The chapters describing Valcour rank among the book's best writing; historians have recognized Roberts's reconstruction of this crucial Revolutionary battle to be startlingly true to life. As Christopher Ward acknowledged, "Kenneth Roberts has told the story [of Valcour], in

great detail and with historical accuracy, in his novel *Rabble in Arms*"
(Ward, 1: 471).

A principle theme of both *Arundel* and *Rabble in Arms* is that the
Revolution was not the conglomeration of patriotic speeches, cheering
crowds, fifes, drums, and waving flags that schoolbooks so often roman-
tically depict. Rather, as Roberts asserts in virtually all of his novels, it
was a senseless madness that leaves no one unscarred, except the "politicians [who place] their own small interests ahead of the truth, ahead of
the army, ahead of their country—just as they always have and just as I
fear they always will." Thus his purpose is "to tell the truth—the truth
as to why wars are fought, and how they are bungled and protracted,
while those who fight them lose their lives and fortunes."[37]

When Peter and Nathaniel Merrill, Steven Nason, Joseph Marie
Verrieul, and the comic figure Doc Means join the army in Canada, the
forces have retreated from Quebec and are scattered around Montreal,
Sorel, and St. John's. Peter is in St. John's and sees nothing but a mob of
dirty, sick, emaciated, and thoroughly demoralized men: "If this was
war, I thought to myself—this muck of hunger, distrust, disease,
raggedness, cowardice—it was different from all my imaginings: so different that a little was already more than enough for me" (*Rabble*,
11/78).

Months later, while marching down a dusty and desolate road in
Bemis Heights just before the Second Battle of Saratoga, Peter looks
around him and wonders if war was supposed to be like this: "Then I
realized that men had lied so often about war that they thought falsely
of it as fine and glorious, whereas it never has been and never can be
anything but a monstrous blend of weariness, disappointment,
heartache, discomfort, injustice, dishonesty, hatred, fear, waste, stupidity, futility, turmoil, misery, sickness, cruelty and death" (*Rabble*, 64/533).

Another central theme, one that Roberts carries over from *Arundel*, is
that Arnold was not the despicable traitor of legend but a fearless military leader and brilliant tactician who was shamefully victimized by
incompetent generals who outranked him; malicious officers who served
beneath him; small-minded politicians who were jealous of him; an
ungrateful, feeble, and inept Congress that hated him; and a host of
other enemies who despised him. "As I get deeper and deeper into
Arnold," Roberts wrote in his diary, "I can't pick up a source book on
the Northern Campaign without finding myself in a fury over the
shockingly raw deal he received from the military peanuts who sur-
rounded him—and over the contemptibly raw deal he has had ever

since from mentally similar persons posing as historians and biographers" (*IWW*, 235).

Roberts also angrily scrawled these convictions throughout the dozens of source books he used for his research, for he was convinced, as he wrote in the margins of Edward Dean Sullivan's *Benedict Arnold: Military Racketeer* (1932), that Arnold's treason colored the thinking of his biographers: "Not *one* of Arnold's biographers has been able to eliminate from his mind the final act of treachery, & judge his preceding career fairly: not one has treated him with a fraction of the courage that Arnold NEVER failed to show."[38]

Roberts begins to clarify these two themes in chapter 10. The Continental Congress—"a pack of fart-wits running things," according to one soldier—has replaced Arnold with General David Wooster, and then Wooster with General John Thomas (*Rabble*, 10/72). Arnold is portrayed by the men loyal to him as the one person bold and smart enough to lead the disillusioned army. When the men from Arundel join Arnold in Montreal, he tells them of the situation that is confronting him:

> He turned to face us. "We're in a mess! We're in as bad a mess as ever was! There's such a mess here, and in Sorel and St. John's, and up and down the river, that no man can comprehend it all. We've got an army, thanks to General Washington; but thanks to Congress it's got nothing to eat, nothing to wear, nothing to put in its guns. There never was an army as sick as this army. It's rotten with smallpox. Half the men are inoculating themselves; and those that don't inoculate themselves are catching it from those that do. We've got no money. We've got no officers worth their salt." (*Rabble*, 13/96)

While Peter and his friends from Arundel are steadfastly loyal to Arnold, Nathaniel questions the American cause and becomes infatuated with Marie de Sabrevois, who is spying for the British. The situation is further complicated when Peter falls in love with her young ward, Ellen Phipps, for he soon realizes that Marie is using both Nathaniel and Ellen to further her own designs as a British informer. Thus Roberts cleverly blends a romantic subplot and one of intrigue and espionage with his central plot of the story of the Northern Army.

With his subplots firmly in place Roberts is free to focus on the plight of the hungry, sick, and discouraged army as it retreats south along the Richelieu River and Lake Champlain to Fort Ticonderoga, before the steady advance of General Guy Carleton. Whereas the personal problems of narrator Steven Nason tend to overshadow the fate of the

Northern Army in *Arundel*, in *Rabble in Arms* the army's misfortunes (and secondarily Arnold's) are of much greater magnitude than the predicament of narrator Peter Merrill. For instance, when the army stops to rest on Isle aux Noix, just south of St. John's, Peter and Doc Means spend two hours disposing of innumerable corpses:

> The dead pits were trenches, shallow and a scant six feet in width. Because of the great number of sick, and the frequency with which they died, the pits were always open, until they were full.
>
> The one to which we came was only partly filled with close packed ranks of swollen carcasses that lay there grinning, as if at some appalling joke. We stood above them, half strangled by the stench, and swung the blanket between us: then tossed the poor body in among the others. A billion flies leaped upward, as if in protest at this new arrival, and such was their buzzing and hissing that the row of dead men seemed to whisper and titter at their uninvited guest. (*Rabble*, 21/159)

After such vivid descriptions of the army's deplorable condition as it retreats southward, the reader cannot help viewing Roberts's colorful depiction of the subsequent conflict at Valcour Island as especially breathtaking and suspenseful. After the battle Sac Indians capture Peter, Doc Means, and Joseph Verrieul, taking them to Wisconsin where they spend the winter of 1776-77. As in *Arundel*, Roberts uses this interval, with the main characters away from the army, to have the narrator relate his experiences with the Indians and give his (and Roberts's) feelings toward them: "Since my opinion is based on my own observation, I am bound to say that all the Sacs and Foxes I saw were more charitable and better companions, after we got to know them, than any of the many Frenchmen and Englishmen I have known" (*Rabble*, 45/356-57).

Although this section of the novel, chapters 41 to 52, was undoubtedly included because of Roberts's passionate interest in eighteenth-century Indians, the interlude seems strangely out of place; moreover, the reader is distracted from the more essential plot—the fate of the Northern Army. As John I. Kitch, Jr., sums it up, "Twelve chapters are too many and needlessly slow down the story" (Kitch, 143).

After the climactic Second Battle of Saratoga at Bemis Heights, New York, Roberts resolves his subplots: Nathaniel realizes how he had been duped by Marie de Sabrevois, Peter and Ellen are reunited, and the three return to Arundel with Steven Nason, Cap Huff, and Doc Means.

Roberts, however, does not settle the controversy surrounding Benedict Arnold so smoothly. By the time he had researched *Arundel* and

Rabble in Arms he was convinced that nearly all Arnold biographies and historical studies were "marred by gross unfairness, misplaced patriotism, inexcusable plagiarism, reliance on untrustworthy evidence, a narrow-minded and confused interpretation of facts, slovenly research, loose thinking, atrocious writing and other grave faults" (*March*, 43). His emotional and impassioned defense of Arnold as a courageous and indomitable military leader—"the most brilliant soldier of the Revolution"—climaxes in the penultimate chapter of *Rabble in Arms*, in which Peter justifies Arnold's treason, insisting that it was inspired by his patriotism:

> I say it was impossible for Arnold, the brilliant soldier, the planner of campaigns, to formulate a sudden angry plan that might have boiled from the addled brain of any spleeny child or shrewish woman—a plan inspired, as the ignorant believe, only by revenge, and with no object save to betray. If he sought to give everything to England until we had regained our strength, it was done to fight a greater threat than England.
>
> Scores of officers who fought with him and thousands who fought under him know in their hearts that Benedict Arnold was a rare and solitary genius—one who, foreseeing the inevitable that was miraculously averted, had the courage to attempt what no other man dared. Other leaders said, "We're beaten: let it be so; let Congress wreck us: let all our states dissolve in Civil War; let France come in to snatch us up again." Arnold said, "No! This imbecile, coward Congress can *not* destroy the freedom *we* have fought to gain!" (*Rabble*, 68/580, 577)

Roberts parrots Arnold's own argument, that it was better to give the colonies back to England than to let them, through an incompetent Continental Congress, fall to France. Roberts's handwritten comments in his reference books indicate that he unhesitatingly accepted this rationale while he was researching *Arundel* and *Rabble in Arms*. In *The Life of General Daniel Morgan* (1856), a biography of the Revolutionary War general who fought with Arnold at Quebec, James Graham states that in 1779 two of the reasons Morgan wanted to resign from the army were his low salary and his "dissatisfaction with the conduct of Congress, which existed so generally among the officers of the army at this time." Roberts wrote alongside this paragraph, "Biographers have sneered at Arnold for feeling as Morgan did, but nobody sneers at Morgan. Note that the dissatisfaction was general. Arnold had good reason to think Congress intended to hand the country over to the French, whom he had always hated, & with good reason."[39]

An equally telling example appears in volume 1 of Thomas Anburey's *Travels through the Interior Parts of America* (1923). Anburey believed that only with the assistance of another power, presumably France, could the Americans achieve "their boasted end," though in the process they might discover that they had exchanged King George for a much more tyrannical and oppressive King Louis. In a bold hand Roberts wrote across both pages, "This is Arnold's argument, & his reason for turning against the Congressional form of gov't of 1775-1785—a terrible gov't. This reasoning of Anburey's is correct, & America was only saved by her accidental Constitution."[40]

Unfortunately for Arnold's—and Roberts's—defense, while Arnold did dislike a number of Frenchmen, he did not voice his opposition to an alliance with France until *after* he betrayed West Point. Concluded Willard M. Wallace in his biography, "There is no surviving record of his antipathy for the [French] alliance before his treason" (Wallace, 265; see also Randall, 574-75).

Most historians and academics agree that Arnold was not only a superb military commander but a man unfortunately maligned by a shortsighted Congress and dozens of jealous, petty individuals. In 1780 when he could not produce missing records to prove to a Congressional Treasury Board that he had purchased supplies and other essentials with the money Washington had given him for his journey to Canada, the board declared that he pay that sum to Congress. Incredibly, the missing records and accounts were discovered more than 200 years later, showing that Arnold was telling the truth—he did use the cash to buy provisions from various Canadian commissaries (Randall, 495-99).

Roberts, quite naturally, saw Arnold in the context of his times and tried to imagine how an ambitious young officer might feel if he were unjustly charged with looting, if various committees ignored his claims for his back salary and the reimbursement of his expenditures, and if Congress promoted younger officers over his head (*Rabble*, 13/94-98, 25/204-5, 34/273-74, 55/427-29, 61/483). Unfortunately, Roberts carried his crusade to portray Arnold as a flawless hero farther than the facts warranted. Some of the officers whom he has his characters belittle as "human shrimps" and "pig-nuts" were not as ineffectual as they are portrayed (*Rabble*, 33/268, 16/21). Furthermore, Roberts presented only one side of Arnold and neglected to mention that while the military commander indeed had to bear many injustices, he was still, as his critics claimed him to be, arrogant, impetuous, avaricious, and a glory seeker. As Willard M. Wallace summarized,

Actually most of what [Roberts] said about Arnold in his novels has a strong basis in fact. Occasionally he did omit facts or shaded them in favor of Arnold. I think this originated less in a calculated manipulation of facts than in an overwhelming conviction that Arnold was right and that it was the critics who were dead wrong—always. Roberts seemed actually to have achieved a kind of identification with Arnold. Personally I continue to be a strong supporter of Arnold up to a point but realize that though he was stout-hearted and a great battle leader, he was also materialistic, opportunistic, and, in the end, traitorous.[41]

Readers of *Arundel* and *Rabble in Arms* occasionally accused Roberts of "vindicating" Arnold, to which he replied that when he was researching and writing his books he had no intention of exonerating or idealizing him. What he wanted to do, he said, was write an accurate history of the Northern Army that everyone could understand and enjoy, portraying each character as true-to-life as possible. "People persist in thinking that in ARUNDEL and RABBLE I was writing Arnold's story," he complained to Herbert Faulkner West. "I wasn't at all. I was writing the story of the Northern Army. I wrote Arnold as I found him—as I tried to write everyone connected with that army."[42]

Book reviewers, however, usually only saw a swashbuckling Benedict Arnold emerge from the two volumes' pages, and only a few took exception to the larger-than-life portrait. The *New York Times Book Review* loudly cheered Arnold and *Rabble in Arms*: "Out of this host of characters . . . stands one dominating and indomitable figure, that of Benedict Arnold, whose name generations of American school children have been taught to abhor. . . . The heroism and tragedy of his career are sufficient in themselves to lift Mr. Roberts's novel to a scale it would be no exaggeration to call epic."[43] "No one reading this novel," contended the *Boston Evening Transcript*, "but must forever recall Arnold as a brilliant leader and a military genius to whom the country owes much."[44] Protested the *New York Herald Tribune* feebly, "[Arnold] is the book's true hero, and though an ill-fated attempt is made to whitewash him completely at the end, and good qualities alone are stressed throughout, he looms big and real."[45]

Evidence suggests that Roberts's steadfast belief in Arnold's patriotism mellowed slightly with the passing years. On the publication of Carl Van Doren's *Secret History of the American Revolution* in 1941, the *New York Sun* asked Roberts if the new book, which the newspaper said "paints [Arnold] even blacker than history has heretofore pictured him," had caused the novelist to change his opinion. Refusing to rise to the

challenge he merely replied, "My novels have dealt only with Arnold's
military achievement. Nothing in Mr. Van Doren's excellent secret history of the American Revolution has any bearing on Arnold as a military
leader so naturally it doesn't affect mine or set me to sizzling with professional jealousy."[46]

Roberts had clearly softened even more on the subject a few years
later, when during a question-and-answer session the subject came up
again:

> Question: A few years ago Carl Van Doren came out with a book, a his-
> tory of the United States. Does that alter your opinion of Benedict
> Arnold?
> Roberts: Not at all. All that stuff you can find elsewhere.
> Question: You still think he was justified in what he did?
> Roberts: Oh, I wouldn't say that. He is justified in his own mind, as every
> fellow is. Hitler is justified in his own mind. [Hideki] Tojo and
> [Tomoyuki] Yamashita, they are also justified in their own minds. We
> are always justified in our own minds in doing what we do. The guy that
> murders his wife, why, he can put up a pretty good case when he is
> telling somebody about it in the bar-room over a couple of beers."
> (Blackington)

Chapter Four

The Glory Years

By the spring of 1934 Kenneth Roberts had published three novels, with *Captain Caution* scheduled to appear in the fall. Unfortunately, *The Lively Lady* and *Rabble in Arms* were selling no better than *Arundel*, and several prominent book reviewers had pointedly belittled the author's abilities as a novelist. Nearly two decades later he reflected on that period of his life: "I'd worked hard on those books for [six] years without any noticeable reward or acclaim; and their reception and sales were discouraging in the extreme—so much so that I was broke and on the verge of abandoning the course I'd charted for myself [six] years before."[1]

A letter the despondent novelist received in April, "at the nadir of my discouragement," changed his plans. Dr. Ernest Martin Hopkins, president of Dartmouth College, invited him to Dartmouth's June commencement exercises to receive an honorary doctor of letters. To a teary-eyed and grateful Roberts Hopkins's letter offered "literary rebirth, resuscitation, [and] rehabilitation." This encouragement was surely reinforced when the author read an editorial in the *Boston Herald* published the day after Dartmouth's graduation ceremony (which was reprinted a few months later on the dust jacket of *Captain Caution*). It affirmed that Roberts's honorary degree was "a proper recognition" of his novels, as "he has proved three times that the historian can be entertaining, and the story teller accurate and instructive."[2]

Other honors soon followed. In January 1935 he was elected to membership in the National Institute of Arts and Letters, and in June Colby College awarded him an honorary doctor of letters. By this time *Arundel*, *The Lively Lady*, *Rabble in Arms*, and *Captain Caution* were all selling well, and Roberts, his spirits buoyed at last, was zealously attacking another novel (*IWW*, 296-98).

Although Doubleday increased his royalties in 1934, he still needed to supplement his income by writing for the *Saturday Evening Post*. During the winter of 1933-34 Roberts sailed to Europe to research two *Post* articles—one on higher education in the United States and England and another on the rise of Adolf Hitler in Germany—for which he was paid $2,000 each (*IWW*, 271). His *Post* earnings grew even more after

Lorimer accepted *Captain Caution* for serialization on 21 May 1934. As he joyfully recorded in his diary, he read the editor's telegram and "spent the rest of the day shouting 'Oh boy! Oh boy! Oh boy!'" (*IWW*, 280).

By autumn Roberts had rewritten a number of his *Post* articles for Doubleday, which were published in book form under the title *For Authors Only, and Other Gloomy Essays*. The lead piece was Roberts's biting criticism of the Pulitzer Prize Committee for what he believed was its blatant refusal to follow Joseph Pulitzer's stipulations that the fiction award be given "'for the American novel published during the year which shall best present the wholesome atmosphere of American life, and the highest standard of American manners and manhood.'"[3] While Roberts stated that he had "nothing whatever" against novels such as Thornton Wilder's *The Bridge of San Luis Rey* (1927) or Pearl S. Buck's *The Good Earth* (1931), he simply believed that if Pulitzer's criteria were strictly followed, then those books did not deserve to win the award:

> Nowhere in *The Bridge of San Luis Rey* have I ever been able to find any-thing remotely suggesting the wholesome atmosphere of American life, or of Peruvian life either. Most of the characters, as a matter of fact, led strikingly unwholesome lives—so much so that although the author per-mitted a gratifying number to be destroyed in the collapse of the bridge, he could probably have allowed nearly all of them to meet the same fate without hurting anyone's feelings. (*FAO*, 20)

Doubleday followed this book with the brief *It Must Be Your Tonsils*, another reprinted essay from the *Post*, which humorously described both Roberts's problems with tonsillitis during his 1933-34 European trip and the subsequent tonsillectomy in Portland, Maine. He entered Maine General Hospital soon after he was honored at Colby College's com-mencement, and a few days after the operation he related to Colby President Franklin W. Johnson how he felt during the tonsillectomy: "Dr. Johnson went after my tonsils and, from the resulting sensation, got not only the tonsils but my Colby, Dartmouth and Cornell degrees as well. I have only now reached the stage where I can eat without shedding tears, and can write a letter without inserting foul and angry phrases."[4]

Northwest Passage

While Roberts was reading the magazine proof sheets of *Captain Caution* and revising the manuscript for book publication, he was also contemplating the subject of his next novel. In preparation for a meeting with Booth Tarkington to discuss this book, on 24 August 1934 he jotted down some subjects that interested him. These included Colonial Indian fighter Robert Rogers, the 1745 military campaign against Louisburg, the Cartagena expedition of 1740-41, and the "third phase" of Benedict Arnold's life. "If I could find a way to do it," he wrote in his notes, "the Rogers story is the one I'd rather do, but there's so much of it, I don't see how a story can be laid against Rogers' life. I can't do it as straight history (even if I wanted to) because the material is too fragmentary."[5]

After his discussion with Tarkington four days later, Roberts decided, despite his initial misgivings, to research and chronicle the career of Major Robert Rogers (1731-95). A commander of Colonial soldiers (Rogers's Rangers) during the French and Indian War of 1754-1763, Rogers gained renown for his daring attack in 1759 on the Abenaki Indian village of St. Francis (now near Pierreville in Canada). In 1765 he went to London to secure financial support for his plan to find the so-called Northwest Passage. Offering a short approach to the trade of the Orient, this was the overland route from the Atlantic Ocean across the Rocky Mountains to the Oregon River and the Pacific Ocean. Several influential people promised him financial backing for the project, and to show its support the English government offered him command of the post at Michilimackinac in the Northwest territory (now Mackinac, between lakes Huron and Michigan). While Rogers was commandant of Michilimackinac from 1766 to 1767, he was charged with disobeying orders, squandering money, deserting to the French, and encouraging the Indians to rebel against the Crown. Although a court-martial acquitted him for lack of evidence, he was ruined financially and his reputation was destroyed. The treachery of others, as well as his own dishonesty and other faults, prevented him from launching his expedition to find the Northwest Passage, and he died in a cheap London rooming house in poverty and obscurity.

Northwest Passage is Roberts's most popular and best-selling novel, and for two reasons it is regarded by many critics as his finest work artistically. First, although Roberts consulted dozens of reference works to ensure the accuracy of his book, he was also concerned that the novel succeed both stylistically and as a work of fiction. As he reminded himself in his notes, the research documents about Rogers's life were scarce and "too fragmentary"; thus, when he found the historical evidence lacking in details, he felt free to elaborate and invent the information he needed, but never in a way as to contradict the implications of his source materials. As Roberts admitted in *I Wanted to Write*, "Robert Rogers in *Northwest Passage*, in spite of having a 'real' name, was created out of a few bare facts and a few scraps of information" (*IWW*, 354-55).

For example, in Robert Rogers's autobiographical *Journals* (1765) Rogers noted that while he and his rangers were en route to St. Francis—about 150 miles due north of Crown Point, New York—one Captain Williams was "accidentally burnt with gun-powder, and several men hurt," and that about 40 had to return to Crown Point. In a later entry Rogers reported that French armed vessels were on Lake Champlain "on purpose to decoy any party of ours, that might come that way." Rogers gave no other details, and Roberts theorized in a page margin that "the loss of these 40 men was either a fight or an ambush of some sort."[6] He subsequently concluded that an argument had broken out among Rogers's men and a fired musket had ignited a bag of gunpowder. When Roberts reprinted sections of the *Journals* and other valuable source documents as volume 2 of the limited edition of *Northwest Passage*, he commented about this incident in a footnote: "There is no way of finding out exactly what happened to Capt. Williams and the others who were injured at the same time. The affair is shrouded in mystery. Whatever happened, both Rogers and General [Jeffrey] Amherst apparently wished to conceal it, 'for the good of the service.'"[7]

The other reason for *Northwest Passage*'s critical success is that Roberts, in his portrayal of Robert Rogers, creates a balanced and believable three-dimensional protagonist. He displays his character's vices as well as his virtues, showing that he is an ordinary person with human frailties and shortcomings as well as a commanding military leader of strength and courage. By not becoming as emotionally involved with his hero as he did with Benedict Arnold, Roberts transcends the weaknesses of his earlier books.

Unlike the fictitious and historical protagonists in *Arundel* and *Rabble in Arms*, both Langdon Towne and Robert Rogers become fully developed characters, for Roberts focuses on not only the physical action in book 1 but also on the character development of the men in book 2. At the end of book 1 Rogers is at his highest and most heroic stature, while Towne is just beginning to mature and develop, both as an artist and as a man. In book 2 Roberts contrasts his two heroes as Rogers falls to disgrace and ignominy while his former secretary and cartographer rises to fame in his profession. Towne becomes a person in his own right and achieves his independence from Rogers, while he simultaneously recognizes and accepts that his erstwhile idol is only human:

> This was like Robert Rogers, I thought; he had more than the two faces of Janus, and all his faces were genuine. It was as if Garrick played a dozen parts—selfless hero, drunkard, daring adventurer, debauchee, generous friend, braggart, rioter, splendid visionary, whiner, conqueror and whatnot—and then as if the audience were told that all these roles were the depiction of but one man. I stood marvelling again, as I so often did when I was with him.[8]

Northwest Passage, therefore, is both a psychological novel and a thriller. To prove in book 2 that Rogers was capable of finding the Northwest Passage, Roberts had him attack and destroy St. Francis in book 1, a similar heroic feat. As the author explained shortly after the novel was published, achieving this end "made it necessary for me to reverse the proceeding ordinarily followed by authors: put my physical climax first; then hold the reader's interest through the true climax, which is a psychological one."[9]

As Roberts traces the downfall of Major Robert Rogers, he portrays him accurately as a tragic hero. Although a fearless and indomitable leader of men while in a woods occupied by Indians, Rogers is impatient with bureaucratic red tape and is unable to adjust to politicians and jealous superiors in a relative peaceful civilization. His ambitious nature and influence with the Indians incur the jealousy and resentment of Sir William Johnson, the royal commissioner for Indian affairs, and General Thomas Gage, two of the most powerful men in British North America. After Johnson tells Rogers that he can no longer buy presents for the Indians, he voices his displeasure to Towne in a tone reminiscent of Benedict Arnold complaining to the men from Arundel: "You don't know what men in the highest positions will do when they see rivals coming too close! They'll steal, lie, buy votes, break their promises and go back on their friends! War's a hard business, but politics is worse. According to a politician's lights, Johnson's justified in bottling me up in Michilimackinac without a penny to spend on presents—not one damned penny!" (*NP*, 467-68).

Rogers's downfall is clearly all the more pathetic because his failure is due as much to the enmity of Johnson and Gage as it is to his own frailties. Although Roberts stresses this theme as he attempts to restore Rogers's reputation, he does not forget his artistic purpose. Thus to depict him sinking below adversity while Towne rises above it, the author portrays Rogers as a hard-drinking gambler and womanizer who may have suffered from syphilis (*NP*, 701). Roberts knew that the latter charge was probably false, and he even defended Rogers in a chapter of his appendix volume titled "Rogers' Morals." Furthermore, while he characterized Rogers's wife, Elizabeth Browne Rogers, as a shrew and a "stinker" and Jonathan Carver as a "liar, trimmer and ingrate" (*IWW*, 327), neither was as contemptible as Roberts indicated. His creative license, however, only complements his growth as a novelist and adds to the dramatic appeal of book 2. As John I. Kitch, Jr., argues, "These and . . . other deviations from historical fact . . . suggest that Roberts used his imagination more fully in *Northwest Passage* than in his other novels, that he actually created rather than retold history" (Kitch, 178).

As in *Arundel* and *Rabble in Arms*, Roberts has his fictitious protagonist relate the story as he accompanies the historical hero on his adventures. Artist Langdon Towne (a composite of Indian painters George Catlin and Paul Kane) lives in Kittery, Maine, where Roberts's forebears emigrated from England in 1639. The Towne family was related to Roberts's Nason ancestors, and in the novel the author unobtrusively includes some of his family genealogy. For example, just as three of Roberts's ancestors—Rebecca, Sarah, and Mary Towne—were all condemned as witches in 1692, Langdon Towne mentions that his great-great-grandfather's three sisters, "Rebecca, Sarah and Mary, all women of probity and good sense, had denounced the vicious children responsible for the beginning of the witchcraft delusion in Massachusetts, and as a result had themselves been put on trial for witchcraft."[10]

Roberts's other subplots and themes, while not as significant as in his other works, still contribute to the story's overall success. Cap Huff makes the requisite appearance as a comic-relief figure, but he is replaced by Hunk Marriner early in book 1, who in turn yields the position to Sergeant McNott in book 2. Just as *Arundel*'s Steven Nason finally realizes how fortunate he is not to have married Mary Mallinson, so does Towne "draw a long inward breath" and sigh with relief when he eventually observes how shrewish Elizabeth Browne has become (*NP*, 461). Ann Potter, the daughter of Rogers's secretary, Nathaniel Potter, provides the love subplot, and when Towne in chapter 77 feverishly tells her that he loves her, the scene seems analogous to *Arundel*'s chapter 36 when Steven Nason confesses his love to Phoebe Marvin. In fact, when Cap Huff commissions Towne to immortalize his battles and triumphs on the walls of his sitting room, he pays for the paintings with the same string of pearls that he took from Marie de Sabrevois in *Arundel* (*NP*, 706).

In *I Wanted to Write* Roberts states that with *Northwest Passage* he "hoped to dispel the fog that obscured New Englanders' understanding of the troubles of our forebears in fighting the French and Indians and the manner in which that fighting was done" (*IWW*, 270). Consequently, his graphic descriptions of Indian warfare, especially the fighting at St. Francis, are among the most descriptive of the book. Also, while Towne studies and paints the Indians, Roberts—as he does in his other novels—discusses them and their customs.

Like Roberts's other protagonists, Towne enlists in the military not by choice but through external circumstances. From the outset the narrator declares that "in telling this story, I would like above all things to be truthful" (*NP*, 3), and he often comments on the reality, and hence the futility, of war:

> There swept over me the feeling that has, at one time or another, almost suffocated most men who have ever been a part of any army. Such home-sickness came upon me that my spirit was ill of it. I wanted no more of imbecile war. I wanted nothing but my own home, my own endeavors, my own friends, my own people—the only things on earth in which I could put faith. To my dying day, I knew, I would refuse to be a part of any other war, even though I should be drawn and quartered for my refusal. (*NP*, 300)

Although *Northwest Passage* received overwhelmingly favorable reviews, some critics, much to Roberts's annoyance, persisted in judging one half of the novel to be better than the other. Roberts's friend Herbert Faulkner West favored book 1, "in which Mr. Roberts describes most vividly Rogers' trip back from the attack on St. Francis, down the Ammonoosuc and Connecticut Rivers to [Fort] Old Number 4 in Charlestown, New Hampshire. The latter part about Rogers in London seems to me to detract somewhat from the artistic whole which Mr. Roberts achieved so well in the first part of his novel" (West 1958, 9). Allan Nevins, who wrote the sketch of Rogers that Roberts used for much of his research, concurred: "The real defects of the second half of the book lie in the disjointed narrative and the inadequate backgrounds. As the narrative swings from the fashionable world and Cabinet Ministers of London to the Minnesota Indians and back again to Fleet Prison in London it becomes unconvincing. We find vigorous narrative bits and spirited scenes. But when Mr. Roberts introduces Hogarth, Sir Joshua Reynolds, Benjamin Franklin and other London characters his dialogue begins to creak."[11]

Other critics have faulted Roberts for his London episodes, for he is clearly laboring with a setting unfamiliar to him. *Saturday Review of Literature* editor Bernard DeVoto, however, particularly singled out book 2 in his complimentary review: "Suddenly Mr. Roberts is animating his material with an imaginative warmth that he had not shown us before. The hunger and desire of the nation just about to break westward into the untrodden lands, the tangle of cupidities and venalities and stupidities that in great part conditioned them—they are in *Northwest Passage* as they have not been in our fiction before."[12]

As DeVoto recognized, book 2 contains some of Roberts's finest writing, particularly in the last several chapters when Rogers is in London's Fleet Prison, his once brilliant career over and his self-respect lost. As Towne leaves the prison after talking with "this garrulous, red-eyed, wheezy derelict" whom the Indians had once feared as the "White Devil," he reflects on not only his friend's life and destiny but his own as well:

> Rogers, I knew, had reached the height of his career—had come to a real grandeur of soul—on that terrible day when, at the end of our retreat from St. Francis, the woodcutters had dragged our raft ashore and helped the three of us to stagger to the stockade at Number Four. I saw him as I had seen him in the flickering firelight of the fort: gaunt, barefooted, covered with bruises, hung with tattered strips of strouding. I remembered the shredded leggins hanging on his emaciated flanks; the ribs and bony chest that showed through his torn rags; the chunk of bread in his scarred, sooty, pitch-stained hands; and as if it had been yesterday I heard his thick voice saying: "Get me some beef—fat beef. I'm going back—back to my men—back to the Ammoonoosuc!"
>
> And now I had seen him so low that a man could go no lower this side of the grave. But far as he had fallen, yet something—some imperishable last glimmer of that old spirit—still survived. There was an inner force that had been warped and twisted by narrow men and a shallow woman, but that had never been wholly crushed and never could be.
>
> More than that, I suspected that even still the man who lay in the mud of the Fleet was better than the mere sodden husk of Robert Rogers. But for Fate and Ann Potter, I suspected, there in that same grime might lie Langdon Towne. There, too, but for the grace of God, might lie any of us, our talents quenched and our best dreams beaten. (*NP*, 693-94, 684)

An unofficial poll among American book reviewers and literary editors showed that *Northwest Passage* was their first choice for the 1938 Pulitzer Prize for fiction.[13] Roberts, however, refused to get his hopes up and merely expressed his dissatisfaction with the award committee's previous selections, much as he had done six years earlier in his essay "For Authors Only." Therefore he was not too disappointed—or surprised—when his friend John P. Marquand received the Pulitzer Prize for *The Late George Apley* (1937). "I warned Doubleday again and again that they were wrong to count on it, and offered to bet against myself on every possible opportunity," he wrote to Ben Ames Williams who had expressed his regrets. "Just received a Stetson, in fact, from a New York rooter. When Esther Forbes offered premature congratulations, I offered her an opportunity to pick up a nice piece of change with the sky the limit, but she failed to seize the opportunity."[14]

Despite this lack of critical acceptance, the immediate public popularity of *Northwest Passage* dramatically increased both Roberts's literary reputation and the sales of his earlier novels. The Book-of-the-Month Club chose the title for its July 1937 selection, and Metro-Goldwyn-Mayer brought him additional publicity when it purchased the motion picture rights shortly after the book's publication in June.

His royalties now enabled Roberts to quit writing for the *Saturday Evening Post* on a regular basis; appropriately, one of his last contributions was book 1 of *Northwest Passage*. He hired his niece Marjorie Mosser to relieve his wife of her typing duties and other secretarial tasks, and he also began drawing plans for a new house he planned to build in the country outside Kennebunkport. In the summer of 1924 Roberts and his wife bought an abandoned livery stable across the street from Stall Hall, their house in Kennebunk Beach, and had it torn down. With Booth Tarkington's help they had designed a New England/Spanish style house that, when completed, they named "Blue Roof" in honor of its brightly colored shingles. Both residences, unfortunately, were adjacent to the local golf course, and Roberts often complained about "golfers knocking balls through windows [and] caddies rattling clubs and screeching" (*IWW*, 221, 168-69).

In March 1939 the Robertses moved into their new two-story, 12-room house near the Atlantic Ocean. Constructed of Maine fieldstone, the house was part of Roberts's working farm, on which he raised vegetables and other produce, cultivated hay, reclaimed marshland, made charcoal from leveled trees, and raised mallards, geese, and other migratory birds. His estate, which he named Rocky Pasture, included a barn, garage, spring house, other outbuildings, and ponds, and he lived on it the rest of his life.[15]

Trending into Maine, Good Maine Food, and *March to Quebec*

Roberts followed *Northwest Passage* with *Trending into Maine,* a collection of 15 essays that celebrate the history, traditions, and people of his native state.[16] Illustrated by N. C. Wyeth, Roberts's informal "book of Maine reminiscences" includes chapters on the shipbuilding and privateer era of the early nineteenth century, the hardships Maine's citizens faced during various American wars, ship captains and their tall tales of the sea serpents they encountered during their voyages, and hunting, fishing, lobstering, and cooking in Maine.

At the end of the first chapter Roberts observes that he has "a profound love and respect for Maine, for its history and for its people; and I'd like everyone to see it as I see it, and to love it as I do" (*Trending,* 15). Because of this pride in his own Marine heritage, he incorporated stories about his ancestors into the book, just as he did with his novels. The arduous journey to Quebec from *Arundel* is re-created in "Road to the Past." "Foundation of a Maine Family" and "Maine Seafarers Speak for Themselves" encompass historical narratives of the Nasons and Townes. The thumbnail sketches of early Arundel residents in "Anthology of a Small Town" are of the real-life counterparts to some of Roberts's fictitious characters. Although he seldom wrote about his own early years, in "A Maine Kitchen" the author fondly recalls how as a boy he loved his grandmother's house and the meals she prepared for her family.

Shortly before *Trending into Maine* was published, "A Maine Kitchen" appeared in the *Saturday Evening Post* under the title "Down-East Ambrosia." Roberts was soon inundated with letters from readers asking why he had failed to include their favorite foods in the article, and he suggested to his secretary that she use the letters and recipes as a foundation of a Maine cookbook. Marjorie Mosser's *Good Maine Food,* with an introduction and notes by Roberts, was published in 1939.[17]

Appearing just a few months after *Trending into Maine, March to Quebec* is Roberts's annotated compilation of 11 of the journal accounts kept by members of Benedict Arnold's Canadian expedition. Also included are biographical sketches of each writer; Arnold's own journal and letters; a casualty list of the Americans who attacked Quebec; the 1761 journal and map of British engineer Lieutenant John Montresor, on which the plans for Arnold's march were based; and a defense of Colonel Roger Enos (written by one of his descendants), who achieved notoriety during the expedition for deserting with his detachment before the journey was completed.

There is less duplication among the journals than might be expected, for the men of different detachments had different experiences. Dr. Isaac Senter often commented on the men's health and medical problems, such as dysentery. No one except Simon Fobes kept a record of the return journey to Maine. The diary of Ephraim Squier, the only journalist from Colonel Enos's division, reflects the company's apathy.

As both readers and reviewers recognized, *March to Quebec* is invaluable not only for its single-volume presentation of more than a dozen significant primary-source documents but also because it shows how Roberts took history and created historical fiction. According to historian Henry Steele Commager, "The journals abundantly substantiate Mr. Robert's [*sic*] interpretation of Arnold in *Arundel*. Historians must be grateful to Mr. Roberts for making available source material not easily accessible and providing it with annotation no less entertaining than informative; laymen can find here historical truth stranger than most fiction and no less exciting than even the best."[18]

Oliver Wiswell

Roberts became interested in the Loyalist side of the Revolution while researching *Arundel*. His interest sharpened when he was writing *Rabble in Arms* and was plotting the characters of Peter Merrill, an American patriot, and his younger brother Nathaniel, who favored the Loyalist cause. Although he read numerous books to try to learn how the Loyalists reacted to the rebellion so he could have Nathaniel effectively present his arguments to his brother, Roberts could find little useful information. He discovered, however, that many of America's intellectual leaders were Loyalists, and he came across references to dozens of well-respected and admired Americans who had become Tories and were consequently forced to flee to England. "Well," he wondered, "if they were admirable, why had they been Tories, when everyone instinctively knew that Tories were fiends in human shape?" (*IWW*, 342).

Roberts answered this question and also climaxed his written convictions on the fundamental idiocy of war in *Oliver Wiswell*, whose title character personifies the Tory attitude toward the American Revolution.

Narrator Wiswell, a Yale student and son of a prominent Massachusetts lawyer, is caught up in the war through his rescue of printer Tom Buell from a rebel mob. Wiswell helps Buell not because of his own loyalties to England but because he abhors the actions of these barbaric men who tar and feather a fellow American, cut him open by forcing him to ride a fence rail, and pry open his horse's mouth so they can viciously cut off its tongue.

In these descriptive passages Roberts dramatically shows that the much-lauded Sons of Liberty actually deserved the appellation coined by Loyalists—the Sons of Tyranny. When Wiswell brings Buell home with him after his ordeal, his father, Seaton Wiswell, angrily speaks his mind: "'I've seen Boston mobs, and I've seen the things they do. I've seen men split up to the middle from being ridden on rails by those lovers of Liberty.' He laughed, and added, 'Those lovers of liberty who won't allow anyone else the liberty of disagreeing with 'em!'"[19]

Roberts asserts in *I Wanted to Write* that "the intellectual cream of America were Loyalists—Tories—and that they had been driven from their country by a wave of intolerance" (*IWW*, 342-43). This statement points out one of Roberts's central theses in *Oliver Wiswell*: the Revolution was essentially a civil war between Americans rather than a conflict between England and the colonies, with the Tories no less patriotic than the rebels simply because they wanted "a friendly adjustment of America's difficulties with England" (*OW*, 102). Many colonists recognized the injustices of King George's oppressive government, but they were neither scoundrels nor villains for not participating in the rebellion, which they viewed as brutal and the work of a demagogic minority. As Wiswell tells Vose Leighton, one of the village's leading rebels and the father of the girl he loves,

> We're all agreed that England'll have to govern these colonies different-ly; but there's considerable difference of opinion about our loss of liberty. I haven't lost any liberty yet under English rule, but I've lost plenty of it under the rule of Americans. Congress has done its best to hide the Galloway Plan from me, so I won't think contrary to what Congress wants me to think. And from what I know about the Sons of Liberty, there's no part of these colonies where freedom of speech hasn't been sup-pressed, the liberty of the press destroyed, and the voice of truth silenced—not by legal means, but by the orders of self-appointed and ignorant committeemen and by little mobs of lawless and equally igno-rant men. (*OW*, 30)

Oliver Wiswell covers the entire Revolution, from two days before the Battle of Lexington and Concord to after the surrender at Yorktown. As Wiswell witnesses the Battles of Bunker Hill and Long Island and fights alongside Colonel John Cruger during the siege of Fort Ninety-Six, his chief objective is to prevent America from being overwhelmed by civil war and fall into the hands of men who beat and banish those who dare to hold thoughts contrary to their own. "You and I and most of our close friends want to avoid war," his father tells him. "More than that, we want to avoid the bitterest of wars—civil war. . . . You'll never again find the Leightons agreeable, Oliver, unless you tell them you're against settling our differences with England by peaceful means" (*OW*, 34).

Another of the novel's themes is that America did not win the war but that England lost it through the incredible stupidity and bungling of its military officers. For instance, at the Battle of Bunker Hill at Charlestown, Massachusetts, Wiswell and his friends watch from the window of a nearby house with frustration as Generals Thomas Gage and William Howe direct their men—who wear full packs on a hot June day—in a ridiculous frontal attack against the fortified rebels. After the British finally take the hill the soldiers fail to pursue the retreating rebels, an action that could have ended the war.

Wiswell, therefore, views the Revolution as a succession of military and criminal blunders, all owing to petty English politics and the failure of the British officers to appreciate the loyal American Tories. He consequently scorns the British for their inept leadership as bitterly as he despises the Rebels for their cowardice and ruthless cruelty. Shortly before the surrender at Yorktown he vents his frustration to General Henry Clinton: "For seven years I've seen things go wrong in this war. For seven years British armies haven't followed up their victories, British ministers have refused to believe what they were told, British fleets have delayed too long, the wrong men have been put in high positions, Loyalists have been treated cavalierly by the very men who should be most grateful to them" (*OW*, 763).

Because Roberts's purpose is to narrate the story of the Revolution from the side of the Loyalists, Wiswell and his friends naturally denounce America's leaders and alleged patriots as well as England's, although they still feel a certain bond to the colonies. Seaton Wiswell labels Samuel Adams a "demagogue" and a "rabble-rouser" (*OW*, 18). Shipowner George Leonard tells Oliver that John Hancock is "a perpetual malcontent! He was at the bottom of his class at Harvard because his father was poor; and because of that he hates everyone with property. He can't make money or keep it, so he argues that everyone who can must be dishonest." Leonard adds that Hancock is "a miserable little over-dressed incompetent," a convicted smuggler, a wastrel who squandered his father's fortune, and an alleged embezzler who "can't account for" 15,000 pounds of Harvard College's money (*OW*, 58, 59). While in Paris Oliver discovers that Benjamin Franklin is a "benevolent old rebel with mistresses up alleys," who has "delighted in forging letters, full of bare-faced lies and foul hints, that destroyed the character and reputa-tion of anyone antagonistic to the rebel cause" (*OW*, 483).

Although the narrators in *Arundel*, *Rabble in Arms*, and *Northwest Passage* all fervently condemned the hopelessness of war, each learned and matured during his military service while serving under a well-respected commanding officer. As John I. Kitch, Jr., points out, war "brought out the best in people, made men out of them, and accomplished some-thing" (Kitch, 198). For Wiswell, Buell, and their other friends, howev-er, no glory or honor was realized because the various battles and struggles accomplished "nothing that couldn't be equally well accom-plished by honest discussion between reasonable men—accomplished without loss of freedom, loss of life, loss of property, loss of all the things men value" (*OW*, 434).

Once again, therefore, a Roberts narrator sees that his duty is to tell the truth about war and the politicians who furthered it. Before Seaton Wiswell's death soon after the Battle of Bunker Hill, his closest friend was Thomas Hutchinson. One of Roberts's historical figures, Hutchinson held many political offices and became chief justice of Massachusetts' Superior Court of Judicature in 1760 and governor of Massachusetts in 1771. In 1765 Hutchinson's Boston home was gutted and its contents destroyed by a rebel mob in a frenzy over the Stamp Tax. When the exiled governor in 1777 meets Oliver in London, he encourages him to write a history of the Revolution:

> "What I'd rather do, Oliver, is make it possible for you to see and under-stand as much of this war as you can, and to write the truth about it—write the truth about the stupidity of those who started it; write the truth about the criminal way in which it has been fought; write the truth about how at any moment it could have been peacefully ended by either side, but wasn't; write the truth about the manner in which America is looked upon as nothing but a means by which European politicians can attain their miserable ends!"

His voice became brittle. "Politicians! There's a great chance for you, Oliver! If only you could write a history of this war that would show our people how easily they'd been used by scheming politicians—how needlessly they'd ruined themselves, killed themselves, brought misery, destruction, hatred to their country just to further the schemes of reckless men—you might be doing something for future generations." (*OW*, 431)

Because Roberts portrayed the Revolution from the Loyalist viewpoint, he was frequently criticized for writing one-sided reactionary propaganda. He received dozens of angry letters, which he promptly consigned to a large manila envelope that he called "the nut file."[20] One of the most bitter public denunciations was a book review in *Catholic World*, whose author sarcastically remonstrated, "The Tories were all good, and Roberts's book ends with all of them going to Canada and thereby removing all goodness from America and leaving it populated only by the execrable rabble he depicts throughout, whose descendants we are."[21]

Roberts's friends Thomas B. Costain and Booth Tarkington predicted this public furor after reading the book in manuscript form, and they both suggested changes so that the novel would not offend its readers. Tarkington, for example, thought that some of the passages in which Wiswell denounces war and the rebels be cut out, and he agreed with Costain that the inflammatory Loyalist opinions of the Declaration of Independence would enrage more readers than just the members of the Daughters of the American Revolution. Costain told Roberts that the book would end on a high patriotic note if Wiswell married Julia Bishop and stayed in the United States instead of marrying Sally Leighton and going to Canada with other Tories.[22]

But Roberts responded—as he often did when confronted with such criticism of *Oliver Wiswell*—by saying that his patriotism was not an issue because his characters' sentiments were not necessarily his own. Wiswell, he declared, was a man of principle who would never abandon the cause for which he had fought for so many years. Consequently, the novel's plot had to remain the way he wrote it because it was vital for fiction—unlike history—to be told from the narrator's viewpoint. In a letter to *New York Herald Tribune* book reviewer Lewis Gannett he commented on his objective:

Naturally my only purpose in writing *Oliver Wiswell* was to tell the loyalist side of the Revolution; and I don't mind saying that for a year or so, I

had great difficulty in holding constantly to the loyalist viewpoint without injecting the beliefs of non-loyalists. However, having embarked on
the loyalist mind, there's no use tampering with it. That's why I couldn't
do anything about it when some pre-publication readers of *Wiswell* urged
me to cut out loyalist opinions of the Declaration of Independence. The
loyalists had those opinions, very strongly, and I'd committed myself to
telling the loyalist side as completely as I could. I was similarly urged to
have the protagonist see the error of his ways, go back to Kentucky and
marry the gal he met on the Wilderness Trail. I couldn't do it because
that wasn't the way things happened. Loyalist regiments, officers and
men too, went as units to New Brunswick, Nova Scotia and Upper
Canada. That's how strongly they felt about it.[23]

While Roberts does not overstate his case for the Loyalist side, the
book can be faulted in other respects. Its major flaw is in terms of scope.
The volume encompasses eight years, covering the Revolution from all
angles—military, economic, social, and diplomatic. Consequently,
Wiswell in a variety of pursuits makes appearances in Boston, Halifax,
New York, London, Paris, Virginia, Maryland, Kentucky, South Carolina,
and New Brunswick. En route to Long Island in book 2, Wiswell and
Buell encounter Colonel Robert Rogers. Attempting to recruit rangers for
England, Rogers is a disheveled and belching "distorted ghost of a one-
time hero" (*OW*, 229). Wiswell meets Benedict Arnold in book 4, who is
still fighting to save the colonies from the Continental Congress and the
French: "He was a great soldier, doing his utmost, singlehanded—which
is in itself held to be a crime—to save America from self-ruin and French
domination" (*OW*, 577). The appearance of Alexander McGillivray, a
Creek Indian chief who helps Wiswell and Buell safely reach the village of
Ninety-Six in book 5, affords Roberts the opportunity to fulminate about
the "ferocious persecution of the Cherokees and Creeks by the avaricious
whites, and the condoning and encouraging of that persecution by the
rebel Congress and government" (*OW*, 655).

Roberts's historical scenes are accurately represented, and his historical figures all appear at the correct places and times. His penchant for
facts, names, and events often clouds his abilities as a novelist, however,
as he shifts his fiction to fit the historical era in which he is working.
Book 3, wherein the action takes place in England and France for four
years, is obviously included so Roberts can explain France's entry into
the war as an American ally. Wiswell could just as easily have learned of
the French alliance if he had stayed in the United States, however, rather
than waste time pursuing melodramatic adventures abroad with numer-

ous American and foreign dignitaries. As Carlos Baker regretfully noted, "There are times in *Oliver Wiswell* when the reader is confronted with a formidable barricade of historical argument, which he must tear down piece by piece before he can proceed" (Baker, 18).

This problem of scope—"a sprawling quality which results in thin and unconvincing passages," according to reviewer Allan Nevins[24]—is also responsible for the weaknesses of Roberts's fictitious characters. Wiswell's whirlwind travels for so many important people render him unconvincing as a real person. His relationship with rebel sympathizer Sally Leighton, who lives the eight years of the war with her patriot family near Boston, has to be projected through letters. As a result the entire love story, while supporting the concept of the Revolution as a "brother against brother" war, seems formulaic and contrived, with Sally never becoming a solid character in her own right.

But as Roberts demonstrated in his other books, especially *Northwest Passage*, he is a master at painting colorful scenes of action-filled battles and military campaigns. Thus, although it seems strikingly coincidental that Wiswell is present at much of the action throughout the Revolution, the author does have him graphically describe what he sees. In a cover story on Roberts on the publication of *Oliver Wiswell*, *Time* noted that the book "is packed with people, battles, sudden flights, escapes, rail-riding mobs, secret service, forlorn defenses, intrigue, massacres, [and] exile."[25] Allan Nevins agreed, contending, "Once more Mr. Roberts proves that his best talents lie in the swift narration of some tale of heroic exertions or resistances. Nobody better than he can bring a battle, a siege, a toilsome march, a wrestle with overmastering moral and material forces, vividly before us" (Nevins 1940, 5).

Roberts's powers of description and narration are possibly best shown in chapters 77 through 86, which dramatize the 22 May to 19 June 1781 siege at the Tory-held Fort Ninety-Six in South Carolina (so named because it was about 96 miles southeast of Fort Prince George on the Keowee River). As Roberts recounts how the beleaguered and vastly outnumbered Loyalists held their own against an entire rebel army, he presents a lifelike chronicle that is, as Revolutionary War historian Mark M. Boatner stated, "better 'history' than most histories"[26]:

> Almost on the instant the ditch beneath us was filled with struggling men. [Captain Thomas] French and [Captain Peter] Campbell came in sight, stabbing and pitchforking with their bayonets at men who stumbled, tried to run and screamed sickeningly.

I saw French slapping his men on the back and pushing them forward. He looked up over his shoulder at the rebels clinging against the face of the stockade and hauling with hooks at the sandbags. He ran to one of them, caught his ankle and pulled. The man came down in a heap, and two of French's men leaped at him and stabbed him with their bayonets. Then they waited like crouched cats for French to pull down two more men from the stockade.

Rebels, escaping by crawling into the traverses, seemed to strike invisible walls against which they crumpled and lay in heaps.

There was something unbearably exciting in the advance of French and Campbell, something shockingly gratifying about the way in which the dodging, scrambling rebels between them grew fewer and fewer, fell beneath the feet of the onrushing Loyalists, raised their hands in surrender and were spewed out into quiet backwaters to stand motionless and dazed. (*OW*, 723)

While Roberts was working on *Oliver Wiswell* in December 1937, Samuel G. Blythe, an old friend from Roberts's *Saturday Evening Post* years, wrote to give him some advice: "You've gotta make a home run when you come up next time. No single or two base hit will suffice. Otherwise, the great Roberts, author of *Northwest Passage*, plainly shows by this new novel that he is on the down grade" (*IWW*, 348). Blythe's concerns were unnecessary. Roberts's fiery passion for justice—a hallmark of his novels—helped create a widely reviewed best-seller that only enhanced his reputation as one of the country's most popular historical novelists.

Lydia Bailey

While Roberts was working on his next novel, Doubleday in 1945 published *The Kenneth Roberts Reader*, a collection of *Saturday Evening Post* essays and excerpts from novels, that the company hoped would attract new readers to the author's works.[27] Doubleday released *Lydia Bailey* in January 1947, and in a brief essay published that month Roberts explained that the "germ of [the story] was planted in 1930, when I was writing *The Lively Lady*." He discovered that the Number Four Prison at Dartmoor, where his great-grandfather was housed, was controlled by a giant black man named King Dick. Also in the prison were a great number of Frenchmen, including a General Le Febvre, who had been captured by the British in Haiti. Roberts wrote, "As I struggled to bring my great-grandfather, General Lefebvre [*sic*], King Dick and other characters to life, I frequently wondered how a French army had got into trouble in Haiti, but couldn't turn from my investigations into the War of 1812 long enough to find out."[28]

Roberts was also interested in the Mediterranean Sea adventures of sailors from Maine and other parts of America, and a few years later he decided to write the story of General William Eaton, who in 1805 had organized an expedition against Barbary pirates in North Africa (*IWW*, 344). As he read about Eaton, he discovered that the campaign was ruined by Tobias Lear, who had once been George Washington's secretary. While reading Lear's correspondence that he obtained from the National Archives in Washington, D.C., Roberts found that Lear was in Haiti with the French army, which partially answered the question he had wondered about in 1930. He also discovered that, in return for French help during the Revolutionary War, the Colonies had promised to defend France's island possessions in the West Indies. When England began attacking these islands during its fight against France, however, the United States refused to intervene. France took hundreds of American ships in retaliation for America's neutrality, and Congress was faced with settling numerous citizen claims for damages.

In addition, Roberts learned that American sea captains, who were worried about these French Spoliation Claims and the Alien and Sedition Acts, were also in Haiti. In his essay Roberts summarized his reasons for including all of these events in his novel: "So one thing led to another—Eaton led to Lear, Lear led to Haiti, Haiti led to American sea captains and French Spoliation Claims, French Spoliation Claims led to French refugees in the United States, French refugees led to Alien and Sedition Laws, Alien and Sedition Laws led to the men who made them" ("Evolution," 6).

Lydia Bailey, whose events take place between 1800 and 1805, is consequently two stories. The first concerns the heroic black leader Pierre François Dominique Toussaint L'Ouverture and the Haitian revolution for independence from France as Napoleon Bonaparte sought to make Haiti a base for his invasion of Louisiana and the United States. The second recounts America's war with the Barbary pirates of North Africa, particularly General Eaton's gallant 600-mile march across the North African desert in his ill-fated attempt to restore the exiled Hamet Karamanli to the Tripolitan throne (an expedition commemorated in "The Marines' Hymn"). Participants in both stories are narrator Albion Hamlin from Gorham, Maine (whom Roberts modeled slightly after his great-great-uncle, sea captain Albion Nason), and the title character, with whom Hamlin falls in love after seeing her portrait.

As one critic has pointed out, throughout *Lydia Bailey* Roberts focuses on Hamlin's fight against "the foolish consistency of ignorant men who refuse to modify their plans in the light of truth."[29] Early in the novel Hamlin stresses that consistency is one of the cardinal faults of many people in power and that "men who make a virtue of consistency" inevitably bring "hell and ruin" on innocent people and countries:

All the great villains and small villains whom I met so frequently in the events I'm about to set down were consistent men—unimaginative men who consistently believed in war as a means of settling disputes between nations; equally misguided men who consistently believed that war must be avoided at all hazards, no matter what the provocation; narrow men who consistently upheld the beliefs and acts of one political party and saw no good in any other; shortsighted men who consistently refused to see that the welfare of their own nation was dependent upon the welfare of every other nation; ignorant men who consistently thought that the policies of their own government should be supported and followed, whether those policies were right or wrong; dangerous men who consistently thought that all people with black skins are inferior to those with white skins; intolerant men who consistently believed that all people with white skins should be forced to accept all people with black skins as equals.[30]

Hamlin's philosophy sets the novel's tone as he confronts the problems brought about by different types of consistent people (Harris, 66-67). A descendant of Loyalists like Oliver Wiswell, the staunchly independent Hamlin agrees to defend Boston newspaper editor Thomas Bailey for allegedly violating the Sedition Act, which the Federalists used to prosecute those who said or printed anything against the government. After talking with Bailey, Hamlin furiously exclaims that it is "sheer wanton brutality" to bring him to trial, to which the editor decries the consistency of politicians: "'Yes,' Bailey murmured, 'sheer wanton brutality. That's politics. Always consistent, politicians are—always descend to sheer wanton brutality, flavored with idiocy, when they're threatened with loss of position or loss of power. Try to ruin everybody who's against 'em!'" (*LB*, 24-25).

Similarly, as Hamlin and King Dick escape from the vicious Haitian General Jean Jacques Dessalines, who has "the face and the body of a giant toad" (*LB*, 194), Hamlin disparages the consistency of the French soldiers who are attempting to gain control of Haiti: "Ah, yes! They were consistent men, those Frenchmen: consistent in their contempt for black soldiers: consistent in their belief in their own invincibility and the superiority of their own logic to other sorts; consistent in their determination to take whatever they wanted from anyone too weak or too ignorant to resist—and for the consistency of a few, hundreds suffered, as must always be the case" (*LB*, 251).

Roberts connects this theme with his observations about war, but with *Lydia Bailey* he departs from his usual message that war inevitably brings futility and hopelessness. Instead, he argues that at times men must fight to overthrow tyranny, to defend their freedom, and to avoid greater suffering.[31] For instance, in Haiti Hamlin encourages the blacks to rebel against the French: "You're arguing that if the Haitians themselves abstain from destruction, there won't be any destruction. The exact opposite is true. People who make war in order to escape slavery may possibly win" (*LB*, 148).

Roberts's theme is also illustrated in the novel's second section. Pasha Joseph Karamanli of Tripoli has usurped the throne of his brother Hamet, who has fled to upper Egypt. In 1801 the ruler decides that the treaty of 1796 between the United States and Tripoli was not sufficiently remunerative, and he declares war on the United States. The American Congress authorizes naval agent Eaton to effect a peace with Tripoli by restoring Hamet Karamanli to power. Eaton finds the exiled pasha, brings him to Alexandria, and with an army of mercenaries, Arab cavalry, and U.S. Marines marches across the desert and seizes the Tripolitan seaport of Derna on 27 April 1805. Eaton and Hamlin soon discover, however, that the U.S. government has withdrawn its support of Hamet and has authorized consular officer Tobias Lear to negotiate a peace treaty with Joseph, the reigning pasha. After the U.S. Navy orders Eaton's forces to leave Tripoli, Hamlin goes to Malta to tell its governor, Sir Alexander John Ball, about the situation and to ask for his help:

> Lear always contrives to think wrong, somehow. . . . He had access to French Spoliation Claims papers in Washington, but he refused to help me get them for my clients, though he damned well knew I was entitled to have 'em. In Haiti he did everything he could to persuade Toussaint L'Ouverture to surrender to the French without a fight—to sell the whole island back into slavery again. Now he means to settle this war with Tripoli in his own way: he's going to sell out the United States Government; he's going to sell out Eaton; he's going to sell out Hamet. The United States Navy in the Mediterranean isn't commanded by Commodore [Samuel] Barron—it's commanded by Tobias Lear; and Tobias Lear's going to run counter to every decent man's opinion! . . . If [Commodore Edward] Preble were in command of our ships in this ocean,

as he ought to be, he and Eaton between 'em would have Joseph Karamanli on his way to exile in a month's time, and Tripoli would be governed by a man who'd guarantee safety and equal rights to the ships of every nation in the world. But that's not how Lear does things! (*LB*, 431)

Roberts's view of war as a necessary evil is rendered more graphic by his realistic and occasionally gory descriptions of bloodshed. During the destruction of Cap François, Haitian women and girls are raped and murdered. In Verrettes General Dessalines orders his men to slaughter hundreds of helpless white men, women, and children. In a battle between Haitians and the French, Hamlin sees "a headless body with blood gushing in a double jet from the raw neck; a whole leg, torn off at the hip, that moved and contracted itself in the moment I watched it; a man, his intestines slipping from a hole in his stomach, who fumblingly tried to stuff them back into himself, as one might try to push eels into too small a bag" (*LB*, 244). These accounts of pillage and carnage were so unlike the descriptions of war in Roberts's earlier novels that a reviewer complained, somewhat unjustly, that "the book is heavily encrusted with profanity, vulgarity, outright obscenity and occasional blasphemy."[32]

Other reviewers and readers had additional objections. The most succinct criticism came from the *Atlantic Monthly*: "I wish Mr. Roberts had a clearer sense of what to eliminate from his first drafts. His novels, even the best of them, have a tendency to sprawl, and in this case, as in *Northwest Passage*, there are a beginning, a middle, and an end, and then without pause for breath, another beginning and middle and end. It adds up to too much, and in the protraction, in the constant shift from one background to the next, the main characters lose their orientation, they become flat rather than forceful, the victims of romance rather than of a reality."[33]

After Allan Nevins, in a generally salutary review, regretted that *Lydia Bailey* contains "a certain excess of richness" and "is stuffed with too many plums," Roberts wrote to thank him for the kind remarks and to explain his problems with writing the second part of the book: "I thought that blasted Eaton expedition had me licked. I gave that story up half a dozen times before it dawned on me that it could only be told from both ends—from the Lear end and the Eaton end, simultaneously. When I told it that way, I couldn't avoid (as you say) stuffing it. What I dropped, hacked and yanked out of that story gave me right-handed-paralysis; and Christ knows I felt that stuffed feeling, even more poignantly than you did, because my feeling lasted for months and months."[34]

As with Roberts's other novels, *Lydia Bailey* includes numerous historical figures, but there are no subtleties in his characterization; heroes are heroes (Toussaint, Eaton, Preble, Hamet Karamanli) and villains are villains (Judge Samuel Chase, Lear, George Lee, Joseph Karamanli), with all persons delineated to one of these two extremes. Although historian Henry Steele Commager praised the book as "a capital tale, packed with action and adventure and with history," he interjected some cautionary opinions from a historian's perspective: "We had not heretofore supposed that Toussaint was quite as admirable a character as he is here painted, that poor [Captain William] Bainbridge was as culpable, Barron as weak, Eaton as heroic, or Lear as despicable as they are here portrayed."[35]

Despite *Lydia Bailey*'s largely favorable reviews, Herbert Faulkner West believed it and *Oliver Wiswell* "were written to satisfy a ready market." He also thought that the two books were "too long, too full of information, and some of the characters, particularly Lydia Bailey, somehow fail to ring true" (West 1962, 97).

West is correct—Roberts's characters do not "ring true." While Lydia Bailey is seen through the eyes of her devoted husband as a strong and wise woman, she nevertheless remains pallid and dull throughout the novel, a caricature with "the soul of a self-satisfied school-marm."[36] Albion Hamlin is overshadowed—and overly protected—by *The Lively Lady*'s formidable King Dick. Part of the problem is that the two never become flesh-and-blood personalities but instead remain puppets. "There is a good deal of talk about 'character,'" contended *Commonweal*'s reviewer, "but little real penetration into the mystery of the human personality" (Connolly, 402).

The novel's melodramatic plot strains the reader's credulity. Wrote the *New York Times Book Review*, "The heroine is dragged into the early chapters by a device that might redden the ears of even an opera librettist—the hero acquires a picture of Lydia Bailey painted by Gilbert Stuart, and falls in love with her though he believes her dead."[37] Hamlin hastily travels to Haiti when he learns that she is still alive and within a few weeks finds her, becomes friends with King Dick and Toussaint L'Ouverture, and is forced to serve as personal secretary to General Dessalines, "the worst man in the world" (*LB*, 197). Hamlin escapes from Dessalines and marries Lydia. When they leave Haiti for France their ship is captured by Barbary pirates through the treachery of

Charles Lee, and the couple is imprisoned in Tripoli. After being held captive for two years Hamlin escapes and enlists in General Eaton's forces, and when Lear thwarts Eaton's plans and negotiates the last-minute appeasement treaty, the two reunited lovers sail for France.

As Roberts admitted to Allan Nevins, *Lydia Bailey* was difficult for him to complete. During his six years of research and writing he had to familiarize himself with the Alien and Sedition Acts and the French Spoliation Claims, read and decipher the letters of Tobias Lear, and translate several French books into English, including Mederic Louis Elie Moreau de St. Mery's *Voyage aux Etats-Unis de l'Amerique, 1793-1798* (1913). He revised the manuscript countless times as he smoothed the transitions between the Haiti and Tripoli sections, and his secretary told him after the book was finished that she had typed more than two million words to get a completed manuscript of 250,000 words.[38]

Although *Lydia Bailey* enjoyed great popular success and was selected by both the Book-of-the-Month Club and the Literary Guild, even Roberts's close friends acknowledged that it was not one of his better works. Just as Booth Tarkington and Ben Ames Williams often helped Roberts with his novels, so did their mutual friend and fellow writer Major Arthur Hamilton Gibbs. In a 1963 interview Gibbs remarked that he thought *Lydia Bailey* should have been two books, one on Haiti and one on Tripoli, for he could see no real connection between the two sections. Gibbs also felt that Roberts, while writing the book, was "in a sense a tired man." The Robertses were in Nassau when it was published, so Doubleday editor Clara Claasen gave Gibbs and his wife two copies to take with them when she learned that they were going to the Bahamas and would see their friends. Roberts was not the least bit interested, however, when Gibbs handed him the books, and he "just shoved them aside."[39] It was shortly after the publication of *Lydia Bailey*, during the notorious Maine forest fires of 1947, that Roberts's passion for dowsing began to supersede his enthusiasm for researching and writing historical novels.

I Wanted to Write and Other Works

Roberts's decidedly vocal opinions and passion for causes were not limited to topics of a national or international nature. In 1926 newspapers across Maine quoted him after he declared that the scenery of his beloved state "is being wrecked by the most atrocious hot dog stands and advertising signs that the world has ever seen." Two years later the first of his several antibillboard articles appeared in the *Saturday Evening Post*. After he observed, however, that Maine still did little if anything to regulate the signs, in 1930 he urged the women of the Arundel Garden Club of Kennebunk to "go forth with rope and grappling irons and tear the offensive billboards down."

Although history does not record whether Roberts's protests inspired the Garden Club members to take up arms against Maine's billboards, his call to action did arouse the ire of former Maine Governor Percival P. Baxter. In a speech to the incoming freshmen of Maine's Bowdoin College Baxter denounced Roberts as "the most recent advocate of the taking of the law into one's hands," adding that "apparently he wishes to pose and become famous as a leader of a sort of modernized Boston Tea Party."

Roberts was hardly one to let Baxter's charges drop unanswered. When the former governor wondered whether "Mr. Roberts would enjoy having some of his neighbors enter upon his property and tear down some building or structure of which they might disapprove," the author quickly retorted, "If I maintained a nuisance, I'd damn well expect to have it torn down."[40]

Although Roberts's efforts probably had little effect on Maine's billboard problem, the author never backed down from his position. Moreover, he seemed to relish the confrontation, for this battle was only the first of numerous statewide controversies that would receive widespread publicity because of his partiality for bluntness and a few well-chosen words.[41]

One of the most notable public furors occurred in 1948. After glancing through a volume of Arnold J. Toynbee's *A Study of History* (1935) Roberts instantly became furious at the British historian's perception of Maine as "unimportant," a state that "survives as a kind of 'museum piece'—a relic of seventeenth-century New England . . . still inhabited by woodmen and watermen and hunters." His scathing and celebrated rebuttal, "Don't Say That about Maine!," was his last essay for the *Saturday Evening Post*. In it he extolled the accomplishments of Maine's citizens while he attacked Toynbee and other historians for their sloppy research. "I have learned," Roberts lectured, "to discard the writings of any historian who errs too grossly. Toynbee's utterances about Maine are so ludicrous that I doubt everything that Toynbee has ever written."[42]

It is not surprising that Roberts chose to focus his wrath on just a few sentences taken out of context from a multivolume scholarly work. In 1951 the Colby College Press of Waterville, Maine, published his article in pamphlet form, and he gave them some 150 letters from readers that the original essay inspired to the college for its library's Roberts Collection. The author's replies indicate that he clearly enjoyed the controversy he stirred up (Kitch, 39).

The crusader in him is also evident in *I Wanted to Write*. This is not an autobiography in the fullest sense of the word but a record of Roberts's literary career, beginning with his college days at Cornell and concluding with the writing of *Lydia Bailey*. In it he presents an account of his evolution as a novelist, describing in detail the planning, researching, writing, and revising that preceded (and often followed) the publication of each of his works of fiction.

Roberts said that he intended *I Wanted to Write* to be an explicit and extensive reply to "Wanta Writers"—the "would-be authors who seem to labor under the delusion that I know a routine, formula or diet that in a half hour's time will transform any aspiring young person who admires his own letter-writing ability into a competent and successful novelist" (*IWW*, 1). Therefore, to illustrate that "no one can become a writer of any standing unless he learns to drive himself incessantly and ruthlessly" (*IWW*, 56), Roberts includes numerous passages from the diaries that he kept over the years. These excerpts show the schedule and progress of each day's work; the accompanying periods of agonizing self-doubt and utter depression; his reading, note taking, and painstaking writing; and the laborious corrections and revisions. He provides accounts of his research in the United States and abroad that enabled him to track down the myriad historical details needed to ensure the accuracy of his novels.

While most reviewers thought that Roberts did an excellent job of showing that good writing necessitates hard labor, they also recognized that the volume is often prosaic and slow moving, marred by such tedious insertions as reprinted book reviews and decades-old newspaper stories. A 90-page appendix and a 10-page list of people to whom Roberts wrote letters in 1935 also seem superfluous. Because the author gives free rein to his prejudices and dislikes throughout the book, both Roberts's and Doubleday's attorneys searched the manuscript for potentially libelous statements (e.g., Arnold J. Toynbee was originally referred to as a "bone-headed British pedant" and Allan Nevins the "sap-headed historian of Columbia").[43] Although Roberts either removed or altered some two dozen of these personal invectives (some were even directed at his own publishing company), the *New York Times* still observed that he "seems to have bellowed with exasperation and ground his teeth with rage for much of his life. . . . *I Wanted to Write* is a blunt, prickly, blustering, belligerent book."[44]

But it is also a vigorously honest and enlightening one, written by a man whom a close friend described as "a hater of shams, pretensions, self-deceptions, [and] fallacies," a person who "is easily aroused to furious indignation."[45] After Doubleday's attorneys pored over the manuscript of *I Wanted to Write*, one of them warned that while Roberts's diatribes against Doubleday were not libelous, the casual reader would undoubtedly infer that there was "something peculiar" about the relationship between the firm and its author.[46] Doubleday editor Kenneth D. McCormick was not particularly worried about the matter. Forty years later he recalled that although Roberts was indeed stubborn and demanding at times, he was "twice as hard on himself as he was on us," and "when you talked with him he could be actually charming." Putting things in perspective, McCormick concluded, "When you have a terrific author who does everything right on paper, you learn not to talk back."[47]

Chapter Five

"How to Lose Friends & Alienate People"

Soon after Kenneth Roberts finished *Lydia Bailey* and *I Wanted to Write*, he turned to a new interest—one that eventually aroused more public criticism than did his admiration for Benedict Arnold. He first wrote about water dowsing—the ability to locate underground water by using a forked stick—in *Rabble in Arms*. When old Doc Means joins up with Steven Nason's scouting detachment for the march to meet Benedict Arnold in Quebec, one item he brings along with his medical supplies is a "hazel wand for finding minerals and water" (*Rabble*, 7/49). One day soon after beginning their journey, the men pitch camp for the night and need to find water: Means "fumbled in his smock until he found what he called his dowsing rod. It was a Y-shaped branch, and he held it by its two arms, gripping it tightly, its stem pointed straight upward. Holding it thus, he shambled aimlessly hither and yon, a living embodiment, it seemed to me, of futility and delusion." After the rod "jerked violently downward," Means marked a spot with his heel and told the men to dig: "We did as he ordered, and unearthed a spring of ice-cold water; so there was more in Doc's dowsing rod than met the eye" (*Rabble*, 8/55).

Henry Gross and His Dowsing Rod

Roberts's interest in dowsing became more personal sometime in the late 1930s when he was building his stone house on his Kennebunkport estate. Because his country home was inaccessible to town water, he had to find his own water supply. When a well driller was unable to penetrate a layer of bluestone, Roberts turned to two local dowsers, who easily located a source of water in a marshy area some 300 yards from his house. In an article a few years later he recounted this dowsing experience: "Now I had no desire to pose as a champion of water diviners; but since two forked twigs in the hands of two amateur water dowsers had uncovered for me a better water supply than I could have obtained from the deepest artesian well or the most elaborate town-water-supply system, I was amiably disposed toward water dowsing, and better than mildly interested in it."[1]

During a widespread summer drought in 1940 Roberts again used water dowsers to locate springs and to fill ponds. By 1947 he had nine springs on his estate, all located by dowsers but all dwindling owing to another summer drought. Furthermore, because much of New England was threatened by forest fires that summer, Roberts needed additional water for firefighting purposes. Henry Gross, a state game warden living in Biddeford, Maine, happened to stop by and quickly located a plentiful supply of water with a dowsing rod. Roberts, impressed with Gross's skill and exceptional talent, encouraged him to develop his dowsing abilities, and the two men began to study water divining and to experiment with Gross's dowsing rod.[2]

They soon determined that water rises from deep in the ground through vertical pipelike spouts called "domes," with water "veins" spreading out from each dome in all directions. Gross learned how to predict the depth of these underground veins and how much water they contained. He mastered the art of "map dowsing," the ability to locate water by merely passing a dowsing rod over a map of the area to be surveyed, pinpointing on the map the spot where one would find water. Gross also found that he was accurate even without a map, as he "had the ability to dowse a locality or a piece of property for veins of water without any information except the name of the locality, or the name of the person who owned the property" (*Henry*, 100).

As local citizens clamored for Gross's dowsing services, Roberts sought to provide a steady income for his friend, whose retirement pay—beginning in January 1951—would be only $61.48 a month. Thus in October 1950 Roberts and Gross founded the organization Water Unlimited, incorporated under the laws of Maine. Its prospectus states that the organization's purpose was "to enable seriously-intentioned persons to seek Henry's help, to stimulate scientific interest in the further development of water dowsing, and to encourage those who have this latent ability—and there are many—to improve their technique through practice and study so that they may become dependable and valuable."[3] At a meeting of the board of directors on 2 January 1951 the corporation voted unanimously to "employ Henry Gross of Biddeford . . . to perform work for the corporation as a water dowser and as teacher and lecturer in the art and science of water dowsing."[4] In return, Water Unlimited guaranteed Gross a minimum salary equivalent to that which he had received as a game warden before his retirement.

To ensure that Gross's dowsing experiences were accurately recorded and preserved and, as Roberts said in a 1954 interview, "to prove to scientists that [dowsing] *is* possible,"[5] the author wrote three books: *Henry Gross and His Dowsing Rod* (1951), *The Seventh Sense* (1953), and the posthumously published *Water Unlimited* (1957). Although *Henry Gross* is not the type of work Roberts's fans were accustomed to, the majority of book reviewers—undoubtedly bearing in mind the author's long-standing reputation for journalistic integrity—reacted favorably to it.[6] "Kenneth Roberts is an accurate reporter," insisted the reviewer for the *New York Times Book Review*. "In all historical researches, he has been a meticulous digger for fact. His veracity cannot be questioned. Otherwise, credulity in his assertions would be strained beyond repair."[7] The *Saturday Review of Literature* similarly praised Roberts's reputation: "Henry Gross, thanks to the writer who has stood up for honesty in historical writing for over two decades, is incorporated now. . . . The crusade is on to incorporate dowsing as the serious profession it has been."[8] And *Booklist* brought up Roberts's meticulous research and attention to detail: "A novelist takes an unconventional step, exploring possibilities, checking results and convincing skeptics of the abilities of an experienced dowser. . . . Readers will fall readily into opposing camps, according to their preconceptions, but the author's purpose is a serious one and his claims well supported by proof."[9]

Some of Roberts's claims, however, were readily questioned by readers and reviewers, including persons who were either strong proponents of dowsing or at least sympathetic to Roberts's water-finding efforts. As Bill Cunningham, a columnist for the *Boston Herald* and a friend of Roberts, admitted in a review of *Henry Gross*, "Personally, I go along with the book until Henry starts talking to his twig—but the twig always, by dipping, gives him the answers, so I don't know."[10] Roberts and Gross first discovered that the rod answered Henry's questions when they were trying to find how a dowsing rod might determine the depth of a water vein and the amount of water running through it:

> The amount of water flowing in [the vein] had always puzzled [Gross]. So one evening, in a sort of desperation, he picked up his rod, said, "How many quarts are flowing in this vein at the present time?" poised the rod above the vein, and said, "Is there a quart a minute flowing at the present

time?" The rod dipped, meaning Yes. He poised it again and asked, "Are there 2 quarts?" The rod dipped. It dipped again at 3 quarts; but refused to dip at 4 quarts. So Henry tried [3.5] and received an affirmative dip; [3.75] and got No. (*Henry*, 71)

Gross's experiments later revealed that he could find people and lost objects by asking his dowsing rod. One day Roberts was working in his home and saw Gross drive up, get out of his car, and swing his dowsing rod from one end of the house to the other, with the rod dipping four times: "Henry said that he had learned, during the winter, that his rod, when asked whether there were persons in a given house or a given area, would dip when it pointed to each person. . . . On driving up to my home on this particular day, he wasn't obliged to do a lot of bell ringing, knocking on doors and questioning as to where I was. The rod told him there were four persons in the house, and he was pretty sure I was one of the four" (*Henry*, 97). Gross said that if the rod had indicated that Roberts was not in the house, he would have swung the rod in a circle around the estate, and it would have dipped when pointed at his friend. Then all he would have had to do would be to ask the rod how far away Roberts was, counting down distances such as 200 yards, 100 yards, 50 yards, and so forth. As long as the rod dipped, he would have continued to ask the questions. When the rod stopped, he would have known that Roberts was within the distance he had last asked, and then could have walked straight to him.

Roberts states that Gross's dowsing rod worked on substances besides just water and people. For example, Gross located an outboard motor that had fallen into deep water, a lost fountain pen, and a coin deliberately tossed into concealing grass. He discovered that if he touched the tip of the rod to any material, it would find any object made of that material until he "sterilized" the tip by washing it in water or rubbing it on the grass. Thus if Gross touched his rod to rye whiskey, it would only work on rye, and not scotch, bourbon, or other liquor. The rod also worked on precious minerals, and the two men debated whether they should go into the treasure-hunting business until they learned that the rod could not differentiate between a single chip of a precious metal and a vast deposit (*Henry*, 63-65, 140-42).

Gross's research also involved the well-known parlor trick of dangling a pendulum over someone's open hand. If the pendulum is over a male's palm, it supposedly moves in circles, while it swings back and forth in a straight line over a woman's. Gross took this theory one step further by holding the pendulum over pregnant women so he could attempt to predict the sex of their unborn children. In October 1949 this experiment received widespread publicity when Gross tested 16 pregnant women in the Maine General Hospital in Portland. When unsure of his predictions using a needle dangling from a thread, he corroborated his findings with his dowsing rod. He was correct in only six instances, however, a success ratio that Roberts admitted was "worse than disappointing." Gross subsequently determined that his technique had been incorrect, and believed that instead of holding the pendulum in one place, he should have moved it over the pregnant woman's entire body.[11]

Surprisingly, the newspaper reporters covering this story treated Roberts's and Gross's experiments as serious research (even after Gross held a dowsing rod over one of the pregnant women in an attempt to predict her delivery date). Not all persons, however, viewed their efforts so sympathetically. One of Roberts's severest critics, waterworks engineer and chemist Thomas M. Riddick, wrote an article on *Henry Gross and His Dowsing Rod* for the *American Philosophical Society Proceedings* and sent a complimentary copy of the published work to Roberts. Riddick's purpose in writing the article was "to set forth some of the principles of dowsing, and subject them to the light of reason and currently accepted science. The personalities of Messrs. Roberts and Gross are injected only because there are no others in America with whom seriously to joust."[12]

Throughout the article Riddick systematically refutes passages from *Henry Gross*. For instance: "Henry's theory of domes, possibly conjectured from the oil fields where domes definitely exist (they impound liquid and gas formed millions of years ago and are totally unrelated to rainfall and runoff which are repetitive and cyclic in nature), is wholly without substantiation." Also, "Henry Gross' location of simple dug wells is not astounding or amazing, except to those who wish to be amazed by treating the commonplace as miraculous. His predictions of yield and quality cannot be taken too seriously since Mr. Roberts gives no indication whatsoever of being even remotely qualified to judge either yield or quality" (Riddick 1952, 533).

As far as Roberts was concerned, scientists like Riddick, as well as others who scoffed at dowsing, had "Closed Minds" because they refused to accept his evidence and research (*Henry*, 268-69). While writing his book, he originally used even stronger language to describe his opponents, singling each out individually. Before *Henry Gross* was published, Doubleday sent a copy of the manuscript to the New York law firm of

Satterlee, Warfield & Stephens—the same one that examined Roberts's *I Wanted to Write*—to check for possibly libelous statements. The firm recommended that Roberts refrain from referring by name to one anti-dowsing geologist as "parrot-brained" and a "boneheaded scientist."[13] The references were removed.

But Roberts's vitriolic outbursts hardly seem justified, for at the same time he publicizes and brags in his book about Gross's "non-water" dowsing talents (finding lost objects, locating gold, differentiating between scotch and whiskey) he fulminates against scientists and skeptics who are interested in those same feats. In 1948, for example, both officials of the American Society for Psychical Research and editors at *Life* asked if Roberts could sponsor a dowsing demonstration at his estate in Kennebunkport, Maine. He readily agreed, and *Life* devoted three pages—including six photographs—to the day-long affair. Roberts, however, complained that "this so-called scientific inquiry was one of the greatest busts since Lillian Russell held Broadway spellbound" (*Henry,* 79). He felt that those present were more curious about seeing a dowsing rod perform such tricks as selecting from mason jars hidden in paper bags the jars containing water and the ones containing sand, than observing Henry Gross locate underground water veins. Furthermore, because Gross was no more successful at selecting jars than he was at predicting the sex of unborn babies, Roberts believed that Gross's reputation as a water dowser had suffered. As Roberts protested to Ben Ames Williams, "I ain't interested in nothing but the action of the rod on water, but the louse who's head of the American Society for Psychical Research is more interested in its action (when tipped with silver) on hidden silver coins."[14]

Roberts admits in *Henry Gross* that during his long association with the dowser he frequently had to admonish him to "stick to water," because in that area "you have never failed" (*Henry,* 271). It is obvious, however, that Roberts did not always follow his own advice, as he often called on Gross to perform dowsing feats that had nothing to do with locating water veins. On the flyleaves of his personal copy of *Henry Gross,* for example, he noted on 16 January 1951 that for a forthcoming autograph session at a bookstore, "the rod said that between 2:30 and 5:00 P.M., 269 people would come in to have H.G.D.R. autographed." On 20 December 1950, two weeks before the book's official publication date, he wrote on another flyleaf, "Henry's rod says this [book] will sell 72,000 in one year. [Roberts later changed this figure to 76,000.] He means *trade* copies. I think it might sell 22,000 if extremely lucky. (June

1, 1956: It has sold abt. 18,000). Can this mean he should divide publishing figures by 4?" (*Henry*, copy 4, Dartmouth College Library). It
seems incongruous, therefore, that if Roberts was not "interested in
nothing but the action of the rod on water," why did he devote so much
time—and so many pages in his book—to experiments with pendulums,
mason jars, and whiskey bottles?

Part of the answer may stem from the fact that just as Roberts heavily researched all of his novels, so did he immerse himself into the thorough studying of dowsing. Furthermore, just as he tended to crowd his
novels with virtually everything he knew on a subject, so did he pack his
dowsing books with superfluous material. His longtime Doubleday editor, Clara Claasen, realized this, and after reading the book in manuscript both she and Kacy Tebbel, the book's copy editor, pointed out
that Gross does not even make his appearance until chapter 4, the first
three chapters being devoted to Roberts's complaints that because of the
"entrenched ignorance" of scientists and others, dowsing is not recognized as a legitimate method of water finding; a history of dowsing and
how the rod works, written by a French professor of physiology; and
anecdotes by a British dowser. Both editors said that the book "really
took hold" with chapter 4 and urged Roberts to relegate chapters 2 and
3 to the back of the book as an appendix.[15] He unfortunately (but pre-
dictably) refused.

Roberts's zealous fidelity to detail is prevalent throughout *Henry
Gross*. Although his and Gross's water-finding exploits do make for
intriguing reading—for believers and nonbelievers alike—he frequently
inserts entire testimonial newspaper articles and correspondence that
detract from his writing. Chapter 8, for instance, merely consists of a few
of the numerous letters Roberts received after the 1948 *Life* article
appeared (*Henry*, 89).

"The greatest water dowsing experiment on record"   Fully
one-third of *Henry Gross* details Roberts's most famous dowsing experience, one that was covered in newspapers and magazines around the
world: the finding in water-starved Bermuda a source of pure, clean
water. Throughout Bermuda's 340-year history its people had relied on
rain as their only source of potable water. On learning this, Roberts had
Gross on 22 October 1949 dowse a map of Bermuda in Kennebunkport,
some 800 miles from the Bermuda Islands. Gross marked on the map
four domes of water, noting that one of them was polluted and unfit to

drink. Excited at the prospect of finding fresh water in Bermuda, the two men went to the islands, and on 6 December 1949 Gross dowsed the water domes he had previously located on a map in Roberts's home. The two sets of calculations coincided, and with the aid of Bermuda businessmen Sir Stanley Spurling and Sir Howard Trott, Gross and Roberts prepared for the drilling of the three wells.

Unfortunately, problems plagued the men from the beginning, such as frustrating delays owing to rusty, antiquated drills and inadequate pumps; the difficulty of finding experienced workmen; and time lags in installing electricity at the site. And even when the three wells were opened—the Royal Barracks well in St. George's Parish on 11 February 1950, the Jennings well in Smith's Parish on 10 March, and the Clayhouse well in Devonshire Parish on 23 March—residents long convinced that no potable water was available in Bermuda refused to believe the water was pure, despite banner headlines to the contrary in the islands' newspapers.[16] As Roberts somewhat bitterly recalled, "Both the *Royal Gazette* and the *Mid-Ocean News* were considerably excited by the copious flowing of the Clayhouse well, and went overboard about it with front-page stories; but the average Bermudian mind . . . continued to dwell on bacteria and the sea water that must be lurking just around the corner" (*Henry*, 246).

Even after the water was analyzed and pronounced safe for drinking, the chief medical officer of the Bermuda Board of Health maintained that "there couldn't be spring water in Bermuda" and that "the Royal Barracks spring was nothing but surface drainage water, and not a dome of fresh water." Furthermore, he insisted that the water Gross found could not be sold as drinking water, as health regulations stated that all well water in Bermuda was contaminated (*Henry*, 225, 252).

Roberts had to return to Kennebunkport at the height of these controversies and before the drilling operations and the installation of the pumps were completed. In a chapter entitled "Bermuda Aftermaths" of his second dowsing book, *The Seventh Sense*, he related that after he left the islands he began hearing false rumors—circulated in Bermuda as well as in Maine—about the wells and their water: "Male and female know-it-alls in the towns of Kennebunkport and Biddeford, Maine, were gabbling delightedly that the water in the Bermuda wells was dark brown and smelled of rotten eggs, that its brackishness was so virulent as to turn teeth green, that it couldn't be used, that Henry was about to be sued by the Bermuda government" (*SS*, 55).

By December 1951 the rumors were so malicious that Roberts asked his friend Robert Choate, the publisher of the *Boston Herald*, if he could send a reporter to Bermuda to examine the wells. Choate, for whom Henry Gross once dowsed a well, readily agreed to the request, and the reporter, Donald Fessenden, published his findings in a series of three articles. After attesting in the first newspaper story that there was no question that the water in the Clayhouse and Royal Barracks wells was potable, Fessenden quoted the commandant of a U.S. naval base near the Clayhouse well as insisting, "We have found absolutely nothing to substantiate that there is any important source of water supply under Bermuda. Seepage water is all there is in Bermuda." In the last article Fessenden stated emphatically that "the facts are that there are two wells yielding fresh water on these beautiful islands where for 340 years men have said it was impossible."[17]

Park Breck, former editor of the Hamilton, Bermuda, *Mid-Ocean News*, also helped to vindicate Roberts publicly by writing two articles on the dowsing venture. In the first, published in a Bermuda magazine, he reported that after *Henry Gross and His Dowsing Rod* was published Gross "located additional and even larger sources of fresh water here; and it now seems safe to assume that, once the ground work has been completed, ample fresh water will be available in Bermuda to anyone who wants it."[18]

Although the groundwork *was* completed, Roberts and Gross continued to face seemingly never-ending frustrations in a venture they once believed to be "the greatest water dowsing experiment on record" (*Henry*, 212). Although water from the Clayhouse well was gratefully used by nearby homes and a few local businesses (and reluctantly by Bermudians during a 1952 summer drought that forced official approval of the water), this well and the two others were abandoned for the most part soon after Roberts and Gross left Bermuda. In March 1956 a representative from the Massachusetts Department of Agriculture traveled to Bermuda to investigate the situation. Although the water from the Clayhouse dome—clearly the purest of the three wells—was still potable, he found the well unprotected (it had bottles and cans floating in it) and the pumping equipment neglected and rusty.[19]

Roberts maintained that the man who owned the land on which the Clayhouse well was sunk let the well fall into disrepair because of pressure brought by people who sold low-quality, "brackish" water to the various Bermuda hotels. The Royal Barracks well, located on British War Department property, was abandoned by Roberts after he received a letter from the British Army Engineers telling him that the digging was being done without their permission. And he contended that water from the Jennings well was slightly salty—though still drinkable—because children had moved the marker originally pinpointing the dome, causing the well to be dug at the wrong spot. In a speech given in September 1956 before a group of New England businessmen, he also complained—perhaps too petulantly—that many of his difficulties were caused by a small group of influential and powerful people in Bermuda who were worried about "the profits somebody would lose if the Clayhouse water were used as freely as it should be" (*WU*, 73).

Some of the scientists who derided *Henry Gross* singled out Roberts's and Gross's dowsing efforts in Bermuda. Thomas M. Riddick, for example, noted, "I have no doubt that moderately non-saline and 'drinkable' water can be withdrawn from many locations in Bermuda, provided the rate of pumpage and overall withdrawal are kept relatively low. I also have no doubt whatsoever that such yields are decidedly limited and that overpumpage would result in a 'salting' of the wells" (Riddick 1952, 533).

Because the abandoned Bermuda wells were scarcely in any danger of being subjected to "overpumpage," it is not surprising that they supplied "non-saline and 'drinkable' water" to local residents. Still, it should be remembered that at one time water from the Clayhouse well was flowing at the pump's capacity of 44 gallons a minute, and that Roberts's supporters were—and are—as strong in their praise as his detractors were in their disparagement. Literary historian and widely published author John Tebbel, who met Roberts while working on a biography of *Saturday Evening Post* editor George Horace Lorimer, offers this unique perspective:

> Ken used to carry on about the goddamned Bermudians, who refused to believe there was any fresh water on their salty little island. In that case, he declared, he would by god bloody well show them they were wrong. He took Henry to Bermuda, the divining rod pointed to a fresh-water source, and Ken imported well-drilling equipment to go down for it. Sure enough, a gushing of spring water appeared and, clearly, it was fresh. Various Bermudians drank it and shook their heads. It was salty, they declared, because as everybody knew, there was no fresh water on Bermuda.
>
> That sent Ken into one of his most spectacular rages. He denounced the citizens of Bermuda as the pinheads of the universe and consigned them to fates far worse than any described in the Apocalypse. They

remained unmoved. Yet, by a curious chance, my wife and I found him
vindicated at last, years later. On one of many vacations in Bermuda, we
happened to ride with a taxi driver one day, and for some now forgotten
reason, I began to tell him this story. He stopped me. The driver knew all
about it, he said; he had been there and the well was now in his backyard.
It was still sending up a good flow of fresh spring water, which he greatly enjoyed after a hard day on the road because it was so cold and pure.
Did his friends or anyone he know admit that he was enjoying the real
thing? we asked. Of course not, he said. They were Bermudians, and as
all Bermudians know. . . . [20]

The Seventh Sense

When Roberts's editor, Clara Claasen, read the manuscript of *Henry
Gross and His Dowsing Rod*, she suggested that he keep his temper in
check and delete such editorial comments as "entrenched ignorance"
when writing about scientists, geologists, and others who belittle dowsing. She stressed to him that his reputation as a "top-notch" reporter
carried considerable weight with readers; therefore, if he would simply
present the facts clearly, report objectively what happened during his
dowsing experiments, draw conclusions impersonally, and refrain from
being belligerent, then his various points would be strengthened, his
book would be more scientific, and readers would be more receptive to
what he had to say (Claasen [ca. 1950]).

Claasen knew Roberts well, having worked with him since 1930, the
year *Arundel* was published. She was, in the words of former Doubleday
editor in chief Kenneth D. McCormick, a "fierce, hard-working editor,"
and until Roberts's death in 1957 she remained intensely loyal to him,
his family, and to his literary interests. Indeed, McCormick also admitted
that "there's no question that she worked for Roberts and not for
Doubleday & Co., but in the end all that evened out."[21]

As the reviews for both *Henry Gross* and *The Seventh Sense* illustrate,
Roberts should have heeded Claasen's warnings as she was almost
prophetic in her initial comments: most reviewers for *Henry Gross* were
charitable because of Roberts's reputation, whereas many of those writing about *The Seventh Sense*—a sequel to *Henry Gross* that was published
after Roberts's readers had barely finished absorbing the novelty of the
first book—took issue with the author for his obvious hostility to those
who disagreed with him. A reviewer for the *New York Herald Tribune*
declared that it "seems to us that by choosing to prove his case in a shrill
scream, pitched on a high note of spite (particularly against professional

water geologists, whom he calls 'Water Babies') Mr. Roberts has done more harm than good to his cause. . . . We think it might be a good idea if Mr. Gross . . . would apply his dowsing rod to Mr. Roberts, and draw off a few gallons from the accumulated veins of bile."[22] The *San Francisco Chronicle* also bluntly criticized Roberts's cantankerousness: "I don't know how [dowsers] do it, and Mr. Roberts admits he doesn't know either. So far all right. But he does not stop there. He says, in effect, 'If you don't agree with every single word I say, then you are ignorant, stupid, and very likely in league with the forces of unrighteousness.' I shouldn't be surprised if he'd do better without his tricky use of name-calling words. Nothing was ever proved yet, just by calling the man who disagrees with you 'ignorant.'"[23]

Roberts argues that the "seventh sense" is the ability of a person to locate flowing underground water by means of a dowsing rod. His book relates—in occasionally tedious detail—many of the 1951 activities of his and Henry Gross's water-finding organization, Water Unlimited, Inc., following the publication on 3 January of *Henry Gross and His Dowsing Rod*. Roberts decided to write about Water Unlimited's dowsing enterprises during its first year of operations because "no experience, no experiment, is of value to a stumbling, fumbling world unless it can be put in print so that the information is available" (*SS*, 1).

In addition, he also wanted to refute the suspicion and skepticism accorded *Henry Gross* by "minor scientists," a term he often uses in *The Seventh Sense* when referring to scientists who question water dowsing (those who are sympathetic to his and Gross's work are called "major scientists"). When he asked these disbelievers to examine objectively his proof of the existence of dowsing, "they behaved, to put it mildly, like timid mid-Victorian ladies confronted by the mangled corpses of persons near and dear to them. They turned away in horror; they cried out in agony; in effect they hid their heads beneath blankets" (*SS*, 5). Early in *The Seventh Sense* Roberts states that scientists "tried to discredit [*Henry Gross*] and destroy it" by contending that he produced no evidence to support his claims, even though "the book was crammed with every sort of evidence" and "full of proof." Consequently, he felt that in his second dowsing book he had to provide "details that must be wearisomely authenticated if they are to be accepted" (*SS*, 3).

Roberts is correct: they *are* wearisome, as he includes minute and extraneous information from the files of Water Unlimited to corroborate his statements—legal documents, reports, statistics, logs, telegrams, affidavits, letters, financial statements, tables, newspaper articles, obituaries, drawings, maps, and even a television script. For the reader who is not a scientist (major or minor), dowser, or geologist, the book reads, as one reviewer aptly put it, "somewhat like the annual report of a major corporation."[24]

Interwoven between Roberts's technical supporting evidence and his truculent attacks on "scientific milquetoasts" (from the book's dust jacket) are numerous "case histories" of his and Henry Gross's water-finding ventures. Their clients for 1951 included 418 individuals, organizations (both private and commercial), and schools (SS, 120). Following is a summary of one of their smaller dowsing cases:

Arthur Davis, chairman of the school board of Hollis, New Hampshire, telephoned Roberts in early November and told him that he and other board members were planning the construction of a new elementary school. Before committing themselves to a site, however, they first needed to know where there was a suitable water supply, and Davis asked if they could hire Gross to help them.

Although the town did not have much money, Roberts had recently received a large check from a satisfied customer, and he offered Gross's dowsing services free of charge. Davis sent the two men a map of the school property, and Gross, by holding his dowsing rod over the map, found six veins of water. The dowser then went to Hollis, pinpointed the veins he had previously located on a map, and told the school board members where to dig their well. In a letter to Roberts, Davis reported that Gross had "hit it 'right on the nose,'" and on the construction of the building, a grateful school board hung a bronze plaque (pictured on the back of The Seventh Sense's dust jacket) in the principal's office proclaiming, "The water supply of this school flows from veins dowsed on a map in Kennebunkport by Henry Gross & Kenneth Roberts November 7, 1951, proved in Hollis November 8, 1951" (SS, 130-31).

Roberts, to his credit, also includes in his book dowsing cases that did not end nearly so happily, and he is quick to point out that "Henry, like all the rest of us, has had failures" (SS, 229). One chapter, for instance, is devoted to the problems the two men encountered while trying to find water on the island of Eleuthera in the Bahamas for a wealthy businessman, Austin Levy. Levy was intensely interested in their dowsing research and experiments, but despite all their efforts, they were not able to locate any potable water for him. When Levy unexpectedly died, nine months after he first contacted Roberts, the author admitted that "we had no theories, no explanation and no excuses as to why this golden chance had crumbled to nothing when it seemed solidly within our grasp" (*SS*, 242).

As both readers and book reviewers pointed out, however, Roberts places most of the blame for dowsing "failures" on other people. As he explained in "Borderline Cases," a chapter of *The Seventh Sense* devoted to case histories of unsuccessful dowsing ventures, "I must pause here to emphasize the fact that the cause of dowsing has suffered its greatest setbacks at the hands of persons who have failed, for one reason or another, to do as they're told. . . . I cannot too often emphasize that the 'failures' blamed on skilled dowsers are usually due to the unpredictable shortcomings of the human race—to the well drillers who shatter rock structures: to property owners who misinterpret or ignore instructions: to water geologists and engineers who say, 'You can't get water in a place like this'" (*SS*, 135).

Roberts's frustrations with "the unpredictable shortcomings of the human race" are evident throughout the volume. He noted on a flyleaf of his personal copy of *The Seventh Sense* that its subtitle should have read, "How to Lose Friends & Alienate People" (*SS*, copy 2, Dartmouth College Library). This conclusion should not have surprised him, as his outbursts—although understandable, particularly coming from someone as choleric as he—alienate even those sympathetic to his efforts to bring water to people who desperately need it. Consequently, readers are likely to wish that they could examine some of these dowsing "failures" from the perspective of someone besides Roberts.

Fortunately, a participant *has* recorded an account of at least one of them, a case Roberts calls "Project A" in chapter 19 of *The Seventh Sense*. Roberts frequently (and derogatorily) refers to this episode as a "charity case"—that is, one for which payment was not expected. He relates that a newspaper reporter in Albany, New York, wrote to ask his and Gross's help in locating water for a friend and colleague who owned a farm near Albany. The colleague's wife had talked to numerous scientists and geologists, with all of them asserting that there was no water on her and her husband's farm. The reporter (unnamed in the book) told Roberts that proving the geologists wrong would be a wonderful opportunity for Gross to display his water-finding prowess.

Roberts agreed to help after Gross long-distance dowsed a map of the property and located a supply of water. The two men went to the farm, readily found the water vein, and after a hole was dug to the depth that Gross specified, water was brought up that was "enthusiastically approved" by those present (*SS*, 199).

Although Roberts considered the case closed after Gross had located the water, the reporter, as detailed in *The Seventh Sense*, began to write disparaging newspaper columns about Water Unlimited's efforts. According to Roberts, "Project A was given blood transfusions, pulmotor treatment and digitalis shots. Other dowsers, working on a charity basis, were dragged in, only to be angered and rejected. Well drillers were lured to the area, put through their paces and consigned to oblivion. Holes were drilled, re-drilled, discarded. An astounding series of claims were made, followed in quick succession by counterclaims, charges, discharges, accusations, disclaimers, sneers at Henry, and reports of speeches made by the reporter before a variety of organizations." These attacks, Roberts claimed, lasted for one and a half years and were "all designed to discredit completely Henry's ability as a water dowser" (*SS*, 200).

The reporter, Cecil R. Roseberry, argued a different story in an article for *American Mercury* (written before the publication of *The Seventh Sense*) and in an unpublished 1967 essay in which he refuted the charges in Roberts's book. Roseberry wrote that soon after *Henry Gross and His Dowsing Rod* was published, he included in his *Albany Times-Union* column some "uncomplimentary remarks about water-witching" by the New York State geologist, Dr. John G. Broughton. Broughton said that dowsing "had been thoroughly discredited by science; that groundwater is to be found beneath approximately 90 per cent of the earth's surface; [and] that there is no such thing as 'veins' of water." Broughton summarized his views in one concise statement: "Dowsing is humbug."[25]

After reading Broughton's remarks, an enraged Roberts, through Roseberry's column, offered $100 to the geologist if he could find in *Henry Gross* "one statement concerning water dowsing that can be successfully controverted." Broughton refused, saying he did not want to advertise Roberts's book through a "publicity stunt" (Roseberry 1953, 26).

Roseberry continued to correspond with Roberts, and the reporter suggested that if Henry Gross in Kennebunkport could map-dowse water in Bermuda, then he easily should be able to find it in Albany, a mere 170 miles away. Roberts agreed to the test, and Roseberry located a couple, Mr. and Mrs. Bob Pauley, whose only supply of water was a well that frequently ran dry. The Pauleys had talked to soil experts and geologists who insisted that because their farm rested on a layer of dense blue clay that was once a glacial lake bed, there was simply no plentiful source of underground water. After learning what the geologists said, Roberts immediately replied to Roseberry, "The whole proposition interests us very much because of the insistence of the local geologists that there can't be any water under Pauley's land. We know different" (Roseberry 1953, 27).

To prove their assertion, Gross dowsed a map of the Pauley farm and traced on it two water veins. He stated that the one on the east side of the farm buildings would yield three and a half gallons a minute and the other on the west side would give two gallons a minute. Roberts suggested to Roseberry that he find a good local dowser to verify Gross's work. Two dowsers quickly found the west vein, but neither located the supposedly better east one.

Roberts and Gross came to Albany in the spring of 1951 to pinpoint the water veins. Roseberry writes that Gross, while dowsing the Pauley land on-site, reached different conclusions from his earlier long-distance map work. He not only preferred the west vein to the east one but traced the former as flowing in a different direction than what he had shown on the map. Nevertheless, Gross indicated where the well should be dug, though on its completion it failed to yield any appreciable amount of water.

Roseberry and his friends asked him to locate a second site, which he did, stating that a 40-foot well would yield seven gallons of water a minute. A well driller, however, gave up after passing the 60-foot mark without finding water; he transferred his equipment to the front yard, where one of the local dowsers had driven a stake 100 feet away from the Gross location.

While the second well was being dug, Roseberry says that he received a telephone call from "a very irate Roberts. He fairly burned the wire for half an hour. . . . 'We told you to dig, not drill,' he vociferated. 'You aren't giving us a fair test. What are you trying to do—crucify Henry?'" (Roseberry 1953, 29).

In his article Roseberry concedes that both Roberts and Gross advised against drilling the well: "A major Roberts tenet is that the 'hammer-type' drill crushes and ruins 'veins,' so that dowsers are discredited. But to dig a forty-foot well in that clay was ridiculous, and would have proved nothing new" (Roseberry 1953, 28).

The well driller finally hit a strong flow of water at the 110-foot mark, but owing to his neglect the clay caved in and ruined the well. At this point another driller (one who had no use for dowsing) volunteered to drill a third well, stipulating only that the site be one that none of the dowsers had selected. He chose a spot convenient for the Pauleys, near the basement wall of their house, drilled, and struck water. The water was piped into the house, "keeping the Pauleys supplied with all the crystal-clear soft water they ever will need" (Roseberry 1953, 29).

Roseberry's unpublished essay offers additional details about this dowsing case. While these accounts are admittedly not from a disinterested observer, they certainly provide a different perspective from that of the "charity case" Roberts so disdainfully relates in *The Seventh Sense*.

Water Unlimited

Roberts's last dowsing book was published on 24 October 1957, three months after his death. Like *The Seventh Sense*, *Water Unlimited* details the activities of Water Unlimited, Inc., and the successes and failures of Henry Gross. With the exception of a few chapters near the end that highlight Gross's experiences in trying to locate oil, uranium, and diamonds, the volume offers no revelations on dowsing. A book reviewer for *Library Journal* echoed these sentiments, emphasizing that "the book adds little to what Roberts has already said on the subject and readers of the earlier works who are not led to believe there is such a thing as dowsing will remain unconvinced."[26]

Unfortunately, Roberts never recognized that most people skeptical of dowsing will not change their minds, and he refused to accept the fact that proving the validity of dowsing had nothing to do with a person's belief in it. "Mr. Roberts' error lies in pursuing proof and disproof in full cry in a hunt where belief and disbelief have little to do with facts," declared a perceptive reviewer of *Water Unlimited* in the *New York Times Book Review*. "He might pleasantly persuade, but he may not convince. He might tease us gently, but he isn't going to beat it through our thick skulls."[27]

With each dowsing book, Roberts became more truculent as he reported his research and attempted to "beat it through our thick skulls." Consequently, his choleric irritability is even more pronounced in *Water Unlimited* than in *The Seventh Sense*. He refers to well drillers as "the most opinionated, fatuous human beings that ever lived, bar none" (*WU*, 61). Geologists are "timid white rabbits, incapable of investigating anything properly or of recognizing the truth" (*WU*, 71). Those who attack dowsing belong to the "League of Ninnyhammers" (*WU*, 49, 55). One lengthy chapter of the book is devoted to a transcript of a speech that the New England Council (an organization of businessmen and community leaders from the New England states) had asked him to give before its Water Resources Committee. During the program's question-and-answer session the moderator asked those in attendance to say "aye" if they believed in dowsing and "no" if they did not. When scattered "no's" were heard, Roberts replied, "You know the world is full of bastards, otherwise they'd have been unanimous" (*WU*, 85).

Public and Private Criticism

Roberts and Gross learned early in their professional relationship that many people laugh at those who believe in and practice "water witching." According to Roberts, "The start of Henry's higher education in dowsing" commenced just a few months after the two men met (*Henry*, 59). On 24 November 1947 the *Boston Traveler* published an article by Professor Ray M. Koon, head of the Waltham Field Station at Massachusetts State College, that ridiculed dowsers. "I have seen these miracle men perform," Koon stated, "and am convinced that it's pure hokum. Dig deep enough anywhere and you strike water. The diviner knows this and cashes in on it."[28]

Roberts, always ready to enter any fight, responded with a rebuttal headed "Nuts to Koon" that was splashed across the front page of the newspaper a few weeks later: "On my farm I have 21 springs, all located by divining rods. The water-supply of my own house comes from a spring dug at the confluence of six veins of water, all traced by water-dowsers. I therefore know that Koon, a professed scientist, hasn't the slightest idea what he's talking about when he says that dowsing rods can't accurately locate underground veins of water. I also say unqualifiedly that Koon is stupidly tossing obstacles in the advancement of human understanding when he, in his profound ignorance, condemns something he has never adequately studied or investigated."[29]

In his article Roberts bet Koon $1,000—a wager circulated in newspapers throughout New England by the Associated Press—that three dowsers could locate a water vein, determine its depth, and by drilling "strike water within one foot of the estimated depth." Koon responded with a proposition of his own: that Roberts's three diviners, after locating a water vein, be blindfolded and led around the spot where they found the water. "If the sticks dip repeatedly on the same and exact location, this stupid, ignorant, narrow minded unbeliever will never again say it's hokum."[30]

Roberts did not publicly respond to Koon's challenge but did write a few years later that "Koon was as wrong in his assumption that Henry (or any other good dowser) wouldn't submit to blindfolding as he was about everything else" (*Henry*, 62). This confrontation was only the first of dozens of occasions that Roberts and his unswerving faith in dowsing would be held up to public ridicule. Bergen Evans wrote in *The Spoor of Spooks and Other Nonsense* (1944) that Roberts believed Gross to have "rhabdomantic powers which, if only recognized and utilized, would flood the earth with life-giving waters and cause the deserts to blossom like the rose."[31] In 1952 the American Philosophical Society gave "a royal roasting to historical novelist Kenneth Roberts for championing water-finding by means of a hooked-stick 'divining-rod'—a technique known as 'dowsing.'"[32] Six months after *Henry Gross* was published the *New Yorker* printed a satirical poem about a dog who could hold a dowsing rod in his teeth and "ask the rod in an undertone, / Where in the world did I bury that bone?"[33]

Roberts's nemesis, Thomas M. Riddick, did not limit his condemnation of dowsing to scientific publications. In an article for *Harper's Magazine* entitled "Dowsing Is Nonsense" he asserted that Roberts's "illogical and unscientific conjectures may do real harm." After Roberts received an advance copy of the article, published in the July 1951 issue, he fired off an angry letter to an editor at *Harper's* in which he referred to Riddick as "a son-of-a-bitch" and denounced the essay as "pretty shoddy stuff to appear in a magazine of *Harper's* reputation."[34]

Although Roberts had his supporters, the antipathy and derision far outweighed the compliments and approval. Furthermore, even some of Roberts's friends, while championing his cause publicly, privately thought he should never have abandoned his historical research and writing. During her career as book review editor of the *Boston Herald* Alice Dixon Bond wrote numerous articles and reviews praising Roberts's works. Although she lauded his dowsing books, a few years after Roberts died she privately referred to the rough, uneducated Henry Gross as "a real boor" and admitted that she was not overly impressed with Roberts's enthusiasm for water divining.[35]

In "Letter to a Friend," a hagiographic "open letter" to Roberts published five years after his death, longtime close friend Arthur Hamilton Gibbs reminisced about Roberts's "magnificent obsession" with dowsing and derided "the nit-wit, anti-dowsing scientists baying at your heels." A few months later, however, he referred to Gross as a "totally ignorant man" who somehow had established a near mystical bond with nature.[36] Another close friend, Dartmouth Professor of English Herbert Faulkner West, greatly admired Roberts's historical novels but had little respect for his dowsing works: "Perhaps the less said the better about his period

of defending the work of his friend, Henry Gross, in the use of the dowsing rod, though it does show his passion for justice and truth as he saw
it. . . . I have always felt that this controversy somewhat embittered
Roberts, and I have always regretted that he ever got mixed up with it"
(West 1962, 98).

Roberts freely acknowledged that even his publishers did not care for
this new avocation. In *Water Unlimited* he remarked that after he completed a number of successful books, "to the distress of my publishers, I
wrote *Henry Gross and His Dowsing Rod*. Since they'd published a number
of my books, they partially concealed their revulsion and published it"
(*WU*, 26).

These misgivings, however, are not reflected in any of the extensive
Roberts-Doubleday papers—including confidential in-house memos—at
the Library of Congress. Furthermore, John Tebbel noted that his wife,
Kacy, who copyedited Roberts's books for 20 years, said that "while she
doesn't doubt Doubleday felt repugnant about publishing *Henry Gross*,
she never heard anyone actually say so, and neither did I. But they could
swallow a lot of repugnance for the sake of Ken's sales figures on other
books. I think . . . that they basically humored him, while retaining the
usual skepticism about dowsing." Tebbel also astutely observed that
"when an author makes as much money for a [publishing] house as Ken
did, he attains the status of a 400-pound gorilla and can do just about as
he pleases."[37]

Former Doubleday editor in chief Kenneth D. McCormick implied
some 40 years after *Henry Gross* was published that, as Tebbel suggested,
he and other Doubleday editors simply humored Roberts and his "obsession on dousing [*sic*]." Roberts was, McCormick recalled, "irrational" and
"pig-headed" on the subject and "really off the deep end on Henry,"
believing that "[Henry] could do no wrong."[38]

Any skepticism that Roberts's publishers may have had about his
dowsing books was well-founded, as none of the volumes sold well. All
three books went out of print in 1965, with total sales of *Henry Gross*
being 20,753; *The Seventh Sense*, 6,944 copies; and *Water Unlimited*,
4,916. As a comparison, Doubleday's records indicate that a few months
after Roberts's death the still-in-print *Northwest Passage* had sold 345,288
copies (not including the more then 160,000 Book-of-the-Month Club
editions) and *Oliver Wiswell* 291,033 copies.[39]

Despite the reservations of his friends, his publishers, and the general
public, Roberts remained a dowsing advocate until his death, maintain-
ing that there lay the solution to the world's water shortage. He often

angrily protested in his books and in personal correspondence that while he and Henry Gross were spending countless hours finding water for persons and businesses, skeptics could do nothing except complain about it:

> Millions of gallons a minute are in use today in many parts of the United States, due solely to Henry's ability to show people, by means of his dowsing rod, where the water could be unearthed. We've worked our heads off to do this; and all the time we were doing it, critics who had made no effort whatever to investigate what we were doing were screaming that it was nonsense, that it couldn't be done, and that the use of a dowsing rod was hokum, the spoor of spooks and a Hindu rope trick. R.C.A. Victor isn't paying $5,000.00 for any Hindu rope trick, but that's what they paid us for showing them the water for their new Cherry Hill and Bridgewater plants in New Jersey.[40]

Why Roberts Turned to Dowsing

In one of Roberts's last memorandums, written the month he died, he asserted, "I can do more good to my country by writing about my dowsing experiences than I can by writing novels, no matter how historically accurate they may be."[41] Five years later Herbert Faulkner West speculated why Roberts forsook his career as a well-known writer of historical novels: "I personally have felt that his energies had been seriously drained by the creation of seven long historical novels, so that almost by necessity he turned to another interest, which was the subject of the national problem of sufficient water" (West 1962, 98).

Arthur Hamilton Gibbs, who also knew Roberts for decades, agreed when he theorized the following year that the author probably "wrote himself out" after completing *Oliver Wiswell* and almost certainly after *Lydia Bailey*. Thus his fascination with dowsing was sort of a "literary holiday" for him that helped relieve his feelings of stress and fatigue (Gibbs 1963).

In 1954 Richard L. Simon, co-founder of Simon & Schuster, repeatedly urged Roberts to research and write for his publishing firm a book to be titled *American Heroes and Heroism*. Roberts's listlessness is evident in a letter to Simon telling him that although he was enthusiastic about the idea, he simply did not have the necessary stamina: "You just have to face the fact that it's impossible for me to work the way I did when I was writing RABBLE IN ARMS, NORTHWEST PASSAGE, OLIVER WISWELL and LYDIA BAILEY—for each of which I had to do my own research and draw my own conclusions, which were markedly different from the conclusions drawn by historians. Each one of those books left me in a state of complete exhaustion; and with the completion of each one, I swore I'd never do it again. Now I *know* that I can't."[42]

Roberts's forceful personality and unwavering convictions contributed as much to his obsession with dowsing as did his need for a "literary holiday." Throughout his life Roberts constantly had to be arguing and battling about someone or something, whether it was the administration at Cornell, immigration, billboards, Benedict Arnold, Loyalists, or historians. A man of action rather than a broad-minded individual of lofty ideals and sentiments, he embraced dowsing with the same passion that he gave his other causes. As Ben Ames Williams understated in 1938, the year following the publication of *Northwest Passage*, "If Ken were not a great novelist he might have been a great crusader" (Williams 1938, 9).

Chapter Six

The Last Years

Boon Island

During the 1950s, as Kenneth Roberts frantically dashed from one water-finding project to another, he found that he had little energy left to write historical fiction. But as he admitted in *Water Unlimited*, "Sandwiched in and among all these dowsing ventures was the worst affliction of all—the effort to find a way of telling a story that had been lurking in the back of my mind for many years." This story "finally emerged" from his mind and pen, and nine years to the day after *Lydia Bailey* appeared Roberts published his last novel, *Boon Island* (*WU*, 215).

During a storm on the evening of 11 December 1710 the British *Nottingham Galley* ran aground and was wrecked on a small, uninhabited island. Although the crew of 14 managed to scramble safely onto the island (little more than a barren pile of rocks measuring 100 by 50 yards), they had few tools, little food, and no shelter except for a makeshift tent. Ten of the castaways, however, managed to survive for 24 days until help arrived, and their struggle is the central focus of much of the novel's drama and suspense.

As Roberts mentioned during an interview shortly before the book's publication, he had long been familiar with both the island, located approximately 14 miles south of Kennebunkport, and the famous shipwreck:

"I've thought about that story for a long, long time—thirty years, say," Mr. Roberts remarked. "As a boy I used to go fishing out there, so probably it dates back even more. But fooling around with the idea, thirty years.

"You'll find the story of Boon Island in footnotes in all Maine histories. They'll keep telling you that you couldn't live twenty-four days on a rock in a Maine winter. These people did. Then I've always wanted to put together a group who had nothing, and see what they'd do."[1]

When Roberts researched his story, the only primary account of the episode he could find was one by *Nottingham Galley* Captain John Dean, which he felt was "a jumbled, garbled, incoherent mass of generalities in which practically no one was named" (Bond 1956). Seeking corroboration of the details, as well as some sort of focus and "lead" to the story, he asked his cousin in Greenwich, England, the city from which the vessel had sailed, to comb through eighteenth-century records for him. His relative found a narrative written by the galley's mate and two of its sailors that claimed Dean deliberately sank the ship so that he could collect the insurance money on it. This journal gave Roberts the angle he was looking for:

> Then, by great good fortune, I found a journal of Dean's first mate. The mate was a liar and a coward. He hated Dean with an abysmal hatred; accused Dean of all sorts of impossible things; but both of these two men, hating each other, agreed in their essential details, so that I knew the *Nottingham* had been wrecked on Boon Island on a certain date, and that the crew had lived under impossible conditions for 24 days.[2]

Boon Island—narrated rather dispassionately by Miles Whitworth, the ship's supercargo—is essentially a morality story of how the essence of a man's character is first tested and then laid bare by the circumstances that befall him. At one extreme is Captain Dean, who while marooned on Boon Island "had washed our ulcerated legs and feet with urine: persuaded his unwilling crew to pick oakum for their own protection: [and] almost paralyzed his hands to dredge up mussels for us."[3] At the other is first mate Christopher Langman, who is described by the narrator as "malice personified" and "a whoreson, beetle-headed, flap-ear'd knave" (*BI*, 192, 47, 156).

As one reviewer indicated, a trademark of Roberts's novels is that "his heroes, as a rule, are thorough heroes; and his villains are unmitigated villains."[4] The men in *Boon Island* are no exception to this dichotomy, and although reviewers criticized the novel for its rudimentary characterization, the shipwrecked men do serve as black-and-white paradigms of virtues and vices. Therefore, just as their isolation and suffering is made particularly vivid to the reader by Roberts's use of dates and days as chapter headings, so do the unremitting conflicts and hardships they face each day increasingly reveal either each man's inner strengths or his basic character flaws.

This is particularly evident when the men discuss whether they should eat the body of Chips Bullock, the ship's carpenter. Narrator

Whitworth observes that Captain Dean "had willingly done physical things that those beneath him hadn't the moral strength to do," but "now I think he foresaw that a worse trial was upon him—one that would require him to ignore standards that civilization builds up within a decent man" (*BI*, 192). William Saver and Charles Graystock, the two "perpetual thorns in the captain's flesh," were initially the two loudest proponents of eating Bullock, but they proved to lack the courage to even help carry the body from the tent (*BI*, 196). Langman, George White, and Nicholas Mellen refuse to consider the idea, arguing that "eating a man would be a sin" (*BI*, 195). After Dean has cut, skinned, and boned out the carcass, however, they change their minds, piously telling him that "it's not a sin to eat beef" (*BI*, 204).

Langman's spite, envy, and malice are particularly noticeable, for regardless of what Captain Dean suggests, he disagrees with the idea and tries to turn it to his own advantage. When the men realize that they are going to have to eat human flesh to survive, Whitworth perceives that Langman tries to make the captain vote in the decision:

> The captain ignored him, and I knew why. The captain didn't want to vote Yes; but if he had, Langman, at the first opportunity, would have taken oath that the eating of Chips Bullock had been done at the captain's suggestion. He might even have implied that the captain killed Chips in order to eat him. That was the sort of person Langman was. Unfortunately there'll always be Langmans in this world, to set people and nations against each other—to condemn the good and extol the bad—to spread sly rumors and spit on the truth. (*BI*, 197)

Thus in *Boon Island* Roberts's "finding the truth" theme refers not only to "what actually happened" but to truth in a deeper, abstract sense of a motivating force. After the men are finally rescued Roberts contrasts England with the United States, portraying the latter as a safe and secure haven where a man can achieve his potential through diligence and hard work, as opposed to a corrupt and amoral eighteenth-century Europe inhabited by scoundrels, thieves, and ne'er-do-wells. As Roberts—the fervent nationalist—summarized in his final paragraph, "How many of us have our Boon Islands? And how many have our Langmans? But doesn't each one of us have an inner America on which in youth his heart is set; and if—because of age, or greed, or weakness of will, or circumstances beyond his poor control—it escapes him, his life, to my way of thinking, has been wasted" (*BI*, 274).

Whereas reviewers were pleased to see a new Roberts novel after a lapse of nine years, many shared the opinion of Herbert Faulkner West, who regarded it as "a failure if judged by the magnificent qualities of his earlier books" (West 1962, 98). A reviewer for the *Chicago Tribune* elaborated on West's evaluation: "This novel lacks the range of character, setting, action, and reflection of Roberts' previous books. Instead of that full fare it offers a somber study in merciless hunger and pitiless cold—and in the greed and endurance, the treachery and loyalty that emerge in men under stress."[5] Roberts's Doubleday editor, Clara Claasen, similarly commented on the novel's "unrelieved emotion," admitting in a 1963 interview that the book was "too stark, too fast without any slowing of pace."[6]

Although *Boon Island* is certainly not one of Roberts's most memorable books, for the author it symbolized the courage and integrity a person needed to confront and overcome life's inevitable adversities. "Boon Island is us fighting the world," he wrote in a memo the month he died. "We aint got a Chinaman's chance—but with guts we can somehow lick the world."[7]

The Battle of Cowpens

In February 1956 *Collier's* magazine asked a Doubleday representative to ascertain if Roberts would be interested in writing a 4,000- to 5,000-word article on the Revolutionary War's Battle of Cowpens, an hour-long skirmish that was fought in a grazing meadow in northwest South Carolina on 17 January 1781. During this brief time an army of only 900 men commanded by General Daniel Morgan routed a larger force of British soldiers led by Colonel Banastre Tarleton. *Collier's* editors planned the article to be included in a series titled "The American Tradition." Each article would recount a dramatic event in American history that influenced American traditions, principles, or institutions. The Battle of Cowpens was chosen because it led to the British surrender at Yorktown.[8]

Roberts's article was published in August 1956, and its writing motivated him to begin a novel on General Morgan, whom he first wrote about in *Arundel* and *Rabble in Arms*. The author's death on 21 July 1957 interrupted his research on this novel, and he unfortunately left few notes on the subject. As his secretary, Marjorie Mosser Ellis, recollected in 1963, "Any plans for such a book were in Mr. Roberts' head at the time of his death."[9]

Shortly before he died, however, Roberts permitted his old friend Herbert Faulkner West to publish his *Collier's* article in book form as a limited edition. In the book's foreword West wrote, "Dissatisfied with a shorter version that appeared in the now-defunct *Colliers* [*sic*] he rewrote *Cowpens: The Great Morale-Builder* just as it appears here."[10] This statement is incorrect. After reading the page proofs of Doubleday's trade edition of the book, *The Battle of Cowpens*, Mosser wrote to Claasen that she was disappointed that Doubleday was including West's foreword in the book. Not only did she dislike his negative comments about *Northwest Passage*, *Boon Island*, and Roberts's three dowsing books, but she stated that "the truth of it" is that the author wrote the work on Cowpens "as it *now* stands and *Collier's* hacked it to pieces: he did *not* rewrite it for Herb West."[11]

In *The Battle of Cowpens*, Roberts's last piece of historical writing, he contends that the clash between the two armies was a turning point in the Revolutionary War. From a military point of view it interfered with Cornwallis's plans to conquer the South and led him to make strategic errors that would prove fatal to the British in Virginia. Psychologically, the battle raised the patriots' morale and helped the North understand the significance of the southern campaign and of "the necessity of supplying their pitiful ghost army in the South with the troops and supplies that eventually made it possible for Cornwallis to be cornered at Yorktown" (*Battle*, 19).

Roberts clearly admired Daniel Morgan. As one reviewer declared, "He was a leader of men, a legendary hero, an unlettered giant with courage and spirit and would have made a great hero for the book Roberts did not live to write."[12] Despite Roberts's enthusiasm for his subject, however, it is obvious that this work was only a mere fragment of his proposed novel. Mark Boatner noted that the book "contains many glaring errors" (Boatner, 291), and it is probably safe to assume that Roberts would have corrected these if he had lived to complete his project. Furthermore, the 16 short sections of the work do not flow together smoothly. After a few introductory passages, Roberts interrupts the story by inserting biographical sketches of Morgan and Tarleton. Shortly before the battle, as another reviewer pointed out, "Roberts falls into the use of invented conversation, as if he was already projecting a scene for his novel."[13]

Unfinished Novels and a Pulitzer Prize

His novel on Daniel Morgan was not the only book Roberts did not live to complete. He also wanted to publish some of the Robert Rogers–Jonathan Carver source material that he used in *Northwest Passage*; the letters that Tobias Lear wrote while a consular officer with the U.S. government; Booth Tarkington's letters to him, spanning the years 1919 to Tarkington's death in 1946; and some of the letters, both to and from him, that were written during the period between when he finished *Oliver Wiswell* and completed *Lydia Bailey*. Roberts's several suggested titles of this latter work were *Between Two Books*, *There Is More to Writing than You'd Think*, and *There's Nothing like a Book*.[14]

Soon after *Boon Island* was published Roberts told an interviewer that he was working on a sequel to *Arundel* and *Rabble in Arms* and on a novel about the expedition against the French fortress of Louisburg during King George's War.[15] Located on Canada's Cape Breton Island, this supposedly impregnable French "Gibraltar of America" guarded the mouth of the St. Lawrence River, but in 1745 land and naval forces managed to capture it after lengthy sieges (*IWW*, 182; *BI*, 275).

Another unfinished novel was *Forty on the Emu*. Taking place in 1813, it focused on 40 women convicts who were on the British ship *Emu* bound for the penal colony in Tasmania. The ship was captured by the American privateer *Holkar*, and the women were put ashore on the uninhabited St. Vincents Island in the Cape Verde Islands. In 1937 after completing *Northwest Passage*, Roberts gave Booth Tarkington a synopsis of this novel, indicating that it "would deal with the life of the women on St. Vincents, and of the association with them of the 2nd officer of the *Holkar*, marooned at the same time for protesting against the marooning of the women."[16]

To prove his theory that book reviews had little long-term effect on book sales, Roberts spent countless hours working on *Reviews and Consequences*, which he intended to be an exhaustive collection of both reviews and sales figures of his books. Although Doubleday wrote a contract for the volume in 1950, the work was never finished or published.[17]

In the *Trending into Maine* chapter "Maine Stories I'd Like to Write" Roberts included ideas for three novels: the 1866 journey of 156 Maine settlers to Palestine in an ill-fated attempt to start a farming community; the Indian massacre at the village of York, Maine, in 1692 (Roberts also noted this subject in his 1937 letter to Tarkington); and Maine Civil War regiments (*Trending*, 16-51).

Although Roberts never won a Pulitzer Prize for any of his books, on 6 May 1957 he was awarded a special Pulitzer Prize citation "for his historical novels which have long contributed to the creation of greater interest in our early American history." Despite his long-standing animosity toward the Pulitzer committee, Roberts was gracious when he learned of the award while playing golf in Kennebunk and remarked that he was "mighty grateful, and I speak not only for myself but for a lot of characters [from my books] who have helped me so faithfully."[18]

Roberts died at his home in Kennebunkport on 21 July 1957, less than three months after receiving his special Pulitzer Prize and soon after he had finished reading the proof sheets of *Water Unlimited*, his third dowsing book. He had suffered a heart attack earlier that month and had been recuperating in bed when he died; the official cause of death was coronary thrombosis. After a private Congregational funeral service his body was cremated, and as he had wished his ashes were buried in Arlington National Cemetery in Virginia.[19]

Newspapers and magazines around the world reported Roberts's death, and copies of editorials and other eulogies poured into Roberts's estate, Rocky Pasture. A respectful but not mawkish tribute—as befitting his nature—appeared in the *New York Times*: "Through exacting, perhaps even loving, research Mr. Roberts produced some of the most distinguished American historical novels of our age. . . . His death leaves us with a definite sadness. We know of no author to fill his place. He was no Dreiser or Thomas Wolfe, but neither were they Kenneth Roberts."[20]

Afterword

In his *Cavalcade of the American Novel* (1952) literary historian Edward Wagenknecht states that "Kenneth Roberts's distinguishing mark as a novelist [is] his capacity to combine really breathless action with a solidity of specification which creates a strong air of reality" (Wagenknecht, 430). Roberts always insisted that accuracy and realism were essential for the readability of his books, and he viewed with contempt any novelist whose works were not illustrative of both attributes. For instance, in December 1931 while reading Robert Raynolds's *Brothers in the West* (1931), published by Harper & Brothers, he noticed that Raynolds depicted a running horse flinging grit into its rider's face. Raynolds also wrote that after the rider put a rifle muzzle in his mouth he tasted "the dull dryness of burnt powder." Neither of these statements made any sense to Roberts. "Burnt black powder is wet and tastes sharp and salty," he observed derisively. "A galloping horse flings grit behind him, and the rider's face is shielded by the horse's neck and body. . . . It was a Harper editor who assured me that *Arundel* wasn't worth writing, but they give this junk a ten-thousand-dollar prize!" (*IWW*, 228-29).

Roberts maintained that historians have an advantage over novelists in that they can state supposed facts without explaining them, while a novelist who is trying to relate a story must be sure that everything is clear to the reader. Without accurate details, Roberts believed, a story seems contrived and the reader is confused (*IWW*, 186-87). For instance, in one of the major research works he used for *Arundel*, *Arnold's March from Cambridge to Quebec* (1903), author Justin Smith admits that he "cannot possibly understand" why some of Arnold's troops suddenly and mysteriously ran out of food on 16 October 1775.[1] As far as Roberts was concerned, however, if *Arundel* were to appear vividly real to the reader then some sort of reason must be given. Thus he reread all of the journal accounts of the Quebec expedition, discovering a brief statement in the entry for 29 October 1775 in James Melvin's diary that "our provisions was stolen by Captain [Daniel] Morgan's company."[2] Roberts consequently clarified the disappearance of the food in chapter 21 of *Arundel*. As he noted in the margin of Smith's book, "Morgan stole [Christopher] Greene's flour on the Great Carrying Place. No other explanation is possible" (Smith, 141).

Roberts elaborated on his method of writing fiction in a letter to
Herbert Faulkner West:

> I have a theory that history can be most effectively told in the form of fic-
> tion, because only in the writing of fiction that stands the test of truth do
> falsities come to the surface. This is an obscure sentence, and my mean-
> ing, I know, is obscure. I don't know whether I can explain it. Your con-
> stant gauge, in writing fiction, is "Is this true: is this the way it
> happened." That gauge is applied to everything—conversation, charac-
> ters, action. The historian isn't bothered by that gauge. He can accept a
> statement made by a reliable man. If [General Arthur] St. Clair says in
> his court martial that the moon was full on July 5, 177[7], Hoffman
> Nickerson naturally feels free to accept it. When I come to writing the
> action of the night of July 5th [during the retreat from Fort Ticonderoga
> in *Rabble in Arms*], however, I find that the night was clear with a high
> hot wind blowing: that the Americans retreated beneath the screen of
> darkness and smoke, and that it wasn't until [General Roche de]
> Fermoy's cabin burned that the British caught sight of the retreat. When
> I say to myself "Is this true: is this the way it happened?", I am at once
> made uncomfortable by this full moon business. Consequently I get a cal-
> endar for 177[7], and find that St. Clair was mistaken. The moon on July
> 5th, 177[7], was a new moon. It went down shortly after sundown.
> There wasn't any moon at all during the retreat.[3]

Roberts argued that a novelist must account for all such details "to
the complete satisfaction of the reader. Otherwise his story doesn't, as
the saying goes, hold water" (*IWW*, 187). Unlike many novelists,
Roberts was unwilling simply to make up explanations, although in
some cases, such as with Robert Rogers's march in *Northwest Passage*, a
paucity of historical information required him to construct his own narrative within the framework of the existing evidence.

Roberts readily acknowledged that poetic license justified this elabo-
ration of his sources. For example, in chapter 49 of *Northwest Passage* he
has Langdon Towne paint portraits of Indians on the walls of the Warner
House in Portsmouth, New Hampshire. After a reader apparently wrote
him to complain that the actual building could not have been painted by
a fictitious character, Roberts produced a passage in Charles W.
Brewster's *Rambles about Portsmouth* (1873) that indicated the decorations
were by an unknown artist. He therefore felt "entitled to ascribe them to
Langdon Towne." As he concluded in his reply to the reader, "In a work
of fiction, an author is entitled to take anything on which he can lay his
hands and weave it into his story."[4]

But Roberts's meticulous fact-finding and attention to detail occasionally detracted from his creativity as a novelist. As shown by his handling of Benedict Arnold in *Arundel* and *Rabble in Arms*, he could not dispassionately view his research and writing, and it often appeared in his books that he felt compelled to relate everything he knew about a subject. "What he sometimes lacked," Herbert Faulkner West declared, "was an artistic power of selection. Seeking to find the whole truth about a character, such as Robert Rogers, he insisted on telling the whole story of his life" (West 1958, 9). Carlos Baker had similar objections, notably with *Oliver Wiswell*, and hypothesized, "I am inclined to wonder whether Roberts' growing reputation as a historian is not working against him as an artist" (Baker, 18). Bernard DeVoto also criticized the exhaustive research that was a trademark of every Roberts novel: "Mr. Roberts's insistence on documenting his novels far more extensively than any other historical novelist I know about seems to me irrational and ritualistic. . . . But, of course, the minute historical accuracies which he insists on, which he must obtain as permission to write a novel, are entirely devoid of importance for a reader."[5]

Perhaps, as his close friend Arthur Hamilton Gibbs suggested, Roberts's constant research and adherence to facts may have stemmed from his uncertainty about his abilities as a creative artist. Although Gibbs could only theorize on this point, he did believe that the many years Roberts spent as a journalist hindered his development as a novelist. Accustomed to hurriedly completing essays, sketches, and other works to meet his deadlines for the *Boston Post* and the *Saturday Evening Post*, he often became impatient when he had to rewrite and polish his novels. Consequently, said Gibbs, he often relied on him, Booth Tarkington, or Ben Ames Williams for assistance (Gibbs 1963). Roberts was well aware of the haste with which he edited his books and struggled with the problem throughout his literary career, admitting while revising *Arundel* that "I had worked for so many years as a reporter that my revisions lacked the necessary care" (*IWW*, 189).

While Tarkington was helping Roberts with his first novel, he encouraged him to rewrite completely one chapter as he thought the love scene was "too explicit and detailed" (*IWW*, 190). Tarkington told Roberts that William Dean Howells had said that "decent people didn't do their love-making on park benches" and that such situations should be left to the reader's imagination. The deleted passages, however, reveal an emotion-charged Nason whose passion is unfortunately missing from the published book.[6]

Because of Tarkington's admonition, Roberts never permitted his heroes and heroines to show any prolonged or heartfelt feelings for each other, which consequently contributed to his occasional flat characterization—especially with women—and constrained love plots. As Carlos Baker summarized, "In the typical Roberts novel, one achieves a speaking acquaintance with the heroine at the start, and bids her farewell at the end. In the lengthy interim, we follow the fortunes of the male protagonist, who has usually undertaken a long and arduous journey during which a female would clearly be excess baggage. The journey completed, we leave the hero with the heroine, aware that he is in good hands" (Baker, 19).

Roberts was aware of his problems with characterization, and his friends often helped him while editing his manuscripts. For instance, as he read *Northwest Passage* Gibbs recommended changes in the book's dialogue that would depict the women more realistically and kindly (Gibbs 1963). The suggested revisions, however, could not alter Roberts's generally weak portrayal of women, and with the exception of *Arundel*'s Phoebe Marvin all of his heroines suffer to some degree. These include Ellen Phipps in *Rabble in Arms*, Ann Potter in *Northwest Passage*, *Oliver Wiswell*'s Sally Leighton, and, most noticeably, the title character in *Lydia Bailey*. As Booth Tarkington remarked to his niece, Susanah Mayberry, Roberts "was incomparable at writing of men on forced marches, as in *Northwest Passage*, but could not write a convincing woman's part."[7]

Roberts's narrators fare better than his heroines. Because they are directly involved in much of the action with their experiences intertwined with those of the novels' historical figures, the reader feels a sense of closeness to them. Although the narrators' motives are usually different from those of the historical characters—such as Steven Nason's quest to find Mary Mallinson and Langdon Towne's desire to paint pictures of Indians—their actions do not adversely affect the books' historicity. At the same time, owing somewhat to the humor of such comic-relief figures as Cap Huff, Doc Means, and Sergeant McNott, the narrators are not eclipsed by the historical events that the author depicts (Kitch, 129).

Although Roberts never explained why he chose the first-person narrative point of view for all of his novels except *Captain Caution*, he probably adopted it because this type of narration presents a sense of reality to readers, drawing them into the action of the novel. Arthur Hamilton Gibbs believed that Roberts's forceful personality and his love of a good argument had much to do with this decision. He much preferred talking to individuals rather than to large groups and tended to dominate conversations, so the first-person narrative was a natural one for him in that it enabled him to communicate directly to the reader. On the other hand, Gibbs also believed that through his use of this point of view Roberts tended to create narrators who simply voiced the author's own conservative opinions, thereby becoming virtual spokesmen for him rather than unique characters in their own right (Gibbs 1963).

But stirring historical novels do not require deep character analysis, and it is Roberts's storytelling abilities that place him among America's best-known writers in this genre. "He set out to rescue certain sectors of American history from inaccuracy and misconception and to tell how the people really lived and what they did," wrote Pulitzer Prize–winning poet Stephen Vincent Benét and his wife, Rosemary. "And, because he told the story with gusto as well as accuracy, readers have flocked to his books. Ph.D.'s may sometimes forget it, but the two things should go together."[8]

It is perhaps Roberts's widespread popularity that provokes these academics to disparage or ignore his works. Usually regarded as mere "escape" literature on a par with mystery stories, historical novels have long been ridiculed as literary potboilers, the products of superficial research, stereotyped plots, and effusive dialogue. In his *American Fiction, 1900-1950* (1974) Tarkington biographer and literary historian James Woodress reported that by the early 1970s Roberts's reputation had "dimmed to third or fourth magnitude importance." Fifteen years later he elaborated on his statement, explaining why Roberts was not included in his book covering the most significant writers of American fiction during the first half of the twentieth century: "It's hard to say why an author's reputation fades, but Kenneth Roberts is in the same boat with lots of authors of second-magnitude importance. How much is Sinclair Lewis or James T. Farrell read today? But Roberts never got any attention from academic critics and hence his books never have been taught in college courses. The result has been that he never gets talked about anymore."[9]

Woodress's statement about academics ignoring Roberts is corroborated by Lee Coyle in the essay "Kenneth Roberts and the American Historical Novel." In the mid-1960s Coyle wrote several well-known historians and asked each for his opinion of Roberts and his novels. Although Allan Nevins remarked that he had "always had the highest opinion of his books," Clinton Rossiter's evaluation was fairly typical of the replies Coyle received: "In general, I would think that [Roberts's] research was very good indeed, but that he made highly selective use of his material. As to his stature among historians, I doubt very much that he has any. It is not that he has a lack of stature, but that he is simply passed over without recognition these days."[10]

Rossiter's conclusion is substantiated by the fact that only a small percentage of the reviews of Roberts's novels appeared in scholarly journals, and most of these were largely negative ones.[11] His vehement defense of Benedict Arnold is probably one reason that Roberts appears to have little credibility among many historians, but as John Tebbel, biographer of *Saturday Evening Post* editor George Horace Lorimer, argues, "No one disputes that Arnold was a traitor, but more recent research has disclosed that he had ample cause, even though many may think that nothing justifies such disloyalty. . . . It's such an unpopular view, of course, that this alone could have queered him with the scholars and a great many critics as well" (Tebbel, 28 February 1988).

Another factor that may account for Roberts's faded popularity is that many present-day readers of fiction have come to expect at least a modicum of sex and indiscriminate violence in their books, both of which are absent from Roberts's novels. Tebbel, however, emphasizes that Roberts was writing at a time "when literary expression even in popular novels was far less free than it is today." Praising his books, Tebbel adds that "his historical descriptions and the evidences of solid research are remarkable. It's only the style and the plotting that date him. But that's the inevitable fate that awaits most authors of popular novels."[12]

Tebbel's favorable assessment of Roberts's literary abilities is shared by many novelists—and even by scholars and historians. Although Benedict Arnold biographer Willard M. Wallace disagrees with the author's interpretation of the military leader, he unhesitatingly affirms that "in other ways Roberts is historically sound. He is especially good in developing the time, place, and action trinity." Wallace particularly admires Roberts's accounts of the attack of Quebec in *Arundel*, the battles at Valcour Island and Bemis Heights in *Rabble in Arms*, and the siege at Fort Ninety-Six in *Oliver Wiswell*. He adds that "it is difficult to fault him on manners, customs, and contemporary interests. He really did his homework on these subjects."[13]

In 1991 Robert Ludlum, an author who dominates the field of spy and espionage thrillers, told a librarian compiling a celebrities reading list that his favorite book was *Northwest Passage*. A few months later he explained that he was "an old Roberts fan" and that the writer's "admixture of academic history with imaginative fiction—in a sense related to Jim Michener's works—had a decided influence on me."[14] James A.

Michener, well known for his epic narratives, thinks highly of the sweeping *Oliver Wiswell* and believes Roberts was a "master craftsman" and a "powerful force in his day": "Many future writers who graduated from college in 1929 when I did, continued their reading education with that splendid chain of books published in those years by Kenneth Roberts. His *Oliver Wiswell* was especially significant in our edification, because of its masterful delineation of the English Loyalist experience in the Revolution. Roberts' thesis was so bold and so well expressed that our eyes were opened."[15]

Although the majority of Roberts's novels are no longer in print, it seems evident that his books will be remembered by those who enjoy reading American history dramatized as rousing adventure fiction. Historian Samuel Eliot Morison acknowledged this in a hortatory essay in which he lamented that although many historical works he had read were scrupulously researched and accurate, nearly all were pedantic and boring, perused by no one outside the profession. "American historians," he chided, "in their eagerness to present facts and their laudable anxiety to tell the truth, have neglected the literary aspects of their craft." He accordingly advised all of them, particularly graduate students and beginning scholars, to bear in mind that writing history is an art and that virtually every historian can learn from the novelist. As Morison declared in an affirmation that recognized the literary abilities of an author who used as much energy and perseverance in writing historical novels as he did in researching them, "When John Citizen feels the urge to read history, he goes to the novels of Kenneth Roberts or Margaret Mitchell, not to the histories of Professor this or Doctor that."[16]

Notes and References

Preface

1. George Gallup, "The Favorite Books of Americans," *New York Times Book Review*, 15 January 1939, 2, 16.
2. Jack Bales, "Letters and Other Documents: A Biographical Essay," in *Kenneth Roberts: The Man and His Works* (Metuchen, N.J.: Scarecrow, 1989), 3-74; hereafter cited in text.

Chapter One

1. Letter to Chilson H. Leonard, 27 November 1935, Phillips Exeter Academy Library, Exeter, New Hampshire; hereafter cited in text. Letter partially quoted in Chilson H. Leonard, "Kenneth Roberts: An Informal Study of America's Best Historical Novelist," in *Kenneth Roberts: A Biographical Sketch, an Informal Study, His Books and Critical Opinions* (Garden City, N.Y.: Doubleday, Doran, 1936), 17-18; hereafter cited in text.
2. Interview with Henry Morgan, 8 July 1937, transcript, Dartmouth College Library, Hanover, New Hampshire; hereafter cited in text. See also "Notes on a Few Nasons Gathered from Various Sources during the Writing of *Arundel* and *The Lively Lady*," in *Arundel*, ltd. ed. (Garden City, N.Y.: Doubleday, Doran, 1931), 621-28; hereafter cited in text as "Notes on Nasons." *Trending into Maine*, rev. ed. (Garden City, N.Y.: Doubleday, Doran, 1944), 83-106; hereafter cited in text as *Trending*. M[alcolm] J[ohnson], "A Biographical Sketch of Kenneth Roberts," in *Kenneth Roberts: An American Novelist* (New York: Doubleday, Doran, 1938), 5; hereafter cited in text.
3. Bales 1989, 3-5; Joyce Butler, "Kenneth Roberts: The Man," *Chapters in Local History* 1, no. 3 (1986): 2; Alice Dixon Bond, "Kenneth Roberts' New Novel Proves Own View, That Writer Must Have 'Stood up to Live,'" *Boston Sunday Herald*, 15 January 1956, sec. 1, p. 2; hereafter cited in text. Genealogical data on Roberts's family in Brick Store Museum, Kennebunk, Maine. Roberts's birthplace was then owned by Charles and Sarah Parsons, relatives of the Tibbets family, who had loaned it to Frank and Grace Roberts.
4. Introduction to *Let Me Show You New Hampshire*, by Ella Shannon Bowles (New York: Alfred A. Knopf, 1938), viii. Frank and Grace Roberts were either separated or divorced by the time Roberts was in college, and an aunt paid his college expenses.

5. Carl Warton, "Kenneth Roberts a Glutton for Truth," *Boston Herald Magazine*, 10 August 1930, 3. See also Box 15, folder 35, Kenneth Roberts Papers, Dartmouth College Library.

6. John Ira Kitch, Jr., "From History to Fiction: Kenneth Roberts as an Historical Novelist," Ph.D. diss., University of Illinois, 1965, 16-17, quoted in Bales 1989, 5; hereafter cited in text.

7. Letter to Chilson H. Leonard, 6 February 1936, Phillips Exeter Academy Library.

8. Edgar S. Wheelan to John I. Kitch, Jr., 25 July 1964, Colby College Library, Waterville, Maine, quoted in Bales 1989, 5; hereafter cited in text.

9. *The Cornell Class Book* (Ithaca, N.Y.: Cornell University, 1908), 158. See also Morris Bishop, *A History of Cornell* (Ithaca, N.Y.: Cornell University Press, 1962), 300, 339-44, 411; Thomas A. Sokol, ed., *Songs of Cornell* (Ithaca, N.Y.: Cornell University Glee Club, 1988), 19-21, 44-48.

10. Gould P. Colman to Jack Bales, 13 June 1989, Dartmouth College Library.

11. *I Wanted to Write* (Garden City, N.Y.: Doubleday, 1949), 9; hereafter cited in text as *IWW*.

12. Jerome D. Barnum to John I. Kitch, Jr., 28 May 1964, Colby College Library, quoted in Bales 1989, 6.

13. "Autobiography," 1919, container 4, Kenneth Roberts Papers, Library of Congress, Manuscript Division, Washington, D.C.; hereafter cited in text as "Autobiography" (reprinted in Bales 1989, 247-50). Romeyn Berry, "Now, in *My* Time!," *Cornell Alumni News* 43 (5 December 1940): 149; hereafter cited in text.

14. Joey Green, ed., *The Cornell Widow Hundredth Anniversary Anthology, 1894-1994* (Ithaca, N.Y.: Cornell Widow, 1981), 9-17; Box 13, Kenneth Roberts Papers, Dartmouth College Library.

15. In later years Roberts never credited his writing talent to Cornell. When an interviewer asked him in 1937, "What one thing in your college days was of the greatest assistance to you in writing books?" Roberts replied, "I don't recall anything" (Morgan). When answering questions before an audience in 1945 he was asked about the value of a college education and answered, "A college doesn't give you anything that helps you write. In fact, I would say a college did more to hurt you in writing than anything" (interview with Alton Hall Blackington, 29 November 1945, transcript, Dartmouth College Library; hereafter cited in text). One possible reason for Roberts's displeasure was that he never received an honorary degree from Cornell and was rebuffed after inquiring if he could submit one of his books as a dissertation and receive a Ph.D. See G. Watts Cunningham to C. L. Durham, 24 April 1948, Colby College Library.

16. Gleeson Murphy to Roberts, 5 October 1908, Dartmouth College Library.

17. Archibald Howard to Roberts, 2 December 1909, Dartmouth College Library.

18. Letter to Julian Street, 31 March 1922, Julian Street Papers, Collection 0036, box 37, folder 12, Princeton University Library, Princeton, N.J. See also Herbert A. Kenny, "Kenneth Roberts: Reporter," in *Newspaper Row: Journalism in the Pre-Television Era* (Chester, Conn: Globe Pequot Press, 1987), 111-19.

19. *IWW*, 25-35. Morton Kilgallen's brother, Milton, later appeared as one of the pseudonyms of Roberts's *The Collector's Whatnot* (1923) and as the pseudonym of his *Antiquamania* (1928).

20. *IWW*, 70. See also "Contemporary Writers and Their Work— Kenneth L. Roberts," *Editor: The Journal of Information for Literary Workers* 48 (25 February 1918): 128. Roberts's first three stories are "Good Will and Almond Shells," *Saturday Evening Post*, 22 December 1917, 12-14+; "With Neatness and Dispatch," *Saturday Evening Post*, 2 February 1918, 12-14+; "Pergola Preferred," *Collier's*, 4 October 1919, 15+.

21. Richard Cary, "Roberts and Lorimer: The First Decade," *Colby Library Quarterly* 6 (September 1962): 111; hereafter cited in text.

22. Cary, 112. Roberts's Siberia report is "The Random Notes of an Amerikansky," *Saturday Evening Post*, 17 May 1919, 3-4+. His two other articles are "The Super Boobs," *Saturday Evening Post*, 7 June 1919, 12-13+, and "Bringing Chaos Out of Order," *Saturday Evening Post*, 12 July 1919, 16+. His play is "The Brotherhood of Man," *Saturday Evening Post*, 30 August 1919, 3-5+. Coauthored with Robert Garland, a medical officer during the war whom Roberts met in Japan, the play was written while they were returning from Siberia on an army transport. It was published separately in 1934 by Samuel French, Inc., in New York.

Chapter Two

1. James Playsted Wood, *Magazines in the United States*, 2d ed. (New York: Ronald Press, 1956), 154; hereafter cited in text. See also John Tebbel, *George Horace Lorimer and "The Saturday Evening Post"* (Garden City, N.Y.: Doubleday & Co., 1948), hereafter cited in text, and Jan Cohn, *Creating America: George Horace Lorimer and "The Saturday Evening Post"* (Pittsburgh: University of Pittsburgh Press, 1989).

2. For example, see "The Threatened Inundation from Europe," *Literary Digest* 67 (18 December 1920): 7. Two excellent studies of American immigration are John Higham, *Strangers in the Land: Patterns of American Nativism, 1860-1925*, 2d ed. (New Brunswick, N.J.: Rutgers University Press, 1988), hereafter cited in text, and Maldwyn Allen Jones, *American Immigration* (Chicago: University of Chicago Press, 1960).

3. For example, see "Self-Preservation," *Saturday Evening Post*, 7

February 1920, 28-29, and "No Admittance," *Saturday Evening Post*, 8 January
1921, 24.

4.   "Bringing Chaos Out of Order," *Saturday Evening Post*, 12 July
1919, 36.

5.   George Horace Lorimer to Roberts, 31 October 1919, Dartmouth
College Library; also quoted in *IWW*, 134-35, and Tebbel 1948, 90-91.

6.   House Committee on Immigration and Naturalization, "Statement
of Kenneth L. Roberts," in *Immigration: Hearings before the Committee on
Immigration and Naturalization*, 67th Cong., 2d sess., 1922, serial 1-B, 98, hereafter cited in text as "Statement"; *Notebooks of a Foreign Correspondent*, Dartmouth
College Library, box 7; *IWW*, 135-43.

7.   "How Cousin John's Getting Along," *Saturday Evening Post*, 13
March 1920, 70.

8.   "The Rising Irish Tide," *Saturday Evening Post*, 14 February 1920, 4;
hereafter cited in text as "Irish."

9.   "Schieber Land," *Saturday Evening Post*, 27 March 1920, 10.

10.   "Husks," *Saturday Evening Post*, 1 May 1920, 3; hereafter cited in
text as "Husks."

11.   "Almost Sunny Italy," *Saturday Evening Post*, 17 July 1920, 18. See
also *IWW*, 142-43.

12.   *Europe's Morning After* (New York and London: Harper, 1921). See
also Kitch, 222-23.

13.   "The Goal of Central Europeans," *Saturday Evening Post*, 6
November 1920, 13; hereafter cited in text as "Goal."

14.   "The Existence of an Emergency," *Saturday Evening Post*, 30 April
1921, 89; hereafter cited in text as "Existence."

15.   "Ports of Embarkation," *Saturday Evening Post*, 7 May 1921, 12;
hereafter cited in text as "Ports."

16.   Madison Grant, *The Passing of the Great Race; or, The Racial Basis of
European History* (New York: Scribner's, 1916), 198; "Ports," 72. See also Gary
Frank Hoffman, "Ethnic Prejudice and Racial Ideology in the Immigration
Articles of Kenneth L. Roberts," M.A. thesis, Michigan State University, 1979,
57-60; Sylvia Choate Whitman, "Dynamic Is the Word: Kenneth Roberts and
the *Saturday Evening Post*, 1919-1938," M.A. thesis, University of Texas at
Austin, 1989, 30-32; hereafter cited in text.

17.   "Plain Remarks on Immigration for Plain Americans," *Saturday
Evening Post*, 12 February 1921, 21.

18.   *Why Europe Leaves Home: A True Account of the Reasons Which Cause
Central Europeans to Overrun America, Which Lead Russians to Rush to Constantinople
and Other Fascinating and Unpleasant Places, Which Coax Greek Royalty and
Commoners into Strange Byways and Hedges, and Which Induce Englishmen and
Scotchmen to Go Out at Night* (Indianapolis: Bobbs-Merrill, 1922); hereafter cited
in text as *WELH*. Roberts's sarcasm is as conspicuous in the book's subtitle as it

was in the original *Post* articles. The book's working title was *What's Coming to America*. See also Kitch, 223-24.

19. "Americanski," *Saturday Evening Post*, 14 May 1921, 20. Lorimer also promoted Madison Grant's and Lothrop Stoddard's books in his editorials. For example, see "The Great American Myth," *Saturday Evening Post*, 7 May 1921, 20. See also Madison Grant to Roberts, 10 April 1922, Dartmouth College Library, in which Grant profusely thanks Roberts for the inscribed copy of *Why Europe Leaves Home*; Lothrop Stoddard to Roberts, 1 July 1921, Dartmouth College Library, in which Stoddard congratulates Roberts on the fine work he is doing to restrict immigration; Roberts to Hewitt Howland, 17 December 1921, Bobbs-Merrill Papers, Indiana University, Lilly Library, Bloomington, Indiana.

20. "Shutting the Sea Gates," *Saturday Evening Post*, 28 January 1922, 11. Roberts often received positive feedback from *Post* readers. Shortly after this article appeared he received a letter from the assistant commissioner of immigration at Ellis Island, thanking him for his efforts to reduce the "hordes" coming into the United States. Byron M. Uhl to Roberts, 9 February 1922, Dartmouth College Library. See also Higham, 309-12.

21. "Meeting of the Senate Committee on Immigration," part of an "8 page pamphlet in press," 5 January 1921 [*sic*, 1922], Bobbs-Merrill Papers, Indiana University, Lilly Library; related letters in Bobbs-Merrill Papers, 1922; "Lest We Forget," *Saturday Evening Post*, 28 April 1923, 3-4+.

22. Eugene S. Bagger, "Ethnology by Ear," *New Republic*, 17 May 1922, 349; Higham, 324; Wood, 159; Kitch, 27-28. The circulation of the *Post* in 1920 and 1921 was 2,061,058 and 2,099,940, respectively.

23. Joe Toye, "Danger That World Scum Will Demoralize America," *Boston Sunday Herald*, 26 June 1921, sec. D, p. 1.

24. Letter to Charles G. Dawes, 4 November 1928, Northwestern University Library, Evanston, Illinois; Letter to Ben Ames Williams, 22 January 1930, Colby College Library; Letter to Williams, 9 September 1926, Colby College Library.

25. "Dalmation—Jugo-Slavia" Notebook, 1920, container 1, Kenneth Roberts Papers, Library of Congress.

26. "Vienna Czecho-slovakia" Notebook, 1920, container 1, Kenneth Roberts Papers, Library of Congress.

27. "Mexican Border Patrol" Notebook, 1927?, container 2, Kenneth Roberts Papers, Library of Congress.

28. Letter to Clara Claasen, 23 November 1937, Kenneth D. McCormick Papers, Library of Congress.

29. John I. Kitch, Jr., "KR Comments in Books in His Library at Roc[k]y Pasture," John I. Kitch, Jr., Papers, Colby College Library.

30. Letter to Ben Ames Williams, 1 January 1948, Colby College Library.

31. "Attacks Roberts for Book on Immigration," *Boston Herald*, 18 March 1922, 18. See also "Roberts Answers Sabath," *Boston Sunday Post*, 19 March 1922, 5.

32. Letter to D. Laurence Chambers, 17 March 1922, Bobbs-Merrill Papers, Indiana University, Lilly Library.

33. Charles H. Joseph, "Random Thoughts," *Jewish Criterion* 63 (18 April 1924): 10. See also Letter to John Tebbel, 7 August 1947, Syracuse University Library, Syracuse, New York; "East Is East," *Saturday Evening Post*, 23 February 1924, 6-7+. In Roberts's letter, one of several he wrote Tebbel while the latter was working on his Lorimer biography, he underplayed his problems with the *Post* editor: "The only jam I was ever in with Lorimer was after the alteration of the words 'Polish Jews' to 'Poles.'" Tebbel followed Roberts's lead and wrote in his book: "Of the 207 articles Kenneth Roberts wrote for [Lorimer], only one was censored and then the change was in two words: 'Polish Jews.' Lorimer made it 'Poles'" (Tebbel 1948, 216). Cary also mentioned this incident and in addition wrote, "Lorimer rarely cut or altered Roberts' work. Roberts remembered only the excision of a paragraph from one of his Hollywood pieces to avoid clamor from the Chamber of Commerce" (Cary, 115). Actually, Lorimer was often open and aboveboard concerning his editing and cutting. See George H. Lorimer to Roberts, 4 June 1924, Dartmouth College Library; Lorimer to Roberts, 30 September 1935, Dartmouth College Library.

34. Letter to Julian Street, 25 August 1922, Julian Street Papers, Collection 0036, box 37, folder 12, Princeton University Library. Robert DeCourcy Ward (1867-1931), a professor of climatology at Harvard, helped found the Immigration Restriction League in 1894. In personal correspondence Roberts seldom used an apostrophe with "won't" or "ain't," believing that the words were not true contractions. The New Jersey Kallikak family (a fictitious surname) was studied by American psychologist and eugenicist Henry Herbert Goddard (1866-1957). In *The Kallikak Family* (1912) Goddard maintained that "feeble-mindedness" was subject to hereditary transmission. See J. David Smith, *Minds Made Feeble: The Myth and Legacy of the Kallikaks* (Rockville, Md.: Aspen Systems Corp., 1985).

35. Question-and-answer session in the Warner House, Portsmouth, New Hampshire, 4 August 1937, transcript, Dartmouth College Library; hereafter cited in text. Roberts's *Post* articles on Washington, D.C., include "Pepper," 6 May 1922, 27+; "Concentrated New England," 31 May 1924, 10-11+, later revised and published in book form as *Concentrated New England: A Sketch of Calvin Coolidge* (Indianapolis: Bobbs-Merrill, 1924); "The Troubles of the House," 3 June 1922, 6-7+; "The Tribulations of the Senate," 16 September 1922, 25+.

36. Roberts's other *Post* articles on Washington, D.C., include "Retrogressives and Others," 3 February 1923, 10+; "The Progressives—What They Stand for and Want," 10 March 1923, 27+; "The Common-Sense

Serum," 9 June 1923, 10+; "Senators and What-Not," 24 March 1923, 27+; "Filibusters," 12 May 1923, 6-7+; "Done in the District of Columbia," 3 March 1923, 3-4+. Flack made his debut in "Three Black Cows," 20 January 1923, 23+.

37. *Black Magic: An Account of Its Beneficial Use in Italy, of Its Perversion in Bavaria, and of Certain Tendencies Which Might Necessitate Its Study in America* (Indianapolis: Bobbs-Merrill, 1924).

38. "The Fight of the Black Shirts," *Saturday Evening Post*, 8 September 1923, 166; hereafter cited in text as "Fight." See also Kitch, 225-28.

39. Letter to Charles G. Dawes, 25 May 1927, Northwestern University Library. See also Tebbel 1948, 151-55.

40. "A Tour of the Bottlefields," *Saturday Evening Post*, 13 November 1926, 24+. See also Tebbel 1948, 277-85; Cary, 119-21.

41. Letter to Roger L. Scaife, 12 February 1922, Harvard University, Houghton Library, Cambridge, Massachusetts.

42. Cornelius Obenchain Van Loot [Booth Tarkington], Milton Kilgallen [Roberts], and Murgatroyd Elphinstone [Hugh MacNair Kahler], comps., *The Collector's Whatnot: A Compendium, Manual, and Syllabus of Information and Advice on All Subjects Appertaining to the Collection of Antiques, Both Ancient and Not So Ancient* (Boston and New York: Houghton Mifflin, 1923), vii; hereafter cited in text as *CW*. The preface bears Van Loot's name; one chapter is by Elphinstone; and Milton Kilgallen's name, surprisingly, does not appear with any chapter. Pseudonyms not on the title page are used with six sections, and the words "compilers' note" follow the title of the remaining essay. See also *IWW*, 34-35; Jack Bales, with Kingsley Kahler Hubby, "Some Notes on the Authorship of *The Collector's Whatnot*," in Bales 1989, 259-64.

43. Letter to Ferris Greenslet, 29 December 1927, Harvard University, Houghton Library.

44. *Antiquamania: The Collected Papers of Professor Milton Kilgallen, F.R.S., of Ugsworth College, Elucidating the Difficulties in the Path of the Antique Dealer and Collector, and Presenting Various Methods of Meeting and Overcoming Them* (Garden City, N.Y.: Doubleday, Doran, 1928).

45. "Wet and Other Mexicans," *Saturday Evening Post*, 4 February 1928, 10. Roberts's other *Post* articles on Mexicans include "Mexicans or Ruin," 18 February 1928, 14-15+; "Docile Mexicans," 10 March 1928, 39+. See also Raymond A. Mohl, "*The Saturday Evening Post* and the 'Mexican Invasion,'" *Journal of Mexican American History* 3 (1973): 131-38. Roberts's *Post* articles on the Southwest and American Indians include "Patient Pimas," 14 June 1924, 29+; "Navaho Land," 13 September 1924, 28+; "Fruits of the Desert," 4 October 1924, 19+; and "First Families of America," 18 October 1924, 23+. See also Sylvia Whitman, "The West of a Down Easterner: Kenneth Roberts and *The Saturday Evening Post*, 1924-1928," *Journal of the West* 31 (January 1992): 88-97.

46. "Florida Loafing," *Saturday Evening Post*, 17 May 1924, 125.

47. *Florida Loafing: An Investigation into the Peculiar State of Affairs Which Leads Residents of 47 States to Encourage Spanish Architecture in the 48th* (Indianapolis: Bobbs-Merrill, 1925). The six articles were collected in *Florida* (New York and London: Harper, 1926). Some of Roberts's earlier *Post* articles on Florida were later published in *Sun Hunting: Adventures and Observations among the Native and Migratory Tribes of Florida, Including the Stoical Time-Killers of Palm Beach, the Gentle and Gregarious Tin-Canners of the Remote Interior, and the Vivacious and Semi-Violent Peoples of Miami and Its Purlieus* (Indianapolis: Bobbs-Merrill, 1922).

48. Donald W. Curl, *Mizner's Florida: American Resort Architecture* (Cambridge: MIT Press for the Architectural History Foundation, 1984), 153-64, and George B. Tindall, "The Bubble in the Sun," *American Heritage* 16 (August 1965): 76-83, 109-11.

Chapter Three

1. Letter to Ben Ames Williams, 31 August 1926, Colby College Library. Williams (1889-1953) published more than 400 pieces in magazines and journals. His many popular novels include *Splendor* (1927), *Honeyflow* (1932), *Come Spring* (1940), *House Divided* (1947), *Owen Glen* (1950), and *The Unconquered* (1953).

2. *IWW*, 151-52; "The Truth about a Novel," *Saturday Evening Post*, 3 January 1931, 29; hereafter cited in text as "Truth." This essay was reprinted in both *For Authors Only, and Other Gloomy Essays*, 177-93, and *The Kenneth Roberts Reader*, 274-86.

3. Letter to Julian Street, 2 November 1931?, Julian Street Papers, Collection 0036, box 37, folder 12, Princeton University Library; hereafter cited in text. The town of Arundel, Maine, was renamed Kennebunkport in 1821. See also Bales 1989, 251-54.

4. Herbert Faulkner West, "The Work of Kenneth Roberts," *Colby Library Quarterly* 6 (September 1962): 92, 91; hereafter cited in text. See also Kitch, 32-35. Useful sources on Roberts as a historical novelist include Ernest E. Leisy, *The American Historical Novel* (Norman: University of Oklahoma Press, 1950), 52-53, 73-75, 87-88, 100-101, and Edward Wagenknecht, "Return to History," in *Cavalcade of the American Novel: From the Birth of the Nation to the Middle of the Twentieth Century* (New York: Henry Holt, 1952), 425-38; hereafter cited in text.

5. "A Patient Waiter," *Saturday Evening Post*, 9 December 1922, 35.

6. Ben Ames Williams, "Kenneth Roberts," *Saturday Review of Literature* 18 (25 June 1938): 8; hereafter cited in text.

7. Letter to Ben Ames Williams, 12 February 1928, Colby College Library. See also Letter to Williams, 5 January 1928, Colby College Library; Letter to Williams, 27 January 1928, Colby College Library.

8. "To Col. Roosevelt, a Letter of Protest," *New York Evening Sun*, 13

April 1918. Photocopies of poem and related letters are in the Dartmouth College Libary. See also Robert B. Beith, "Kenneth L. Roberts, Who Wrote Arundel, Was First Encouraged to Write Book by Col. Roosevelt," *Portland (Maine) Sunday Telegram*, 23 March 1930, sec. C, p. 11; hereafter cited in text. Another possible connection between Roberts and Roosevelt stems from the former's membership in Chi Psi fraternity at Cornell. While Roosevelt was governor of New York his secretary was a Cornell graduate and Chi Psi member. In 1899 Roosevelt made the Chi Psi fraternity house his headquarters while visiting the university, and in 1906, while Roberts was at Cornell, President Roosevelt sent Chi Psi his condolences after several members burned to death during a terrible fire at their fraternity house. See H. Seger Slifer and Hiram L. Kennicott, eds., *Centennial History and Biographical Directory of the Chi Psi Fraternity* (Ann Arbor, Mich.: Chi Psi fraternity, 1941), 336.

    9. *IWW*, 185-86; "Notes on Nasons," 623-25; *Trending*, 70-72. Roberts's annotated copies in the Dartmouth College Library of the following works (which all contain references to Harding) show his use of family and local history: Charles Bradbury, *History of Kennebunk Port, from Its First Discovery by Bartholomew Gosnold, May 14, 1602, to A.D. 1837* (Kennebunk, Maine: James K. Remich, 1837), hereafter cited in text; Edward E. Bourne, *The History of Wells and Kennebunk, from the Earliest Settlement to the Year 1820, at Which Time Kennebunk Was Set Off, and Incorporated* (Portland, Maine: B. Thurston, 1875), hereafter cited in text; and Daniel Remich, *History of Kennebunk from Its Earliest Settlement to 1890* (Portland, Maine: Lakeside Press, 1911), hereafter cited in text.

    10. Roberts named his Italian retreat the "Half-Baked Palace," the wing he added on the "American Wing," and the entire estate "Lividonia." His *Post* articles on his experiences of living in Italy have been reprinted in *For Authors Only* and *The Kenneth Roberts Reader*. See *IWW*, 176-81; Letter to Charles G. Dawes, 17 January 1928, Northwestern University Library; Letter to Ben Ames Williams, 12 February 1928, Colby College Library.

    11. *IWW*, 320-21; Kitch, 74-77; James Woodress, *Booth Tarkington: Gentleman from Indiana* (Philadelphia: Lippincott, 1954), 275-77, hereafter cited in text; "A Gentleman from Maine and Indiana," *Saturday Evening Post*, 8 August 1931, 14-15+, reprinted as appendix in *IWW*, 361-74.

    12. Letter to Street, 1931? Former Doubleday editor in chief Kenneth D. McCormick, who knew both Roberts and Tarkington, recalled in 1990 that Roberts "adored [Tarkington] and with reason because Tarkington took him in hand and made him a novelist. He was a successful non-fiction writer for the SEP but he had so much to learn about fiction that he was lucky to have Tarkington around to tell him, in T's funny way, what was wrong with everything he did wrong, which was plenty" (Kenneth D. McCormick to Jack Bales, 2 July 1990, Dartmouth College Library; hereafter cited in text).

    13. Letter to Charles G. Dawes, 27 December 1928, Northwestern University Library.

14. *Arundel* (Garden City, N.Y.: Doubleday, 1956), 3; hereafter cited in text as *Arundel*. This is a later printing after the two Doubleday revised editions of 1933 and 1956 and the British revised edition of 1936.

15. Roberts marked passages throughout a "working copy" of the first edition of *Arundel*, noting the sources he used while writing the book. *Arundel* (Garden City, N.Y.: Doubleday, Doran, 1930), 1/16, Dartmouth College Library.

16. *March to Quebec: Journals of the Members of Arnold's Expedition*, compiled and annotated by Kenneth Roberts (Garden City, N.Y.: Doubleday, 1953), 569; hereafter cited in text as *March*. Writing about his youth, Roberts noted that his mother was an Episcopalian, his grandmother a Congregationalist, and his grandfather a Baptist, so "they tolerantly divided me, so to speak, between them," taking him to alternate churches each Sunday. See the Introduction to *Let Me Show*; Bales 1989, 5.

17. Willard Sterne Randall, *Benedict Arnold: Patriot and Traitor* (New York: William Morrow, 1990), 99; hereafter cited in text. See also Willard M. Wallace, *Traitorous Hero: The Life and Fortunes of Benedict Arnold* (New York: Harper, 1954), 42-54; hereafter cited in text. Christopher Ward, *The War of the Revolution*, vol. 1 (New York: Macmillan, 1952), 63-72; hereafter cited in text; Kitch, 117.

18. Letter to Ben Ames Williams, 20 June 1930, Colby College Library.

19. "*Arundel* and Some Other Recent Works of Fiction," *New York Times Book Review*, 12 January 1930, 8.

20. Dorothea Lawrance Mann, "Benedict Arnold on His Way to Canada," *Boston Evening Transcript Book Section*, 25 January 1930, 2.

21. Letter to Ben Ames Williams, 9 July 1928, Colby College Library.

22. Letter to Ben Ames Williams, 22 November 1929, Colby College Library. Roberts's income substantially dropped when he quit the *Post*. In 1926 he earned $27,250, not including a $1,000 advance for *Florida*; in 1927 his salary was $22,750; in 1928, $17,250; and in 1929, $12,750. Adding to his problems, in March 1924 his aunt, Lucy Tibbets Russell, wrote not only to thank him for the copy of *Black Magic* that he had sent her but also to tell him that she had lost most of her money and that she would be unable to continue to support his mother. That would now be his responsibility.

23. Letter to Marion Cobb Fuller, 30 August 1929, Maine State Library, Augusta, Maine.

24. "Chronicles of Arundel" include *Arundel* (1930), *The Lively Lady* (1931), *Rabble in Arms* (1933), and *Captain Caution* (1934).

25. *Trending*, 305-6; "Motor Routes," in *Kenneth Roberts: An American Novelist*, 19-22.

26. Letter to Chilson H. Leonard, 19 December 1935, Phillips Exeter Academy Library.

27. *The Lively Lady: A Chronicle of Arundel, of Privateering, and of the Circular Prison on Dartmoor* (New York: Doubleday, Doran, 1938), 3/24-25;

hereafter cited in text as *LL*. This is a later printing after the revised 1935 edition. Before publication in book form, *The Lively Lady* was condensed and serialized in six consecutive issues of the *Post*, from 7 March 1931 to 11 April 1931.

28. *Captain Caution: A Chronicle of Arundel* (Garden City, N.Y.: Doubleday, Doran, 1934). Before publication in book form it was condensed to 80,000 words and serialized in six consecutive issues of the *Post*, from 18 August 1934 through 22 September 1934. It was accepted after being rejected five times by the *Post* and turned down by a number of other leading magazines as well. According to Kitch (58), about one-third of the original manuscript of *The Lively Lady* was deleted before the book's final draft, and about three-quarters of this leftover material was used in *Captain Caution*.

29. Janet Harris, *A Century of American History in Fiction: Kenneth Roberts' Novels* (New York: Gordon, 1976), 73; hereafter cited in text. See also *LL*, 32/365.

30. Carlos Baker, "The Novel as History: Kenneth Roberts," *Delphian Quarterly* 24 (January 1941): 17; hereafter cited in text.

31. "The War of 1812 in Historical Romance," *New York Times Book Review*, 10 May 1931, 9.

32. William Rose Benét, "In the War of 1812," *Saturday Review of Literature* 11 (10 November 1934): 273.

33. Herschel Brickell, "Kenneth Roberts Writes a Lively, Lusty Novel of the War of 1812," *New York Post*, 6 November 1934, 9.

34. Letter to Marion Cobb Fuller, 1 July 1933, Maine State Library. See also *IWW*, 243, 249.

35. "Bibliography of Kenneth Roberts's *Rabble In Arms*," compiled by Chilson H. Leonard, Phillips Exeter Academy; Clara Claasen, "Literary Detective Work in Kenneth Roberts' Novels," in *Kenneth Roberts: An American Novelist*, 17; hereafter cited in text. Notes Ward, "Before [Roberts's] discovery, no description of the galleys had been obtainable" (1: 472).

36. Letter to Mildred and Madeleine Burrage, 12 February 1933, owned by Earle G. Shettleworth, Jr. of Augusta, Maine.

37. *Rabble in Arms* (Garden City, N.Y.: Doubleday, 1947), 68/577; hereafter cited in text as *Rabble*. This is the revised edition after the first edition of 1933.

38. Edward Dean Sullivan, *Benedict Arnold: Military Racketeer* (New York: Vanguard, 1932), ix, Dartmouth College Library. On the inside flyleaf Roberts wrote, "It's vilely written, unsound, untrue, unreliable, careless, reckless. There isn't a fragment of original research in it; his material is nothing but a rewrite job, & a damned bad one."

39. James Graham, *The Life of General Daniel Morgan* (New York: Derby and Jackson, 1856), 228-29, Dartmouth College Library.

40. Thomas Anburey, *Travels through the Interior Parts of America*, vol. 1 (Boston and New York: Houghton Mifflin, 1923), 160-61, Dartmouth College Library. See also Leonard 1936, 11.

41. Willard M. Wallace to Jack Bales, 18 February 1990, Dartmouth College Library.

42. Letter to Herbert F. West, 26 July 1935, Dartmouth College Library; hereafter cited in text. Letter partially quoted in Herbert Faulkner West, foreword to *The Battle of Cowpens: The Great Morale-Builder* (Garden City, N.Y.: Doubleday, 1958), 10-15; hereafter cited in text as *Battle*. When Roberts was once asked, "Why did you whitewash [Arnold]?" he replied, "I didn't whitewash him. I only wrote what he did. That automatically made him a hero. Every statement made about him in any of my books can be documented. Not one of 'em is untrue. That's not whitewashing. He was a great man, and you should be glad to claim him as a fellow citizen—gladder to claim him than some of the miserable politicians who have achieved higher places in history, but done far more to wreck the fortunes of America, and not one-tenth as much to further them" (question-and-answer session, Warner House).

43. Margaret Wallace, "An Epic Tale of the Revolution," *New York Times Book Review*, 19 November 1933, 8.

44. D[orothea] L[awrance] M[ann], "Benedict Arnold as a Colonial Leader," *Boston Evening Transcript*, 29 November 1933, sec. 4, p. 2.

45. Otis Ferguson, "Leading Recent Fiction," *New York Herald Tribune Books*, 19 November 1933, 16.

46. "Still Defends Arnold's Ability," *New York Sun*, 10 October 1941, 17. According to Carl Van Doren, Arnold was "bold, crafty, unscrupulous, unrepentant: the Iago of traitors" (*Secret History of the American Revolution* [New York: Viking, 1941], v).

Chapter Four

1. "Roberts Also Loves Green: Dr. Hopkins' Inspiration Leads to Historical Find," *Boston Herald*, 30 September 1950, 5. In these reminiscences Roberts mistakenly gave 1935 instead of 1934 as the year he received his honorary degree. Thus he worked on his books for six years, not the seven he indicated. Also, contrary to Roberts's implication, reviews of his books were largely favorable. See also Jack Bales, "'At the nadir of my discouragement': The Story of Dartmouth's Kenneth Roberts Collection," *Dartmouth College Library Bulletin*, n.s., 30 (April 1990): 45-53.

2. "Dr. K. L. Roberts," *Boston Herald*, 19 June 1934, 12; see also Ernest Martin Hopkins to Roberts, 5 April 1934, Dartmouth College Library.

3. "For Authors Only," in *For Authors Only, and Other Gloomy Essays* (Garden City, N.Y.: Doubleday, Doran, 1935), 18; hereafter cited in text as *FAO*. See also Kitch, 230-37.

4. Letter to Franklin W. Johnson, 26 June 1935, Colby College Library. "It Must Be Your Tonsils," *Saturday Evening Post*, 12 October 1935, 10-11+; *It Must Be Your Tonsils* (Garden City, N.Y.: Doubleday, Doran, 1936).

5. "Notes for a Discussion with Booth," 24 August 1934, Adams Manuscript Collection, Indiana University, Lilly Library.

6. Robert Rogers, *Journals of Major Robert Rogers* (London: J. Millan, 1765), 151, 146, Dartmouth College Library.

7. *Northwest Passage*, ltd. ed., vol. 2 (Garden City, N.Y.: Doubleday, Doran, 1937), 18; see also Kitch, 46. In Roberts's "working copy" of the novel (now in Dartmouth College Library), he wrote beneath the passage about the fight (p. 126): "Had to invent this. Originally wrote it so that one of the boatloads tackled one of the French decoy-boats, but threw it away & re-did it." Roberts also had difficulty retracing Rogers's march to St. Francis and his retreat, and the errors in *Northwest Passage* can be justified by the lack of available reference material. For example, decades after Roberts wrote his book scholars have argued about the location (and even the existence) of Fort Wentworth, the stronghold where Rogers's Rangers supposedly stopped for provisions during their trip back from the attack. See John R. Cuneo, *Robert Rogers of the Rangers* (New York: Oxford, 1959), 286; John R. Cuneo, "Mysterious Fort Wentworth," *Historical New Hampshire* 12 (June 1962): 18-25; Philip N. Guyol, "Fort Wentworth: The Mystery Compounded," *Historical New Hampshire* 12 (June 1962): 26-48; Robert E. Pike, "Where Was the Site of Fort Wentworth?" *Vermont History* 36 (Summer 1968): 144-49.

8. *Northwest Passage* (Garden City, N.Y.: Doubleday, Doran, 1937), 431; hereafter cited in text as *NP*. While Roberts mulled over the book in 1932 his tentative title was *The White Devil*, the Indians' name for Robert Rogers.

9. Alfred T. Hill, "The Class Finds a Northwest Passage," in *Kenneth Roberts: An American Novelist*, 30.

10. *NP*, 5. See also *NP*, 77; Bales 1989, 254. The idea of Langdon Towne is mentioned in "Elizabeth Browne, Joseph Blackburn and 'Northwest Passage,'" *Art in America* 41 (Winter 1953): 5-6; Blackington.

11. Allan Nevins, "Rousing Tale of the French and Indian War," *New York Herald Tribune Books*, 4 July 1937, 1-2. Nevins (1890-1971), a well-respected historian, wrote "The Life of Robert Rogers," in *Ponteach; or, The Savages of America: A Tragedy*, by Robert Rogers, ed. Allan Nevins (Chicago: Caxton Club, 1914), 17-174. After one of Roberts's researchers located a copy of Rogers's court-martial in a repository of British Colonial Office papers in Canterbury, England, Roberts often congratulated himself for having found the document, while deriding Nevins for stating "unequivocally that no copies existed" (*IWW*, 284). Nevins, however, never made this claim, and Roberts could have easily found the court-martial himself by consulting Charles M. Andrews's *Guide to the Materials for American History, to 1783, in the Public Record Office of Great Britain* (Washington, D.C.: Carnegie Institution of Washington, 1914), 2: item 4957. While working on his dissertation John I. Kitch, Jr., corresponded with Robert Rogers scholars Nevins and John R. Cuneo and their letters are in Colby College Library.

12. Bernard DeVoto, "Roberts Ranges," *Saturday Review of Literature* 16 (3 July 1937): 5. Carlos Baker remarked that "Roberts is notoriously uncomfortable in cities" (Baker, 17).

13. "Critics Vote on Best Books of 1937 in Country-Wide Poll," *Saturday Review of Literature* 17 (2 April 1938): 8-9.

14. Letter to Ben Ames Williams, 5 May 1938, Colby College Library. Esther Forbes (1891-1967) was a Massachusetts biographer and historical novelist who won the 1942 Pulitzer Prize for *Paul Revere and the World He Lived In*.

15. Roberts despised the "motion picture treatment" of *Northwest Passage*. For example, see *IWW*, 5; Letter to Orson Welles, 4 March 1940, Welles Manuscripts, Indiana University, Lilly Library. Book 1 of *Northwest Passage* appeared under the title "Rogers' Rangers" as a seven-part serial in successive issues of the *Post* from 26 December 1936 through 6 February 1937. For information on Roberts's first house see "The Little Home in the Country," *Saturday Evening Post*, 30 June 1928, 16-17+. For information on his second house see "The House with the Blue Roof," *Country Life*, December 1927, 71-73. For information on his third house see Mary Carpenter Kelley, "Author of *Arundel* Builds 12-Foot Wall to Bar Visitors," *Christian Science Monitor*, 12 September 1939, 3. Roberts began planning his estate in 1938 and that year purchased 50 acres of land. By the time his house was built a year later he had acquired an additional 26 acres, and by the end of 1952 he owned 171 acres. See *The Rescued Fields of Rocky Pasture* (painting), Brick Store Museum.

16. *Trending* was first published by Little, Brown & Co. in Boston in 1938. Doubleday did not publish it because Roberts was dissatisfied with the way the company handled his last nonfiction book, *For Authors Only*, and he particularly disliked its title. Therefore, because "I'm a great believer in competition," Roberts offered the book to his close friend and neighbor, Little, Brown publisher Alfred McIntyre (Letter to Clara Claasen, 6 November [1937?], Kenneth D. McCormick Papers, Library of Congress). When Roberts signed the book contract with Little, Brown on 25 October 1935, the tentative title was *Along the Rocky Coast of Maine*. Several of the essays in *Trending* originally appeared in the *Saturday Evening Post*. Doubleday, Doran published an enlarged edition of *Trending* in 1944. Added was "Invitations to Idlers," which originally appeared as "That's Hay, That Is!," *Country Gentleman*, May 1943, 12+, and "Enemies Nobody Knows," which was accepted by *Country Gentleman* in February 1944 under the title "My Enemy the Great Horned Owl" but was not published by the magazine after Doubleday requested it (Clara Claasen to Sally Baker, 15 February 1944, Kenneth D. McCormick Papers, Library of Congress).

17. Marjorie Mosser, *Good Maine Food*, with an introduction and notes by Kenneth Roberts (New York: Doubleday, Doran, 1939). In Roberts's introduction he writes, "I've scrutinized *Good Maine Food* with care, and I am happy to see that it contains all the dishes I like, with rules for cooking them in the

way they ought to be cooked" (xviii). A revised edition was published in 1947, and another revision was published as *Foods of Old New England* in 1957.

18. Henry Steele Commager, "Source Materials for *Arundel*," *New York Herald Tribune Books*, 16 October 1938, 2. The third edition of *March*, with John Pierce's journal added, was published by Doubleday, Doran in 1940. In 1953 the book was reprinted by Doubleday with "Arnold's Account Sheets of the Quebec Expedition" added.

19. *Oliver Wiswell* (New York: Doubleday, Doran, 1940), 13; hereafter cited in text as *OW*. The working title was *Current of Destiny*.

20. These letters are in the Dartmouth College Library. Many have "File with Nuts" or similar phrases scrawled across them.

21. Charles Willis Thompson, "Debunking Our Revolution," *Catholic World* 152 (February 1941): 526.

22. Booth Tarkington, "Preliminary Generalization," [March 1940?], Kenneth D. McCormick Papers, Library of Congress; Thomas B. Costain to Roberts, 26 March 1940, McCormick Papers, Library of Congress; *IWW*, 353-55. Costain (1885-1965) was at this time an advisory editor at Doubleday, having been chief associate editor of the *Post* from 1920 to 1934. He would later gain fame as the author of numerous historical romances and the nonfiction four-volume "Pageant of England" series.

23. Letter to Lewis Gannett, 18 October 1941, Harvard University, Houghton Library.

24. Allan Nevins, "Young Man in a Revolution," *Saturday Review of Literature* 23 (23 November 1940): 5; hereafter cited in text.

25. "Angry Man's Romance," *Time*, 25 November 1940, 94.

26. Mary Mayo Boatner III, *Encyclopedia of the American Revolution* (New York: McKay, 1966), 805; hereafter cited in text.

27. *The Kenneth Roberts Reader* (Garden City, N.Y.: Doubleday, Doran, 1945); hereafter cited in text as *KRR*. See also Kitch, 230-37. Roberts thought that the poor sales of *For Authors Only* were due largely to its poor title, and he wanted Doubleday to bring out a new edition under a different title. Because the firm thought that this would not be "considered ethical," it added several new essays and some excerpts from his novels and published *The Kenneth Roberts Reader* (Clara Claasen to Kenneth D. McCormick, 7 April 1954, Kenneth D. McCormick Papers, Library of Congress).

28. "On the Evolution of *Lydia Bailey*," *Wings: The Literary Guild Review*, January 1947, 4; hereafter cited in text as "Evolution."

29. Ray Martin Bertram, "The Novel of America's Past: A Study of Five American Historical Novelists, 1925-1950," Ph.D. diss., University of Michigan, 1954, 154.

30. *Lydia Bailey* (Garden City, N.Y.: Doubleday, 1947), 1; hereafter cited in text as *LB*.

31. Harris, 67; Andrew R. Supplee, "Kenneth Roberts: An Historical

Novelist," B.A. paper, Department of English, Princeton University, 1961, 13, 16. Copy in Dartmouth College Library.

32.   Review, *Best Sellers* 6 (1 January 1947): 160.

33.   Edward Weeks, "Hell in Haiti," *Atlantic Monthly*, February 1947, 130.

34.   Letter to Allan Nevins, 27 December 1946, Allan Nevins Papers, Columbia University Library, New York. Allan Nevins, "The Past as a Pageant," *Saturday Review of Literature* 30 (4 January 1947): 15.

35.   Henry Steele Commager, "A Breathless Vista of Forgotten History," *New York Herald Tribune Weekly Book Review*, 5 January 1947, 2.

36.   Francis X. Connolly, "Books of the Week," *Commonweal* 45 (31 January 1947): 402; hereafter cited in text.

37.   Robert van Gelder, "When the Republic Was Young," *New York Times Book Review*, 5 January 1947, 1.

38.   Marjorie Mosser Ellis, interview by John I. Kitch, Jr., February 1963, Colby College Library; "Evolution," 7. Roberts's and his wife's translation of Moreau de St. Mery's work was published as *Moreau de St. Mery's American Journey (1793-1798)* (Garden City, N.Y.: Doubleday, 1947).

39.   Arthur Hamilton Gibbs, interview by John I. Kitch, Jr., 7 February 1966, Colby College Library; hereafter cited in text. Gibbs (1888-1964) was born in London and served in Flanders, Egypt, and France during World War I. He published 14 novels, including at least four best-sellers: *Soundings* (1925), *Labels* (1926), *Harness* (1928), and *Chances* (1930).

40.   Emma W. Moseley, "Hot Dog Stands and Billboards Mar Scenery, Says Kenneth L. Roberts," *Portland (Maine) Evening Express*, 21 September 1926, 11; "Baxter Hits Roberts' Stand on Billboards," *Portland Evening Express*, 23 September 1930, 1; "Roberts Aims Attack at Baxter after Criticism for Stand on Billboards," *Portland Evening Express*, 26 September 1930, 11; "Roberts like Spoiled Child, Resenting Reproof, Says Baxter," *Portland Evening Express*, 3 October 1930, 2. Roberts's *Post* antibillboard articles include "Travels in Billboardia," 13 October 1928, 24-25+; "Revolt in Billboardia," 2 November 1929, 14-15+; "Roads of Remembrance," 7 December 1929, 24-25+; "Billboard-Dammerung," 6 September 1930, 20-21+; "Scenery Wreckers," 2 May 1931, 25+.

41.   For examples see Jack Bales, "The Irascible Mr. Roberts," *Down East* 38 (August 1991): 38-39, 70-74.

42.   "Don't Say That about Maine!," *Saturday Evening Post*, 6 November 1948, 136. Toynbee's original statements appear in his *A Study of History*, vol. 2, 2d ed. (London: Oxford University Press, 1935), 295.

43.   James C. Stephens to Clara Claasen, 3 August 1948, Kenneth D. McCormick Papers, Library of Congress. See also Letter to Robert Hale, 31 January 1949, Dartmouth College Library. Hale was a Maine congressman and Roberts's attorney.

44. Orville Prescott, "Books of the Times," *New York Times*, 22 April 1949, 21.

45. Ben Ames Williams, Introduction to *The Kenneth Roberts Reader*, ix, viii.

46. James C. Stephens to Clara Claasen, 21 September 1948, Kenneth D. McCormick Papers, Library of Congress.

47. Kenneth D. McCormick, interview by Jack Bales, 30 May 1990, Dartmouth College Library; McCormick 2 July 1990.

Chapter Five

1. "The Mystery of the Forked Twig," *Country Gentleman*, September 1944, 12. This was revised and published as "Experiments with a Forked Twig" in *The Kenneth Roberts Reader*.

2. *Henry Gross and His Dowsing Rod* (Garden City, N.Y.: Doubleday, 1951), 43-51; hereafter cited in text as *Henry*.

3. Water Unlimited, Inc., *Suggestions to Prospective Clients: Revised Work Sheet* (Kennebunkport, Maine?).

4. Water Unlimited, Inc., "Meeting of Directors," *Records* 3 (May 1950-January 1951): 158, Dartmouth College Library.

5. Interview by Arlene Francis, 19 July 1954, transcript, Dartmouth College Library.

6. "It was reviewed at some length in 437 newspapers. News stories on the book appeared in 188 newspapers. Magazine articles on it were written for 41 magazines with national circulations. Of the reviews, 408 were favorable. Of the news stories, nearly all seemed to have a distinctly friendly flavor. Of the magazine articles, 28 were generous and appreciative" (*The Seventh Sense* [Garden City, N.Y.: Doubleday, 1953], 40; hereafter cited in text as *SS*).

7. Samuel T. Williamson, "Water, Water Everywhere," *New York Times Book Review*, 7 January 1951, 6.

8. Robert P. Tristram Coffin, "Homer Didn't Tell Lies," *Saturday Review of Literature* 34 (6 January 1951): 16.

9. Review, *Booklist* 47 (15 February 1951): 214.

10. Bill Cunningham, "Roberts' Book Great Reading," *Boston Herald*, 2 February 1951, 28.

11. *Henry*, 142-45. See also Richard Hallet, "Roberts' Friend Very Successful Finding Water, Tries New Field," *Portland (Maine) Press Herald*, 6 October 1949, 1-2; Harry T. Foote, "Doctors, Nurses, Expectant Mothers Skeptical, Willing to Be Convinced," *Portland Press Herald*, 6 October 1949, 1-2; Foote, "Dowser's Time Prediction Wrong, but Wait and See!," *Portland Press Herald*, 7 October 1949, 1, 12; Foote, "Gross Can Rest on Laurels after Predicting Right," *Portland Press Herald*, 8 October 1949, 2.

12. Thomas M. Riddick, "Dowsing—an Unorthodox Method of

Locating Underground Water Supplies or an Interesting Facet of the Human Mind," *American Philosophical Society Proceedings* 96 (October 1952): 527; hereafter cited in text.

13. Satterlee, Warfield & Stephens law firm to Clara Claasen, 21 September 1950, Kenneth D. McCormick Papers, Library of Congress.

14. Letter to Ben Ames Williams, 6 September 1948, Colby College Library. See also "Can He Find Water? . . . Kenneth Roberts Says Yes," *Life*, 4 October 1948, 119-20, 122.

15. Clara Claasen to Roberts, n.d. [ca. 1950], Kenneth D. McCormick Papers, Library of Congress; hereafter cited in text.

16. For example, see "Water from St. George's Well Analysed As Fresh," (Hamilton, Bermuda) *Mid-Ocean News*, 13 February 1950, 1, 18; "Hundreds Watch as Royal Barracks Well Pours Forth Fresh Water," *Mid-Ocean News*, 20 February 1950, 1, 4; Reginald Wells, "Plan to Form Company to Distribute Fresh Water," (Hamilton, Bermuda) *Sunday Royal Gazette*, 5 March 1950, 1.

17. Donald Fessenden, "Bermuda Reacting Very Slowly to Discovery of Fresh Water," *Boston Sunday Herald*, 30 December 1951, 10; Fessenden, "Small Group of Enthusiasts Best Hope for Bermuda's Water," *Boston Herald*, 1 January 1952, 40. Fessenden's second article is "Bermuda's Fresh Water Project Now Awaits Further Equipment," *Boston Herald*, 31 December 1951, 1-2.

18. Park Breck, "Drought, Doubt and Dowsing," *Bermudian*, July 1951, 41. Breck's second article is "Bermuda Drops Phobia on Wells," *Boston Herald*, 24 June 1952, 1, 23.

19. *Water Unlimited* (Garden City, N. Y.: Doubleday, 1957), 70-73; hereafter cited in text as *WU*.

20. John Tebbel, Foreword to Bales 1989, ix-x.

21. Kenneth D. McCormick to Jack Bales, n.d. [March 1990], Dartmouth College Library; hereafter cited in text.

22. Margaret Parton, "Book Review," *New York Herald Tribune*, 9 July 1953, 19.

23. Joseph Henry Jackson, "Bookman's Notebook: This Water-Dowsing Business," *San Francisco Chronicle*, 26 June 1953, 13.

24. John Moore, "Kenneth Roberts Defends Dowsing," *Houston Post*, 12 July 1953, sec. 7, p. 7.

25. Cecil R. Roseberry, "A Report on Water Dowsing," *American Mercury* 77 (July 1953): 25-26; hereafter cited in text. See also Roseberry, "The Angry Man of Kennebunkport," n.p., [1967], Dartmouth College Library; "Roberts Offers $100 Wager to Back Dowsing Rod Story," *Boston Herald*, 25 January 1951, 10. In a letter to a close friend, Roberts refers to Roseberry as a "pure louse," stating that "he has been after us for two solid years with a malevolence I've never seen equalled. God knows why; but he has apparently dedicated his life, after we broke our necks and went far out of our way to help him, to proving we're a couple of bums, liars, bastards, phoneys, etc., with other

grave faults, and to making a living out of doing it" (Letter to Romeyn "Rym" Berry, 15 June 1953, Romeyn Berry Papers, Cornell University Library, Ithaca, New York).

26. Jack E. Brown, review, *Library Journal* 82 (15 October 1957): 2538.

27. John Gould, "Other Wells Are Deeper," *New York Times Book Review*, 27 October 1957, 43.

28. Ray M. Koon, "Cynic Ray Koon, with Poor Jud in Mind Says Water 'Divining' Is Pure Hokum," *Boston Traveler*, 24 November 1947, 10.

29. "'Nuts to Koon': Kenneth Roberts Stakes 'Rep' on Divining Rod," *Boston Traveler*, 18 December 1947, 11.

30. Ray M. Koon, "Koon Stands by Broadside at Diviners," *Boston Traveler*, 19 December 1947, 27. In a letter Roberts wrote to a friend a year later he refers to Koon as a "damned fool" and states, "I hate to waste any time trying to convince a congenital idiot, in face of his preconceived wrong-headedness, that a dowsing rod infallibly points to flowing water" (Letter to Eleanor Nickerson, 29 January 1948, owned by Nickerson of Kennebunkport, Maine).

31. Bergen Evans, *The Spoor of Spooks and Other Nonsense* (New York: Knopf, 1944), 12.

32. "Kenneth Roberts' Water Dowsing Beliefs Panned by Ancient Club," *Portland (Maine) Press Herald*, 25 April 1952, 44.

33. Robert A. Kissack, Jr., "On First Looking into Roberts' 'Henry Gross and His Dowsing Rod,'" *New Yorker*, 14 July 1951, 30.

34. Thomas M. Riddick, "Dowsing is Nonsense," *Harper's Magazine*, July 1951, 68. Letter to Horace A. Knowles, 28 June 1951, Dartmouth College Library. *Time* publicized Riddick's article (and ridiculed Roberts) in "Why Dowsing Works," 16 July 1951, 48.

35. For example, see Alice Dixon Bond, "The Case for Books," *Boston Sunday Herald*, 7 January 1951, sec. G, p. 3; "Henry Gross' Dowsing Rod Again Finds Water Miles Away," *Boston Sunday Herald*, 27 September 1953, sec. 1, pp. 1, 6. Bond, telephone interview by John I. Kitch, Jr., 10 February 1963, Colby College Library.

36. A[rthur] Hamilton Gibbs, "Letter to a Friend," *Colby Library Quarterly* 6 (September 1962): 88. Gibbs 1963.

37. John Tebbel to Jack Bales, 27 March 1990, Dartmouth College Library; also, Tebbel to Bales, 28 February 1988, Dartmouth College Library; hereafter cited in text.

38. Kenneth D. McCormick to Jack Bales, 8 July 1991, Dartmouth College Library; McCormick [March 1990].

39. Clara Claasen to Clifford Deveroux, David Replogle, and LeBaron Barker, 25 November 1968, Kenneth D. McCormick Papers, Library of Congress; Claasen, record of "Kenneth Roberts Titles in Print," 21 October 1957?, McCormick Papers, Library of Congress; *WU*, 25-26.

40. Letter to Robert Hale, 28 April 1955, Dartmouth College Library. The yearly gross income of Water Unlimited, Inc., was as follows: 1951,

$20,125.27; 1952, $13,742.41; 1953, $11,413.42; 1954, $16,353.59; 1955, $18,207.82; 1956 (through 10 November), $26,235.86 ("Daybook of Dowsing Cases," 4, Dartmouth College Library, box 27). In January 1958, six months after Roberts's death, Water Unlimited, Inc., was dissolved. An extensive study of Henry Gross (1895-1979) appears in Berthold Eric Schwarz, "Psychic Aspects of the Art of Dowsing: Notes on Henry Gross, Successful Dowser," in *Psychic-Dynamics* (New York: Pageant Press, 1965), 91-161.

   41.   Memorandum, July 1957, Dartmouth College Library.

   42.   Letter to Richard L. Simon, Richard L. Simon Papers, 2 August 1954, Columbia University Library.

Chapter Six

   1.   Lewis Nichols, "A Visit with Mr. Roberts," *New York Times Book Review*, 1 January 1956, 3.

   2.   Bond 1956, 2. The captain's name was actually "Deane," though it is spelled both with and without the "e" in the various editions of his narrative. In the text I have retained Roberts's spelling to avoid confusion. Similarly, while the galley's name was simply *Nottingham* I have kept Roberts's version, *Nottingham Galley*. Roberts examined at least three editions of Dean's account, and two editions annotated by him are in the Dartmouth College Library. The work's first edition is John Dean, *A Narrative of the Sufferings, Preservation and Deliverance, of Capt. John Dean and Company; in the Nottingham-Galley of London, Cast Away on Boon-Island, Near New England, December 11, 1710* (London: R. Tookey, 1711). *The Magazine of History with Notes and Queries* published Dean's work in 1917 as extra no. 59, pt. 2 (vol. 15), pp. 199-217. In 1968 the Provincial Press of Portland, Maine, reprinted the 1762 edition of Dean's narrative in a limited edition. Mason Philip Smith's brief introduction gives a physical description of Boon Island, noting that it "lies 5.7 miles southeastward of Cape Neddick, Maine and 12 miles east-northeast of Portsmouth, New Hampshire." The mate's version of the shipwreck is Christopher Langman, Nicholas Mellen, and George White, *A True Account of the Voyage of the Nottingham-Galley of London, John Dean Commander, from the River Thames to New-England, Near Which Place She Was Cast Away on Boon-Island, December 11, 1710, by the Captain's Obstinacy, Who Endeavour'd to Betray Her to the French, or Run Her Ashore; With an Account of the Falsehoods in the Captain's Narrative* (London: Printed for S. Popping, 1711).

   3.   *Boon Island* (Garden City, N.Y.: Doubleday, 1956), 192; hereafter cited in text as *BI*.

   4.   Lewis Gannett, "Book Review," *New York Herald Tribune*, 2 January 1956, 11.

   5.   Walter Havighurst, "Kenneth Roberts' Somber Tale of Cold, Desperation," *Chicago Sunday Tribune Magazine of Books*, 1 January 1956, 3.

6. Clara Claasen, interview by John I. Kitch, Jr., February 1963, Colby College Library.

7. Memorandum, July 1957, Dartmouth College Library.

8. Various letters between William F. Berger and Clara Claasen, February 1956, Kenneth D. McCormick Papers, Library of Congress; Claasen to Roberts, 27 February 1956, McCormick Papers, Library of Congress.

9. Kitch, 60. See also Clara Claasen to Kenneth D. McCormick, 15 March 1956, Kenneth D. McCormick Papers, Library of Congress. Roberts's article is "Battle of Cowpens: Nine Hundred Men Who Shook an Empire, *Collier's* 138 (17 August 1956): 58-67.

10. Herbert Faulkner West, Foreword to *Cowpens: The Great Morale-Builder* (Hanover, N. H.: Westholm, 1957), v.

11. Marjorie Mosser to Clara Claasen, 28 December 1957, Kenneth D. McCormick Papers, Library of Congress. West's unfavorable comments about Roberts and his works were deleted from his Foreword in Doubleday's trade edition but are in his limited edition volume.

12. R. W. G. Vail, review, *New-York Historical Society Quarterly* 43 (January 1959): 123-24.

13. Howard H. Peckham, review, *William and Mary Quarterly*, 3d ser., 15 (October 1958): 530.

14. Various letters between Roberts and Clara Claasen, February 1955, Kenneth D. McCormick Papers, Library of Congress; Claasen to Kenneth D. McCormick, 21 August 1957, McCormick Papers, Library of Congress.

15. John K. Hutchens, "Kenneth Roberts Says It Was Like This," *New York Herald Tribune Book Review*," 8 January 1956, 2.

16. Letter to Booth Tarkington, [1937], Colby College Library. See also *IWW*, 430-33.

17. "Reviews and Consequences: A Reference Book, Compiled for the Benefit of Publishers, Authors, Would-be Authors and Aspiring Reviewers," 4, Dartmouth College Library. The manuscript numbers 107 pages and deals mainly with *IWW*. It lacks both reviews and sales figures, although the Dartmouth College Library has a series of letters Roberts wrote to publishers and editors requesting permission to include the reviews in his work. See also Clara Claasen to Roberts, 22 June 1950, Kenneth D. McCormick Papers, Library of Congress; Letter to Claasen, 11 February 1955, McCormick Papers, Library of Congress.

18. "Maine Novelist Kenneth L. Roberts Awarded Special Pulitzer Citation," *Portland (Maine) Press Herald*, 7 May 1957, 1. See also *IWW*, 355, 356.

19. "Kenneth Roberts Dies at Kennebunkport," *Portland (Maine) Press Herald*, 22 July 1957, 1-2.

20. "Kenneth Roberts," *New York Times*, 23 July 1957, 26. Excerpts from obituaries and tributes are in Bales 1989, 238-43.

Afterword

1.   Justin H. Smith, *Arnold's March from Cambridge to Quebec: A Critical Study* (New York: G. P. Putnam's Sons, 1903), 141; hereafter cited in text. Annotated copy in Dartmouth College Library.

2.   James Melvin, *The Journal of James Melvin, Private Soldier in Arnold's Expedition against Quebec in the Year 1775*, with notes and an introduction by Andrew A. Melvin (Portland, Me.: Hubbard W. Bryant, 1902), 51, annotated copy in Dartmouth College Library. In a footnote beneath Melvin's entry in *March to Quebec* Roberts added, "This entry provides the key to the hitherto unexplained loss of provisions by Greene's division on October 16. Morgan's men halted temporarily on October 14 and permitted Greene's men to pass. On October 17 Morgan's company caught up to Greene's men and passed them. Most of Greene's food vanished in the meantime. Evidently Morgan's men, like most old soldiers, were confirmed food-stealers" (*March*, 439). See also *IWW*, 186-87; Kitch, 46; Claasen 1938, 16-17.

3.   Letter to West 26 July 1935. In Roberts's letter he stated incorrectly that the retreat from Fort Ticonderoga took place in 1776. Hoffman Nickerson wrote *The Turning Point of the Revolution* (Boston: Houghton Mifflin, 1928), a book Roberts consulted for *Rabble in Arms*.

4.   Letter to A. L. Barden, 9 August 1956, Dartmouth College Library. Also, Charles W. Brewster, *Rambles about Portsmouth: Sketches of Persons, Localities, and Incidents of Two Centuries*, 1st ser. (Portsmouth, N.H.: Lewis W. Brewster, 1873), 140-43. Letter tipped in the Dartmouth College Library's copy. Roberts occasionally corrected his novels when readers pointed out errors. For example, in chapter 43, page 382, of *Oliver Wiswell* Wiswell and his friends pass through the town of Millis, Massachusetts. At that time it was part of Medway, as one reader told Roberts, who replied, "I think the error happened because I was working with a modern map, intending to re-check on the old maps: then, with eight million points to check in the last three or four months before publication, overlooked that particular one. At all events, it was changed [to Medway] last November, and has now run through several editions in the corrected form. Letters from distressed Millisers continue to trickle in, however; and each one makes me wince" (Letter to George L. Smith, 5 March 1941, Colby College Library). See also George L. Smith to Roberts, 3 March 1941, Colby College Library. Many readers objected to Roberts mentioning tomatoes in *Arundel*, claiming that in the 1770s they were called "love-apples" and were regarded as poisonous. Although he produced evidence to support his use of the word, Roberts still deleted the references from the novel, "saying that even though a fact might be correct, it should be removed from a book if too many readers considered it an anachronism. A story should *sound* true, he says, as well as *be* true" (Claasen, 1938, 23).

5.   Bernard DeVoto, *The World of Fiction* (Boston: Houghton Mifflin, 1950), 75.

6. *IWW*, 190. Although Roberts wrote that chapter 34 contains a "love scene between Steven and Phoebe," it actually describes Steven's encounter with Mary Mallinson in Quebec. The manuscript in the Dartmouth College Library contains nothing "explicit"; one sentence that Roberts deleted refers to Steven's thoughts after seeing Mary: "I remember thinking that I had waited all my life for this moment, and . . . there came to me all the thoughts I had had each day for countless years about kissing her: how I should hold her in my arms, and how her hands would draw my face to hers" (p. 219). Another omitted sentence notes that Mary "was vastly pleasant in my hands, nor did it seem a repulsive matter to me to press my lips against the velvety white skin of her neck, where it rose out of the collar of her blue dress" (p. 220). Roberts echoes Howells's advice to Tarkington in *Lydia Bailey*: "She never liked public lovemaking, either, whether in life or in books. She said it was like making love in broad daylight on a park bench" (*LB*, 474).

7. Susanah Mayberry, *My Amiable Uncle: Recollections about Booth Tarkington* (West Lafayette, Ind.: Purdue University Press, 1983), 97. See also Kitch, 210-11; West 1962, 93. Roberts was aware of his limitations. After reading Tarkington's *The Heritage of Hatcher Ide* he wrote his friend that Sarah Florian is "a terrible lady, beautifully done. I wish to God I could do it a quarter as well" (Woodress 1954, 308).

8. Stephen Vincent Benét and Rosemary Benét, "Kenneth Roberts: Historian of His People," *New York Herald Tribune Books*, 8 December 1940, 7. Stephen Vincent Benét (1898-1943) won his first Pulitzer Prize for poetry for the book-length poem *John Brown's Body* (1928). He posthumously received his second Pulitzer for *Western Star* (1943), the first part of a proposed epic poem.

9. James Woodress, *American Fiction, 1900-1950: A Guide to Information Sources* (Detroit: Gale Research, 1974), xvii. James Woodress to Jack Bales, 18 November 1989, Dartmouth College Library.

10. Lee Coyle, "Kenneth Roberts and the American Historical Novel," in *Popular Literature in America: A Symposium in Honor of Lyon N. Richardson*, ed. James C. Austin and Donald A. Koch (Bowling Green, Ohio: Bowling Green University Popular Press, 1972), 71. The other historians questioned include Henry Steele Commager and Samuel Eliot Morison. In 1992 *American Heritage* asked a wide range of novelists, journalists, and historians to answer the question, "What is your favorite American novel, and why?" Of the more than 100 who responded, most listed more than one author and title. Five persons mentioned Roberts, including historian and novelist Thomas Fleming, who credited *Oliver Wiswell* "with turning me into a historian." See "My Favorite Historical Novel," *American Heritage* 43 (October 1992): 84-94, 97-107. For additional comments on Roberts by historians and authors see Bales 1989, 67-71.

11. For examples, see C. P. Stacey, review of *Northwest Passage*, *Canadian Historical Review* 18 (December 1937): 435; Arthur Pound, "Notices and Reviews of Books," review of *Oliver Wiswell*, *New York History* 22 (April 1941):

214-15; Orville Prescott, "Outstanding Novels," review of *Lydia Bailey*, *Yale Review*, n.s., 36 (Spring 1947): 573. See also Bales 1989, 67.

12.   John Tebbel to Jack Bales, 17 January 1990, Dartmouth College Library.

13.   Willard M. Wallace to John I. Kitch, Jr., 9 June 1963, Colby College Library.

14.   "Small-town Librarian Gains Media Attention with Celebrities List," *American Libraries* 22 (June 1991): 475; Robert Ludlum to Jack Bales, 8 August 1991, Dartmouth College Library.

15.   James A. Michener to Jack Bales, 10 July 1990, Dartmouth College Library.

16.   Samuel Eliot Morison, "History as a Literary Art," in *By Land and By Sea: Essays and Addresses by Samuel Eliot Morison* (New York: Knopf, 1953), 289. In mid-1992 Doubleday had no Roberts titles listed in *Books in Print*. Several novels were noted as being published by Fawcett Crest in paperback.

Selected Bibliography

PRIMARY WORKS
Novels

Arundel. Garden City, N.Y.: Doubleday, Doran, 1930. Revised edition. Garden City, N.Y.: Doubleday, Doran, 1933. Revised edition. London: Lane, 1936. Revised edition. Garden City, N.Y.: Doubleday, 1956. Paperback. Greenwich, Conn.: Fawcett, 1963.

Boon Island. Garden City, N.Y.: Doubleday, 1956. Paperback. Greenwich, Conn.: Fawcett, 1967.

Captain Caution. Garden City, N.Y.: Doubleday, Doran, 1934. Paperback. Greenwich, Conn.: Fawcett, 1964.

The Lively Lady. Garden City, N.Y.: Doubleday, Doran, 1931. Revised edition. Garden City, N.Y.: Doubleday, Doran, 1935. Paperback. Greenwich, Conn.: Fawcett, 1966.

Lydia Bailey. Garden City, N.Y.: Doubleday, 1947. Paperback. Greenwich, Conn.: Fawcett, 1963.

Northwest Passage. Garden City, N.Y.: Doubleday, Doran, 1937. Paperback. Greenwich, Conn.: Fawcett, 1963.

Oliver Wiswell. New York: Doubleday, Doran, 1940. Paperback. Greenwich, Conn.: Fawcett, 1963.

Rabble in Arms. Garden City, N.Y.: Doubleday, Doran, 1933. Revised edition, Garden City, N.Y.: Doubleday, 1947. Paperback. Greenwich, Conn.: Fawcett, 1964.

Other Fiction

Antiquamania. Garden City, N.Y.: Doubleday, Doran, 1928. Includes material that originally appeared as follows: "Notes on an Antique Weevil," *Saturday Evening Post*, 21 January 1922, 8-9+; "Antiquamania," *Saturday Evening Post*, 14 March 1925, 12-13+; "A Tour of the Bottlefields," *Saturday Evening Post*, 13 November 1926, 24+; and "How to Instruct the Little Tots in Antiques," *Saturday Evening Post*, 21 July 1928, 40-42+.

The Collector's Whatnot, by Cornelius Obenchain Van Loot [Booth Tarkington], Milton Kilgallen [Kenneth Roberts], and Murgatroyd Elphinstone [Hugh MacNair Kahler]. Boston & New York: Houghton Mifflin, 1923. Humorous essays and drawings.

Nonfiction

Black Magic. Indianapolis: Bobbs-Merrill, 1924. Contents originally appeared as
follows: "The Ambush of Italy," *Saturday Evening Post*, 25 August 1923,
6-7+; "The Fight of the Black Shirts," *Saturday Evening Post*, 8
September 1923, 19+; "The Salvage of a Nation," *Saturday Evening Post*,
22 September 1923, 20-21+; "Suds," *Saturday Evening Post*, 27 October
1923, 10-11+; "The Constitution Busters," *Saturday Evening Post*, 23
September 1922, 23+; "The Inarticulate Conservatives," *Saturday
Evening Post*, 21 July 1923, 25+.

Concentrated New England: A Sketch of Calvin Coolidge. Indianapolis: Bobbs-
Merrill, 1924. Originally appeared as *Saturday Evening Post* article, 31
May 1924, 10-11+.

Cowpens: The Great Morale-Builder. [Hanover, N.H.]: Westholm, 1957 [limited
edition of 400 numbered copies]. *The Battle of Cowpens: The Great Morale-
Builder*. Garden City, N.Y.: Doubleday, 1958. Paperback. Garden City,
N.Y.: Doubleday, 1976.

Don't Say That about Maine! Waterville, Maine: Colby College Press, 1951.
Originally appeared as *Saturday Evening Post* article, 6 November 1948,
30+.

Europe's Morning After. New York & London: Harper, 1921. Contents originally
appeared as follows: "Poland for Patriotism," *Saturday Evening Post*, 17
April 1920, 10-11+ (about Poland); "Husks," *Saturday Evening Post*, 1
May 1920, 3-4+ (about Austria); "Handing It Back," *Saturday Evening
Post*, 29 May 1920, 8-9+ (about Czechoslovakia); "For Over a Thousand
Years," *Saturday Evening Post*, 12 June 1920, 18-19+ (about Hungary);
"Almost Sunny Italy," *Saturday Evening Post*, 17 July 1920, 18-19+
(about Italy); "The Mysteries of Paris," *Saturday Evening Post*, 3 April
1920, 3-4+ (about France); "How Cousin John's Getting Along,"
Saturday Evening Post, 13 March 1920, 18-19+ (about England);
"Schieber Land," *Saturday Evening Post*, 27 March 1920, 10-11+ (about
Germany).

Florida. New York & London: Harper, 1926. Contents originally appeared as
follows: "Florida Fever," *Saturday Evening Post*, 5 December 1925, 6-7+;
"Good Warm Stuff," *Saturday Evening Post*, 9 January 1926, 12-13+;
"Florida Prophets," *Saturday Evening Post*, 13 February 1926, 20-21+;
"Florida Fireworks," *Saturday Evening Post*, 23 January 1926, 12-13+;
"Tropical Parasites," *Saturday Evening Post*, 2 January 1926, 6-7+;
"Florida Diversions," *Saturday Evening Post*, 20 February 1926, 24-25+.

Florida Loafing. Indianapolis: Bobbs-Merrill, 1925. Originally appeared as
Saturday Evening Post article, 17 May 1924, 20-21+.

For Authors Only, and Other Gloomy Essays. Garden City, N.Y.: Doubleday,
Doran, 1935. Includes material that originally appeared as follows: "The
Circumspect Seventies," *Saturday Evening Post*, 24 January 1925, 17+;

"The Lure of the Great North Woods," *Saturday Evening Post*, 12 September 1925, 5+; "The Little Home in the Country," *Saturday Evening Post*, 30 June 1928, 16-17+; "Roads of Remembrance," *Saturday Evening Post*, 7 December 1929, 24-25+; "The Truth about a Novel," *Saturday Evening Post*, 3 January 1931, 29+; "How I Don't Play Golf," *Saturday Evening Post*, 24 January 1931, 10-11+; "The Half-Baked Palace," Part I, *Saturday Evening Post*, 18 April 1931, 12-13+; "The Half-Baked Palace," Part II, *Saturday Evening Post*, 25 April 1931, 33+; "Twinkle, Twinkle, Little Star," *Saturday Evening Post*, 23 April 1932, 11+; "Country Life in Italy," *Saturday Evening Post*, 7 May 1932, 14-15+; "Dogs in a Big Way," *Saturday Evening Post*, 28 May 1932, 14-15+; "For Authors Only," *Saturday Evening Post*, 24 September 1932, 14-15+; "An Inquiry into Diets," *Saturday Evening Post*, 15 October 1932, 14-15+; "Confessions of a Small Investor," Part I, *Saturday Evening Post*, 18 March 1933, 12-13+; "Confessions of a Small Investor," Part II, *Saturday Evening Post*, 25 March 1933, 8-9+; "A Few Remarks on Exercise," *Saturday Evening Post*, 18 November 1933, 26-27+; "Sport and Play at Oxford," *Saturday Evening Post*, 7 April 1934, 10-11+; "An American Looks at Oxford," *Saturday Evening Post*, 16 June 1934, 16-17+.

Henry Gross and His Dowsing Rod. Garden City, N.Y.: Doubleday, 1951. Paperback. New York: Pyramid Books, 1969.

It Must Be Your Tonsils. Garden City, N.Y.: Doubleday, Doran, 1936. Originally appeared as *Saturday Evening Post* article, 12 October 1935, 10-11+.

I Wanted to Write. Garden City, N.Y.: Doubleday, 1949. Paperback. Camden, Maine: Down East, 1977.

The Seventh Sense. Garden City, N.Y.: Doubleday, 1953.

Sun Hunting. Indianapolis: Bobbs-Merrill, 1922. Contents originally appeared as follows: "The Time Killers," *Saturday Evening Post*, 1 April 1922, 6-7+; "The Sun Hunters," *Saturday Evening Post*, 15 April 1922, 27+; "Tropical Growth," *Saturday Evening Post*, 29 April 1922, 8-9+.

Trending into Maine. Boston: Little, Brown, 1938. Augmented edition. Garden City, N.Y.: Doubleday, Doran, 1944. Includes material that originally appeared as follows: "The Lure of the Great North Woods," *Saturday Evening Post*, 12 September 1925, 5+; "Roads of Remembrance," *Saturday Evening Post*, 7 December 1929, 24-25+; "Potato-Poor," *Saturday Evening Post*, 23 November 1935, 23+ (republished partially); "Quoddy," *Saturday Evening Post*, 19 September 1936, 16-17+ (republished partially); "Down-East Ambrosia," *Saturday Evening Post*, 19 March 1938, 18-19+. The enlarged 1944 edition includes "Invitations to Idlers," which originally appeared as "That's Hay, That Is!" *Country Gentleman*, May 1943, 12+, and "Enemies Nobody Knows," which was accepted by *Country Gentleman* in February 1944 under the title "My

Enemy the Great Horned Owl" but was not published by the magazine after Doubleday requested it.

Watchdogs of Crime. Chicago: Chicago Crime Commission, 1927. Originally appeared as *Saturday Evening Post* article, 8 October 1927, 45+.

Water Unlimited. Garden City, N.Y.: Doubleday, 1957.

Why Europe Leaves Home. Indianapolis: Bobbs-Merrill, 1922. Contents originally appeared as follows: "The Goal of Central Europeans," *Saturday Evening Post*, 6 November 1920, 12-13+; "The Worth of Citizenship," *Saturday Evening Post*, 18 February 1922, 3-4+; "Ports of Embarkation," *Saturday Evening Post*, 7 May 1921, 12+; "The Existence of an Emergency," *Saturday Evening Post*, 30 April 1921, 3-4+; "Plain Remarks on Immigration for Plain Americans," *Saturday Evening Post*, 12 February 1921, 21-22+; "Shutting the Sea Gates," *Saturday Evening Post*, 28 January 1922, 11+; "Waifs of an Empire," *Saturday Evening Post*, 2 July 1921, 14-15+; "The Constantinople Refugees," *Saturday Evening Post*, 16 July 1921, 10-11+; "They Sometimes Come Back," *Saturday Evening Post*, 10 September 1921, 12-13+; "The Beer Worshippers," *Saturday Evening Post*, 19 February 1921, 6-7+; "Scotland for Scotch," *Saturday Evening Post*, 5 March 1921, 3-4+.

Collections

The Kenneth Roberts Reader. Garden City, N.Y.: Doubleday, Doran, 1945. Reprinted essays and selections from novels. Includes material that originally appeared as follows: "The Lure of the Great North Woods," *Saturday Evening Post*, 12 September 1925, 5+; "The Little Home in the Country," *Saturday Evening Post*, 30 June 1928, 16-17+; "Roads of Remembrance," *Saturday Evening Post*, 7 December 1929, 24-25+; "The Truth about a Novel," *Saturday Evening Post*, 3 January 1931, 29+; "The Half-Baked Palace," Part I, *Saturday Evening Post*, 18 April 1931, 12-13+; "The Half-Baked Palace," Part II, *Saturday Evening Post*, 25 April 1931, 33+; "Country Life in Italy," *Saturday Evening Post*, 7 May 1932, 14-15+; "Dogs in a Big Way," *Saturday Evening Post*, 28 May 1932, 14-15+; "For Authors Only," *Saturday Evening Post*, 24 September 1932, 14-15+ (republished partially); "An Inquiry into Diets," *Saturday Evening Post*, 15 October 1932, 14-15+; "Sport and Play at Oxford," *Saturday Evening Post*, 7 April 1934, 10-11+; "An American Looks at Oxford," *Saturday Evening Post*, 16 June 1934, 16-17+; "It Must Be Your Tonsils," *Saturday Evening Post*, 12 October 1935, 10-11+; "Down-East Ambrosia," *Saturday Evening Post*, 19 March 1938, 18-19+; "The Mystery of the Forked Twig," *Country Gentleman*, September 1944, 12+.

Other

The Brotherhood of Man, with Robert Garland. New York, Los Angeles, Toronto & London: French, 1934. One-act play. Originally appeared in the *Saturday Evening Post*, 30 August 1919, 3-5+.

Check List, for Use of Whisky Tenors and Back-room Quartets. Kennebunkport, Maine. Revised edition. *Revised Checklist, 400 Songs for Boys in the Back Room*. Kennebunkport, Maine: n.p., 1944. Song list.

Good Maine Food, by Marjorie Mosser; introduction and notes by Kenneth Roberts. New York: Doubleday, Doran, 1939. Revised edition. Garden City, N.Y.: Doubleday, 1947. Paperback. Camden, Maine: Down East, 1974. Revised edition. *Foods of Old New England*. Garden City, N.Y.: Doubleday, 1957. Cookbook.

Know New England: Eighty Cities and Towns. Boston: Boston Herald-Traveler, 1950? Historical anecdotes. Contents originally serialized in the *Boston Herald* and the *Boston Traveler*, beginning in March 1950.

March to Quebec: Journals of the Members of Arnold's Expedition, compiled and annotated by Kenneth Roberts. New York: Doubleday, Doran, 1938. Augmented edition. New York: Doubleday, Doran, 1940. Paperback. [Camden, Maine]: Down East, 1980. Augmented edition. Garden City, N.Y.: Doubleday, 1953. Historical journals.

Moreau de St. Mery's American Journey (1793-1798), by Mederic Louis Elie Moreau de St. Mery; translated and edited by Kenneth Roberts and Anna M. Roberts. Garden City, N.Y.: Doubleday, 1947. Diary.

Panatela: A Political Comic Opera, book and lyrics by Kenneth Roberts and Romeyn Berry. Ithaca, N.Y.: Cornell Masque of Cornell University, 1907. Song book.

SECONDARY WORKS
Bibliographies

Albert, George. "Bibliography of Kenneth Lewis Roberts." Parts 1-4. *Bulletin of Bibliography* 17 (September-December 1942): 191-92; 17 (January-April 1943): 218-19; 18 (May-August 1943): 13-15; 18 (September-December 1943): 34-36. A checklist of works by and about Kenneth Roberts, covering the years 1920 to 1941. Continued by Stemple.

Bales, Jack. "Kenneth Roberts." In *Bibliography of American Fiction, 1919-1988*, vol. 2, edited by Matthew J. Bruccoli and Judith S. Baughman, 424-26. New York: Facts on File, 1991. Primary and secondary bibliography of major works published between 1919 and 1988.

_____. *Kenneth Roberts: The Man and His Works*. Foreword by John Tebbel. Scarecrow Author Bibliographies, no. 85. Metuchen, N.J.: Scarecrow, 1989. A biobibliography that includes a 74-page biography, a 988-item annotated bibliography of criticism, and six appendices.

Ellis, Marjorie Mosser. "Supplementary Bibliography of Kenneth Roberts." *Colby Library Quarterly* 6 (September 1962): 99-105. Roberts's niece and longtime secretary continues and updates George Albert and Ruth Stemple and also lists works published before 1920, editions and translations of Roberts's novels, and items the two other bibliographers had missed.

Murphy, P. *Kenneth Lewis Roberts: A Bibliography*. Privately printed, 1975. Partly annotated bibliography of works by and about Roberts.

Stemple, Ruth. "Kenneth Roberts: A Supplementary Checklist." *Bulletin of Bibliography* 22 (September-December 1959): 228-30. Continues and updates George Albert, listing primary and biographical works. Continued by Marjorie Mosser Ellis.

Books

Harris, Janet. *A Century of American History in Fiction: Kenneth Roberts' Novels*. New York: Gordon, 1976. A detailed and sympathetic study of Roberts's works, analyzing themes, characters, plots, and other elements. Includes bibliography.

Kenneth Roberts: An American Novelist. New York: Doubleday, Doran: 1938. A 40-page promotional booklet, issued by Roberts's publishers, similar to that of Chilson H. Leonard.

Leonard, Chilson H. *Kenneth Roberts: A Biographical Sketch, an Informal Study, His Books and Critical Opinions*. Garden City, N.Y.: Doubleday, Doran, 1936. A 32-page illustrated pamphlet issued by Roberts's publishers as a promotional item. Includes a brief biography, a description of Roberts's research methods, and plot summaries of novels and excerpts from reviews.

Mayberry, Susanah. *My Amiable Uncle: Recollections about Booth Tarkington*. West Lafayette, Ind.: Purdue University Press, 1983. Tarkington's niece reminisces about her uncle's longtime friendship with Roberts.

Tebbel, John. *George Horace Lorimer and "The Saturday Evening Post."* Garden City, N.Y.: Doubleday, 1948. Traces Roberts's lengthy relationship with *Saturday Evening Post* editor Lorimer.

Articles and Parts of Books

"Angry Man's Romance." *Time*, 25 November 1940, 91-92, 94, 97-98. Cover story surveying Roberts's literary career, with emphasis on the just-published *Oliver Wiswell*.

Baker, Carlos. "The Novel as History: Kenneth Roberts." *Delphian Quarterly* 24 (January 1941): 15-20. Excellent article that presents biographical information on Roberts and critical analyses of several of his novels.

Benét, Stephen Vincent, and Rosemary Benét. "Kenneth Roberts: Historian of His People." *New York Herald Tribune Books*, 8 December 1940, 7. Summarizes Roberts's life and praises his books.

Cary, Richard. "Roberts and Lorimer: The First Decade." *Colby Library Quarterly* 6 (September 1962): 106-29. Examines the business association and strong friendship between Roberts and *Saturday Evening Post* editor George Horace Lorimer.

Coyle, Lee. "Kenneth Roberts and the American Historical Novel." In *Popular Literature in America: A Symposium in Honor of Lyon N. Richardson*, edited by James C. Austin and Donald A. Koch, 70-77. Bowling Green, Ohio: Bowling Green University Popular Press, 1972. Discusses Roberts as a historical novelist, with brief, critical assessments by several historians.

Gardner, Martin. "Dowsing Rods and Doodlebugs." In *In the Name of Science*, 101-15. New York: G. P. Putnam's Sons, 1952. Denouncement of the "pseudo-science" of dowsing, singling out Roberts and Henry Gross.

Hutchens, John K. "Kenneth Roberts Says It Was like This." *New York Herald Tribune Book Review*, 8 January 1956, 2. During an interview Roberts discusses his books, particularly his latest, *Boon Island*.

Kelley, Mary Carpenter. "Author of *Arundel* Builds 12-Foot Wall to Bar Visitors." *Christian Science Monitor*, 12 September 1939, 3. In an interview Roberts talks about his estate and the work schedule he has to maintain to write his books.

Nichols, Lewis. "A Visit with Mr. Roberts." *New York Times Book Review*, 1 January 1956, 3, 21. Interview with Roberts in which he talks about his various interests, including his love of Maine, dowsing, and his just-published *Boon Island*.

Riddick, Thomas M. "Dowsing Is Nonsense." *Harper's Magazine*, July 1951, 62-68. Points out "fallacies in reasoning" and "illogical and unscientific conjectures" in Roberts's *Henry Gross and His Dowsing Rod*.

Roseberry, Cecil R. "A Report on Water Dowsing." *American Mercury* 77 (July 1953): 25-29. A newspaper reporter relates his unfavorable impressions of dowsing, Roberts, and Henry Gross.

Schwarz, Berthold Eric. "Psychic Aspects of the Art of Dowsing: Notes on Henry Gross, Successful Dowser." In *Psychic-Dynamics*, 91-161. New York: Pageant Press, 1965. Extensive though overly warmhearted study of Henry Gross, the central figure in Roberts's three dowsing books.

Shepard, Brooks. "Firsthand Report on Dowsing." *Harper's Magazine*, September 1951, 69-75. A friend of Roberts's describes how Henry Gross found water by dowsing.

West, Herbert Faulkner. Foreword to *The Battle of Cowpens: The Great Morale-Builder*, by Kenneth Roberts, 7-16. Garden City, N.Y.: Doubleday, 1958. Memorial tribute to Roberts, objectively written by a longtime friend.

_____. "The Work of Kenneth Roberts." *Colby Library Quarterly* 6 (September 1962): 89-99. Assesses Roberts's literary career from both a broad perspective and from analyses of his individual books.

Williams, Ben Ames. Introduction to *The Kenneth Roberts Reader*, vii-xi. Garden City, N.Y.: Doubleday, Doran, 1945. Personal reminiscences.

_____. "Kenneth Roberts." *Saturday Review of Literature* 18 (25 June 1938): 8-10. A tribute by one of Roberts's closest friends.

Dissertation

Kitch, John Ira, Jr. "From History to Fiction: Kenneth Roberts as an Historical Novelist." Ph.D. diss., University of Illinois, 1965.

Index

The Author

Jack Bales is a reference and bibliographic instruction librarian at Mary Washington College. He received his B.A. in English from Illinois College in Jacksonville, Illinois, and his M.S. in library science from the University of Illinois in Urbana-Champaign. He is the author of *Kenneth Roberts: The Man and His Works* (1989), and his writing on Roberts has appeared in publications as diverse as the *Dartmouth College Library Bulletin*, *Down East*, and the *Bibliography of American Fiction, 1919-1988*. In 1991 he was awarded a Distinguished Alumnus citation from Illinois College for his books and articles on Roberts and other literary topics. He lives in Fredericksburg, Virginia.

The Editor

Joseph M. Flora earned his B.A. (1956), M.A. (1957), and Ph.D. (1962) in English at the University of Michigan. In 1962 he joined the faculty of the University of North Carolina, where he is now professor of English. His study *Hemingway's Nick Adams* (1984) won the Mayflower Award. He is also author of *Vardis Fisher* (1962), *William Ernest Henley* (1970), *Frederick Manfred* (1974), and *Ernest Hemingway: A Study of the Short Fiction* (1989). He is editor of *The English Short Story* (1985) and coeditor of *Southern Writers: A Biographical Dictionary* (1970), *Fifty Southern Writers before 1900* (1987), and *Fifty Southern Writers after 1900* (1987). He serves on the editorial boards of *Studies in Short Fiction* and the *Southern Literary Journal*.